TEACHING
the
MALE
Brain

In Memory of Two Great Teachers:
Elizabeth Copeland Norfleet
and
R. Fillmore Norfleet

TEACHING the MALE Brain

How Boys Think, Feel, and Learn in School

Abigail Norfleet James

CORWIN PRESS
A SAGE Publications Company
Thousand Oaks, CA 91320

For information:

Corwin Press
A Sage Publications Company
2455 Teller Road
Thousand Oaks, California 91320
www.corwinpress.com

Sage Publications India Pvt Ltd
B 1/I 1 Mohan Cooperative
  Industrial Area
Mathura Road, New Delhi 110 044
India

Sage Publications Ltd.
1 Oliver's Yard
55 City Road
London EC1Y 1SP
United Kingdom

Sage Publications Asia-Pacific Pte Ltd
33 Pekin Street #02-01
Far East Square
Singapore 048763

Printed in the United States of America

Library of Congress Cataloging-in-Publication Data

James, Abigail Norfleet.
Teaching the male brain: How boys think, feel, and learn in school/Abigail Norfleet James.
    p. cm.
Includes bibliographical references and index.
ISBN 978-1-4129-3662-0 (cloth)
ISBN 978-1-4129-3663-7 (pbk.)
  1. Boys-Education. 2. Boys-Psychology. 3. Sex differences in education.
4. Academic achievement. I. Title.
LC1390.J36 2007
371.823-dc22   2006034140

This book is printed on acid-free paper.

07   08   09   10   11   10 9 8 7 6 5 4 3 2 1

Acquisitions Editor:	Allyson P. Sharp
Editorial Assistant:	Nadia Kashper
Production Editor:	Beth A. Bernstein
Copy Editor:	Glenn Wright
Typesetter:	C&M Digitals (P) Ltd.
Proofreader:	Word Wise Webb
Indexer:	John Hulse
Cover Designer:	Lisa Miller

Contents

Foreword

In recent years, there has been a remarkable amount of new research regarding teaching and learning styles as they apply to persons of all ages. At the same time, research has led to new thinking about whether there are differences in the way girls and boys learn. Girls seem to mature earlier than boys, on average, and studies suggest that there are biological differences that influence, if they do not determine, developmental process and educational achievement. These are controversial ideas, because, until recently, prevailing acceptable opinion has been that girls and boys should be treated in exactly the same way—that they should be taught in the same manner and in the same classrooms, and that every effort should be made to avoid any hint of difference so as to avoid prejudice or role stereotyping. These worthy goals have nevertheless proven complex because, despite efforts to achieve an evenhanded approach, there is evidence to suggest that it makes sense to recognize that differences do exist between the genders and that they may be biologically influenced.

This book offers a helpful overview of recent work in the fields of gender studies, education policy as it applies to girls and boys, debates about single-sex classrooms and schools, and brain research. All educators need to be familiar with these issues and the academic studies that explore them. The author gives special attention to the biological research on the human brain and writings in the field that suggest implications for education. The chapter on the brain provides a thoughtful analysis of current thinking among researchers using the most advanced techniques to study this most amazing of human organs.

Abigail Norfleet James is a psychologist with a PhD from the University of Virginia and an undergraduate degree from Duke. She has done years of clinical research. What is important about the author's credentials for this book, however, is that she began her doctoral studies and came to her advanced research after many years of classroom teaching with students at the middle and secondary level. Here is an author who really knows what it is to do the daily work of lesson preparation and teaching, of evaluating, encouraging, and challenging students. To use the jargon of the day, she is schooled and practiced in classroom management. Moreover, much of her experience was in teaching boys. Her practical experience suggested that style, setting, attitude, materials, length of class periods, furniture, lighting, and even temperature all have an impact on the effectiveness of teaching and learning. Her research has suggested why this is so, and has given theory to good practice.

What is special about this book is that the author not only provides the intellectual foundation for new thinking about the way boys learn, but also offers very practical advice about how these new ideas and insights, derived from advanced research about the brain and learning, can be applied to actual classroom settings. This book will help teachers do a better job not only with boys, but with girls as well. The book makes us think about how all of the assumptions we bring to our teaching have an impact on what our students learn.

Anyone interested in education will find this book stimulating. It will make one think in new ways, especially about boys. In particular, this book will help those who teach on a daily basis bring the fruits of pathbreaking research into classroom styles and projects. It will also help parents who have puzzled about why their boys and girls come at certain problems and challenges in such different ways. I also think that persons interested in the social policy questions of education in our time will find this book stimulating.

We are in a time when prevailing assumptions about education are being regularly challenged because there is unease about how well we are doing in all areas, and at all levels, of education. One of the areas that must be explored is whether single-sex education should be more widely available. For the most part, only those who can pay for independent school education can allow their children that option. If recent research suggests anything, it is that multiple styles of teaching and learning are necessary, because we all learn in different ways. For many boys and girls, single-sex education serves well, giving them the opportunity to learn in ways that this book suggests are very important.

Teaching the Male Brain, then, will be read on many levels by many different persons, but perhaps its greatest significance is in its practical application to the actual needs of students and teachers. Most of all, it is a worthy contribution because it has the potential to be a positive force in improving education for boys at a time when that is a particularly urgent need.

—Dennis M. Campbell

Dennis M. Campbell, Headmaster of Woodberry Forest School, Woodberry Forest, Virginia, holds AB and PhD degrees from Duke University and a BD from Yale University. He is the former dean of the Divinity School and Professor of Theology at Duke, and author of eight books and numerous articles and reviews.

Acknowledgments

This manuscript is the product of a lifetime of being around boys After all, my first home was a boys' dorm. Years later, as a teacher at that same school, I became concerned by the pressure to admit girls to the school. Fortunately, at that time, both the head of school and the Board of Trustees did not yield to suggestions that admitting girls would assist the school in providing a better education to its students. Even though the calls for coeducation were quelled for a while, I felt sure that they would return unless we could demonstrate that what happened in the classroom at boys' schools was fundamentally better for boys than what they experienced in a coed classroom.

As a lifelong academic, I started my search for this information in the library at the University of Virginia's Curry School of Education. What I found was that most of the substantive research on boys' education was being done in Australia, New Zealand, and England. There were some studies from the United States, but little of the research examined the differences in attitudes toward education for boys and girls. I reasoned that if boys' schools were not to go the way of dodoes and carrier pigeons, I'd have to do the research myself. Fortunately, I found Herbert C. Richards, who wasn't exactly sure of what I was trying to study, but who had the instincts of all good teachers—let the student try to prove his point. I will never forget the day when he brought me a copy of *Scientific American* in which there was a report on the increasing number of countries around the world where more women were graduating from colleges than were men (Doyle, 1999). He pointed to the article and asked me if that was what I was talking about—he just needed to see some data before he was convinced. Dr. Richards has been my teacher, my friend, and my coauthor. He helped me learn to "tell the story," and if any of this makes sense, you have him to thank.

If the research on cognitive gender differences is understandable, thank Elana Farace. I met Dr. Farace when I took her psychology class in gender-based cognition, and she has been a valuable mentor and model ever since. In an undergraduate class, she put up with me even though I was a graduate student who was the same generation as her parents, and she helped me understand how neurobiology applies to cognition. My postdoctoral fellowship was in her lab sponsored by the American Pediatric Brain Tumor Foundation (thank you all) where I learned the fine points of good research and report writing.

While in graduate school, I was supported by two friends whose company, wise counsel, and lunchtime conversations made graduate school survivable. Marlie McKinnon (now Eversole) and I met on our first day in graduate school, in Statistics I, and discovered that we approached the world the same way. She is young enough to be my daughter, but she has an old head on her shoulders and has done me the honor to call me friend.

The other member of the Three Chicks is Lori Howard, and this book would not exist were it not for her. She has read every word, provided countless notes and suggestions, and interpreted the world of special education for me. Her wise counsel enabled me to frame this manuscript so that it makes sense and flows. She should be a coauthor, but she refuses to accept that label. We have written together before and will do so again. We work well together, and our collaboration produces countless ideas, some of which have come to fruition.

If you have not read Leonard Sax's book *Why Gender Matters* (2005), you need to do so. His experiences as a family practice physician have led him to become a leading expert on cognitive gender differences in children. He believes so much in this cause that he founded the National Association for Single Sex Public Education (www.singlesexschools.org), which is the leading proponent of gender-separate classes/schools. Some of the research cited in this manuscript came to me through Dr. Sax's friendship and collegiality.

Those at the Woodberry Forest School have also had a hand in this. Emmett Wright gave me a job in spite of his better judgment and eventually agreed that I did a good job with the boys. Dennis Campbell, the present head of the school, has supported me in this endeavor as well and has provided the foreword. Ben Hale and David McRae provided a place for me to teach in summer school and allowed me to teach the study skills class in which I tried out many of the suggestions you will find here. Jim Reid has long been a model of what excellent teaching looks like and gave me the freedom to teach science my way.

The journey from the day I left teaching at the boys' school until now was made possible by my family. My parents were my first teachers, and I owe a great deal of what I know about teaching to listening to them discuss what they did in their classrooms. The contrast in their approaches always fascinated me. My father taught boys and my mother taught girls, and they were the first who opened my eyes to the fact that good teaching should be gender specific. My son has been good enough to let me use him as an example (not that he had much choice in the matter) and has provided many suggestions for this work. My husband has been a rock of support for thirty-five years and his sense of humor has made my world a better place. His ability to clarify problems is astounding.

Others who have helped include Fred Nichols, Charles Stilwell, John Sanderson, Harold Burbach, Samuels Real Estate, Germanna Community College, Orange County High School, and Marcus Hamilton. In addition, Dan Grogan has generously allowed me to use some of his pictures and Sanford Wintersberger, aka the starving artist, provided all the drawings.

Most important, I thank every one of my students, both boys and girls. I learned much more from you all than I ever taught you. You trusted me to open the world of science to you, and in return we explored what actually works in the classroom. If you think you recognize yourself in some of the stories, you should know that all the stories are made up (except the ones about my son), but they are based on what did happen in my classrooms. I used the underlying grain of truth to make new stories. Without that grain, there would be no authenticity to these words.

Corwin Press gratefully acknowledges the contributions of the following reviewers:

Dr. Tim Hawkes
Headmaster
The King's School
Parramatta, Australia

Michael E. Ingrisani
Dean of Faculty and Head of English
The Browning School
New York, NY

Helane Smith Miller, CPA
Assistant Principal
District of Columbia Public Schools
Washington, DC

About the Author

**Abigail Norfleet James** taught for many years in single-sex schools and consults on the subject of gendered teaching to school systems, colleges, and universities. Her area of expertise is developmental and educational psychology as applied to the gendered classroom. Prior to obtaining her doctorate from the University of Virginia's Curry School of Education, she taught general science, biology, and psychology in both boys' and girls' secondary schools.

Her previous publications include reports of research comparing the educational attitudes of male graduates of coed schools and single-sex schools, and research describing the effects of gendered basic skills instruction. In addition, she has written on differentiated instruction at the elementary school level. She has presented workshops and papers at many educational conferences and works with teachers and parent groups in interpreting the world of gendered education.

Her professional affiliations include the American Educational Research Association, the American Psychological Association, the Association for Supervision and Curriculum Development, the Gender and Education Association, the International Boys' School Coalition, and the National Association for Single-Sex Public Education (advisory board member).

Introduction

DENNIS THE MENACE   HANK KETCHAM

"SO, WHAT DID WE LEARN IN SCHOOL TODAY?" "TO SIT DOWN AND KEEP MY MOUTH SHUT."

SOURCE: Dennis the Menace ® used by permission of Hank Ketcham Enterprises and © North America Syndicate.

The ninth-grade physical science class was hard at it one day. They heated thin strips of wood in a test tube and found that when they were finished, the wood had shrunk and turned a dark gray. A thick, dark brown smelly substance was stuck to the walls of the test tube, and a colorless, odorless gas had been produced. There were lots of giggles when they discovered that the gas was methane and that it did indeed burn, but there was some discussion in the back of the room as to whether methane was actually odorless. The dark smelly substance turned out to be tar and that started a conversation about where tar on the roads came from and whether it was the same tar as in cigarettes. The gray wood was charcoal, and a debate ensued about the relative merits of charcoal versus wood for barbecuing. At the end of the lab period, the classroom stunk, most of the boys had a bit of tar on them somewhere, and they had used open flames. One boy turned to me as he left and said, "Mrs. James, this has been more fun than I have ever had in class in my life."

◆◆◆

This lab is part of a science course that was designed expressly for boys. Each day the students find a bin with materials and a lab sheet. The teacher spends no more than five minutes helping the boys set up the exercise before they begin. The lab sheet helps structure the collection of data and provides some direction about what the boys are to do. The teacher helps with troubleshooting by asking questions to help the boys figure out what they are doing. At the end of the lab, with prompts from the teacher, the class discusses the findings and figures out what happened and why. For most lab exercises, a written lab report is required.

This course works because boys in the ninth grade learn best by being active, by putting their hands on the materials, and by talking about the material once they have some context to work with; they like doing something in class, and they can better grasp concepts when they have a concrete visual reference. When I developed the course, I didn't know why this approach worked with my students. I knew what worked with boys, but I wasn't always sure why. Consequently, it was hard for me to convince other teachers to try this course because I couldn't explain to them the reasons for the way the course was constructed. I can now explain why this course works for boys.

Would this method work for you? How does your brain work?

To determine how you best process information, read the following statements and select the choice that most nearly describes you.

1. When putting something together, you are more likely to
   A. Read the directions first
   B. Look at the diagrams first

2. When working together with others, you are more likely to
   A. Choose to work with people you know you get along with
   B. Choose to work with people who know a lot about the subject

3. When you have to learn a skill, you are more likely to
   A. Read about how to do it
   B. Ask someone to show you how to do it

4. How important is the teacher in how well you do in a course?
   A. I work hard regardless of the teacher
   B. I am more likely to do well if the teacher and I get along

5. When you are bored in class or in a meeting, you are more likely to
   A. Daydream
   B. Doodle

6. When watching TV with other people, you are likely to find that the sound is
   A. Too loud
   B. Not loud enough

7. If you had a choice you would rather
   A. Write a poem to be given to everyone to read
   B. Recite a poem in front of a group

8. If you give directions, you are more likely to describe the route
   A. Using landmarks
   B. Using mileage and compass directions

9. You are more likely to select a book to read that is
   A. A sensitive treatment of family relationships in turmoil
   B. A thriller about daring exploits

10. How easy is it for you to understand how someone feels by looking at their facial expression and body language?
    A. Easy
    B. Difficult

If you select more A choices, you are likely to be a reflective learner whose auditory/hearing and verbal/reading skills make experiential/hands-on learning a problem, but who will shine in a traditional classroom where reading and writing are important.

If you select more B choices, you are likely to be an active learner whose kinesthetic/physical and iconic/visual skills make learning in a traditional classroom more difficult, but who will shine in laboratory exercises and other hands-on tasks.

The "B" brain is usually described as the Male Brain because more men appear to think and reason in this fashion. There are women who think this way as well, although not nearly as many as men. As a female with a male brain, I had a hard time in school because my teachers assumed that I should be able to work like my female classmates. What helped me realize how I learned best was working with my male students, especially when I taught them in coed environments. It was there that I began to understand how the methods I had learned in a single-sex environment—both boys' schools and girls' schools—could make a difference for my "B" brain students in a coed environment. From this point on, I'll refer to the "B" brain as a male brain even though the methods will work just as well with girls who learn this way.

What follows is a discussion of the unique ways that most boys learn, together with some applications for schools and classrooms. This book addresses the belief that boys and girls do not always learn in the same way and different approaches to teaching benefit both. As schools are presently configured, girls appear more successful in school settings. In 1998, the results from the writing portion of the National Assessment of Educational Progress indicated that at grades 4, 8, and 12, girls had a 16- to 20-point advantage over boys. In 2002, the same test showed that the girls' advantage had grown to 17 to 24 points. On the reading test in 2002, 38 percent of eighth-grade girls attained proficiency, whereas only 27 percent of eighth-grade boys were proficient. In the same year, 44 percent of the twelfth-grade girls reached proficiency in reading while the twelfth-grade boys were not much different from the eighth graders, with a proficiency of 28 percent (National Assessment of Educational Progress [NAEP], 2006).

Some boys have no trouble in school, but others are failing, dropping out, or not continuing in education past high school. Data from the National Center for Education Statistics showed that in 2001, 57 percent of those receiving bachelor's degrees and 59 percent of those receiving master's degrees were women (National Center for Education Statistics [NCES], 2006). Colleges are concerned with the lack of male applicants (Gose, 1997). It is for the boys who are having

trouble that this book is written, or rather for their teachers and families. Boys who are not succeeding in an educational setting are not necessarily unable to learn, but it is likely that they learn in very different ways than those for which classrooms are now structured.

One caveat. Not all boys will fit the model used for this work. More important, cognitive differences within gender—girls compared to girls and boys to boys—are far greater than differences between the two genders (Halpern, 2000). These differences in how children process information are largest at birth and shrink over time, but never really disappear. However, differences in other areas, such as hearing and smell, are large and remain that way throughout life. Additionally, differences between genders can be magnified in a school setting. Stereotyping, peer pressure, social expectations, and environmental influences from families, peers, and teachers, as well as the media and entertainment industry, all work together to intensify the importance placed on gender differences. Students enter your classroom with beliefs about gender-appropriate behavior for them and for their classmates and for you. Understanding those beliefs and helping children cope with how those beliefs affect classroom performance is preferable to pretending that the beliefs don't exist.

All of those influences are what makes it hard to determine exactly which differences are due to biology and which are due to environment. We will begin with biological factors that are the source of gender attributes and then show how those factors are influenced by the world. For example, it is generally thought that boys, ages 20 to 36 months, are more active than girls. Research has shown that when children are very young, the difference in activity level is related more to the amount of space allowed each child than to the child's gender (Maccoby, 1998). Boys may be noisier and more active than girls because of expectations and not biology, but most are still noisier and that can have a deleterious effect on their classroom experience.

Certain terms are used extensively in this book and what follows are brief definitions of how those terms are used here.

Cognition refers to all of our mental functions, such as thinking, remembering, dreaming, and problem solving. If a child's cognitive skills are not a good fit for the academic activity at hand, the child may appear to be learning disabled. For example, if a child does not learn well from auditory information, the child is going to have trouble in a conversational Spanish class. However, the same child may have little trouble learning Spanish when the material is presented in written form. Some cognitive abilities and weaknesses are typical of boys, but you will find girls with the same cognitive patterns and the information presented here will help them as well. Remember, the information included here is typical for most boys, but not necessarily for all boys.

Stereotype refers to beliefs that we have about the way people behave as a result of their membership in a group. What facts those beliefs are based on and where they begin is the subject of much speculation. Many stereotypical beliefs have no basis in fact; for example, blondes are not thought to be academically capable in spite of many examples to the contrary. Other stereotypical beliefs do have some factual basis—for example, the view that males don't like to read. In fact, many men do like to read, but the learning curve for reading is different for girls and boys. In general, girls learn to read earlier than boys, and the stereotype of males not liking to read begins there, even though boys will catch up to girls later.

What is the difference between sex and gender? *Sex* is a biological descriptor and refers to areas that apply to individuals because of their genetic makeup. During puberty, the growth pattern of girls tends to be slow and steady and the growth pattern of boys tends to be in rapid bursts (Berk, 1997). Those growth patterns reflect the different hormonal levels present in girls and boys as a result of their sex. One result of these sex-determined growth patterns is vocal change. Girls' voices drop gradually and usually only the choral teacher is aware of their changing vocal ranges. Boys' voices can change rapidly, and the resultant squeaks and cracks may be embarrassing. That is one reason why some middle-school boys stop participating in class discussion.

Gender is a sociological descriptor and refers to areas that apply to individuals because of their membership in society. Many boys do not see school success as a masculine trait. Their belief is that school is for girls, and many girls would agree. The difference between the way that boys and girls view school is based on gender stereotypes. Just because the beliefs are based on stereotypes does not make them any less real or any less of a problem in the classroom. Acknowledging these beliefs about what is gender-appropriate behavior will allow the student and teacher the chance to address the issues. Ignoring these gender differences will not make them disappear. Part I of the book will cover material based on sex differences and references will be made to brain and neurological research. Part II will cover material based on gender differences and references will be to survey and opinion research.

SUBSTANTIATING RESEARCH

In the past 100 years, the process of teaching has changed a great deal. Our attitudes about appropriate classroom activities have changed and continue to change. Part of the reason for the changes is that educational research shows that different teaching methods and approaches produce better results. Teachers and families hear the experts say that new methods will produce superior outcomes, and five years later hear that the experts now think some other way is better. Does that mean that educational research is somehow flawed or unreliable? Not at all. Our ideas about what are good outcomes for education change over time, leading us to reevaluate what we do in the classroom. In addition, new methods affect other aspects of the learning environment, prompting further changes in methods or curricula.

You will not be asked to believe the assertions in this book, and the suggestions based on those assertions, simply because another teacher suggested that you might try them. The assertions are based on research, which comes in three categories:

1. Classic research that was done more than ten years ago, but that has been replicated and whose findings are generally agreed upon.

2. Recent research that has been replicated and whose findings have been found to be useful by teachers of boys.

3. Cutting-edge research that has not been replicated but that has been carefully designed, and whose findings are being applied in all-male classrooms right now.

The evidence for sex differences is based on neurobiological research, which generally involves passive information from brain sections, electroencephalograms (EEGs), and magnetic resonance imaging (MRI), and active information from responses to challenges to the neurological system. This active information comes from reflex responses to stimuli such as discrimination of colors or sounds, physiological responses such as differences in pain thresholds or attention, and biological maturational differences such as pubertal timing.

The evidence for gender differences is based on more qualitative research because gender has to do with how behavior is affected by environment and those differences do not necessarily show up in brain structures. A great deal of this information comes from survey and opinion research and, as such, is open to questioning and differences in interpretation. If there is no definitive opinion in a particular area, you will find all of the major opinions included. For example, it is generally agreed that boys have an advantage in spatial rotation ability; what is in question is whether or not that is the reason boys usually do better in math. Some experts in the field are very sure that the spatial ability makes the difference; others are just as sure that it does not.

HOW THE BOOK IS STRUCTURED

The first part starts with information on basic brain differences. If the idea of neurobiology seems a bit overwhelming, do not worry. I include research that uncovers areas that make a difference in the learning process and how the educational environment can be responsive to those differences. I will describe sex differences in neurobiology and how those differences affect learning, but you will not find sex differences that, while substantiated by research, do not seem to have merit for the educator. Following this will be an examination of sex and gender differences in sensory, physical, and cognitive systems and how those affect what happens in the classroom.

The second part explores the relationship between society and biology on boys in school. We will begin with a discussion of Attention Deficit Hyperactivity Disorder (ADHD) and learning disabilities. There is no question that ADHD and other learning concerns are brain based, but the problems that result are exacerbated by social concerns and so this information will be found here. This will be followed by a study of emotional and social factors, together with information on students who have cultural, linguistic, and socioeconomic differences. The discussion and suggestions are based on stereotypes, and while these stereotypes are common for the United States they may not apply in your particular situation. Please know that I have tried to cover as many bases as possible, but won't cover them all.

The final part offers specific strategies for the classroom teacher. This section begins with some suggestions for classroom management of boys, particularly focusing on the issue of discipline. This will be followed by subject-specific suggestions providing strategies for teachers across the curriculum. These ideas are presented not as models for you to emulate, but as possibilities for you to use in enlarging your teaching strategies. Finally, we will address how to integrate the boy learning style with other learning styles because most boys are in classrooms with students who do not learn in this way—either other boys or the majority of girls. Don't forget, some girls learn more like boys and much of what follows will help them as well.

Just because boys and girls are in the same classroom we cannot assume that they learn in similar ways. In fact, in the rest of the book you will find out how very different they are. It is important to approach teaching from a gendered perspective, as not all students learn the same way and teaching them as if they did will not change that fact. "The first priority of schools must be education. Social engineering comes second" (Sax, 2005, p. 112).

LEARNING OBJECTIVES

I have to admit that I really like teaching boys. Partially, it is because I learn the same way that many of them do, but primarily it is because it is so exciting to see boys come alive in a classroom when the lesson is structured for them. In my attempt to make sure that I've covered all the bases and that there are appropriate references for each suggestion, I may not have conveyed that enthusiasm. However, I know that teachers who try a few of the ideas here will also find that teaching boys is really rewarding.

My purpose in writing this book is to show how boys learn, how those learning patterns affect what happens in the classroom, and how schools and teachers can modify the classroom experience to help boys (and therefore all students) learn better. Consequently, there are three learning objectives:

1. To gain an understanding and awareness of the sociological and neurobiological foundations of cognitive gender differences as they relate to education

2. To look critically at curricula and teaching practices with respect to their responsiveness to cognitive gender differences and to uncover areas where changes can and should be made

3. To develop educational approaches based on research and classroom practice to provide an instructional climate responsive to cognitive gender differences.

PART I

Sex and Gender Differences in the Classroom

1

Brain Basics

One of my advisees came to visit me during a free period. Sam flung himself down in a chair and asked me what I thought about the colleges to which he wanted to apply. He and his parents were disagreeing about his choices; he wanted to apply to smaller colleges with access to wilderness areas where he could climb and kayak and his parents wanted him to apply to traditional, East Coast private universities. He and I had gone over this ground for months and the real problem was that he and his parents did not view college in the same light. He saw college as a time to expand his horizons, to have adventures, and eventually to figure out what he wanted to do with himself. His parents saw college as a place to lay the groundwork for his future career in business or law. I asked Sam what more I could say on the subject and he replied, "Oh, probably nothing, but I need to hear you talk. I never can think of what to say to my parents, and after listening to you, I get all filled up with words and phrases and I can make a better argument."

Sam was referring to what is known as the "female advantage" in verbal skills. This advantage is the ability of women to talk freely and to say a great deal on any subject. The stereotype is pervasive in our culture, and you find references to it in every sitcom on TV; men complaining that women talk too much, and women complaining that men talk too little.

The matching stereotype is the "male advantage" in spatial rotations, the mental skill that enables men to find their way and not get lost. Women complain that men won't ask for directions while men report that they are not lost, they just need to go a bit further and then they will find their way. Are there bases for these stereotypes? Are there actual differences in male and female brains, or is it just so much hype?

ARE BRAINS GENDERED?

If you have never seen a human brain, it really is not all that exciting. A beating heart in a chest is an amazing sight because it is working all on its own and you know that if it stops, there will be disastrous consequences. But the brain just sits there looking like gray scrambled eggs. The volume of the brain is about the size of a medium cantaloupe, and it sits in the skull surrounded by cerebrospinal fluid. The fluid acts as a cushion, so if you get a blow to the head the fluid dampens its effect. However, if the blow is severe, your brain will slosh in the fluid and bump up against the other side of the skull and may get bruised. This may well cause a concussion (see Chapter 4 for further information on concussions).

If you look at a brain, can you tell if it belongs to a man or a woman? The only superficial difference is size, as female brains are a bit smaller on average than male brains. There are two viewpoints on this dichotomy. One is that of course women's brains are smaller, because women's bodies are smaller and the difference in volume is simply due to the different relative body sizes. The other view is that no, even if you use relative brain size, men's brains are bigger (Halpern, 2000; Kimura, 2000). What this slightly larger brain size means is the subject of a great deal of discussion. What is causing the larger size and what difference, if any, does it make to the thinking capacities of the individual?

Part of the controversy is a difference of opinion as to who has more brain cells. A study found that males have more cells in the brain as a whole than do women, and used that larger number to explain the larger size of male brains (Pakkenberg & Gundersen, 1997). Men's slightly larger brains have been cited as possibly explaining the observation that men score, on average, four points higher than women on the Wechsler Adult Intelligence Scale (Lynn & Irwing, 2002), a standard test of intelligence. It has also been suggested that the larger number of cells is what allows men to be more detail oriented, for instance in detecting movement and features in a landscape (Baron-Cohen, 2003), but this is just a thought.

Even though men have larger brains, some studies have found that women have as many or more cells, just in a more dense arrangement.

In the brain, there are two kinds of cells: neurons, what we typically think of as brain cells, and neuropil, which has two functions. Some of the neuropil contains the connections between neurons, and some contains cells that help provide structure, nutrition, and healing to the neurons. One study found that women had more neuropil in their brains than did men, which led to the conclusion that women had more connections between their neurons (de Courten-Myers, 1999). The stereotype is that women either can't make decisions or change their minds once they make a decision, and it has been suggested that this increased connectivity may be the source of that stereotype. Again, just a suggestion.

A different study found that female brains have more brain cells, at least in one area of the brain devoted to language (Witelson, Glezer, & Kigar, 1995). It would be tempting to point to this finding as the source of the "female verbal advantage," but the research is correlational not causational. What that means is that while the two phenomena coincide, there is no indication that one causes the other. This is similar to the observation that when skirts are short the stock market is up and when skirts are long, the stock market is down. No one would suggest that the length of skirts affects the direction of the stock market, but there may be some other factor that affects both. The problem with correlational data is that it may be difficult to determine what causes the relationship. While women may have more neurons in the area devoted to language, there is no research that definitively demonstrates that this particular area is the source of their verbal advantage, any more than we can say that men's greater number of cells is the source of their four-point lead on a test of intelligence. There is a great deal of variation in brain volume, and no one is proposing that we use hat size as a measure of intelligence. *What this means is that we don't yet know the answer to the question of whether or not the differential size of brains makes a difference in thinking.* While this information on the cellular differences between male and female brains does not yet explain gender differences in brain function, it is interesting that there are differences even though the studies do not concur.

ANATOMY OF THE BRAIN

The brain is divided into two roughly equal hemispheres, with the right hemisphere sending and receiving information from the left side of the body and the left hemisphere sending and receiving from the

Figure 1.1   View of Left Exterior and Right Interior of Brain

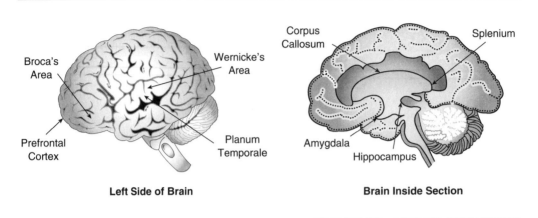

Left Side of Brain

Brain Inside Section

SOURCE: Reprinted with permission of Sanford Wintersberger.

right side. For the most part, the brain works the same for men and for women, but there are a few major areas of interest where sex differences have been found.

The *corpus callosum* contains the nerve fibers that connect the two halves of the brain. The reason this area is of interest is that, if one sex uses one side of the brain more than the other for a task, the connections between the two sides should show some difference for that sex. There are a great many studies on sex differences in the shape of the corpus callosum.

Regarding the *splenium*, the rounded back portion of the corpus callosum, one group believes that it is rounder in women and the other side is just as sure that it is not, attributing any difference to a natural variation in shape unrelated to sex (Bishop & Wahlsten, 1997; Oka et al., 1999; Witelson, 1989). The jury is still out on this one, but there probably is some difference.

The *isthmus*, which is in the front of the corpus callosum, appears to be larger among individuals who are not consistently right-handed. Additionally, among right-handed individuals, the isthmus is larger in women (Witelson, 1989). The implication is that this difference might result from the fact that men tend to use only the left side of the brain for language, while women use part of the right side in addition to the left (Hines, 2004), but there is no way of being sure.

There is general agreement that another group of connecting fibers, the *anterior commissure*, a very small bundle of connecting fibers below the corpus callosum, shows significant differences by sex, being larger in women. This might mean that, with more connections in this area between the two halves of the brain, women would be better able to use information from both sides, making more information available for decisions. On the other hand, this might make the decision process lengthier than if there were fewer connections (Kimura, 2000). This is all conjecture.

The *planum temporale* is a section found on both sides of the brain at the top of the temporal lobes. For all of us, the left side is slightly larger than the right, but for men the difference is greater and for women the two sides are more balanced (de Courten-Myers, 1999; Witelson & Kigar, 1988). We know that this area is involved with speech and it is one structure included in discussions of the source of the verbal advantage enjoyed by women. If women use both sides of their brain for language, their brains are more balanced whereas, since men use primarily the left side of their brain, the language part is larger on the left for them.

The areas called *Wernicke's area* and *Broca's area* are found on the left side of the brain, in the temporal and frontal lobes respectively. Wernicke's area is thought to be responsible for the acquisition and understanding of words, and Broca's area is thought to be responsible for grammar and the production of words. At least one study found that these regions were larger in women than in men (Harasty, Double, Halliday, Kril, & McRitchie, 1997). There is general agreement that girls acquire words faster than boys (Maccoby, 1998), so it has long been accepted that these areas involved in language and speech develop sooner in girls than in boys. Research has shown that for both 3- and 6-month-old girls, the left hemisphere shows higher response to stimuli, whereas for their male age-mates, the right hemisphere shows higher response (Shucard & Shucard, 1990), suggesting a difference in maturity rates. In addition, research using adult subjects involved in a language task found that males used their Broca's area almost exclusively, whereas females activated the Broca's area as well as the corresponding area on the right hemisphere (Shaywitz et al., 1995). Additionally, damage to the left side of the brain in men is likely to cause aphasia (disruption of language skills). However, women with similar injuries are more likely to recover language skills to some extent (Kimura, 2000). These findings demonstrate that males are lateralized for language. What that means is that men appear primarily to use their left hemisphere for language while women also use the corresponding areas on their right hemisphere. Because females have the advantage in verbal fluency, the laterality of males for the production of language has been cited as the reason that males are not as good at this skill as are females. Yes, men show laterality for language and yes, men are not as verbally fluent as women, but men have other verbal strengths, and we are not precisely sure exactly how laterality affects language development.

The *amygdala* and *hippocampus* are structures deep within the brain that show significant differences by sex. The amygdala connects sensory information with emotions, and the hippocampus is involved with making memories. Findings indicate that as children mature, the amygdala increases in size more for males and the hippocampus more for females (Giedd, Castellanos, Rajapakse, Vaituzis, & Rapoport, 1997; Yurgelun-Todd, Killgore, & Cintron, 2003). In addition, the latter study found that increases in the amygdala were associated with academic strengths in the areas of vocabulary, basic arithmetic, reading single words, and total estimated intellectual ability. Increases in the left hippocampus were associated with academic strengths in spelling, reading, and verbal intelligence, and increases in the right hippocampus were associated with academic strength in mathematical calculations.

The areas comprising the *prefrontal cortex* are at the very front of the brain, roughly behind the eyes, and are thought to mediate between emotions and decision making. This particular part of the brain continues to develop and mature through adolescence (Davies & Rose, 1999). Because girls mature sooner than boys—and this is true of brains as well as bodies—it has been inferred that earlier development of the prefrontal cortex in girls may be the source of their better self-control (Baron-Cohen, 2003; Giedd et al., 1999).

SEX DIFFERENCES IN BRAIN FUNCTION

The Senses

Differences in the senses are included in a discussion of the brain because the information from the senses—hearing, vision, touch, smell, and taste—goes to the brain. There, the sensory information is registered and the process of understanding what that information means takes place. All experiences in the classroom, in fact all experiences anywhere, enter the brain through one or more of the sense organs. There are sex differences in sensory experience, and this makes a difference in the way that educational information is best presented to boys and to girls. Later, in the discussion of each system, you will be reminded of the basics of the sensory differences.

The ear. For the most part, boys' and girls' ears are very similar, but the innermost part of the ear, the cochlea, shows significant sex differences. The cochlea is the part of the ear where sound energy is transformed into neural energy, or in other words where sound becomes a nerve signal. This structure is a fluid-filled, coiled tube

Figure 1.2   View of Structure of Ear

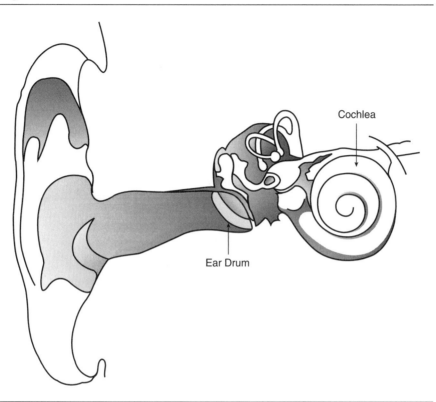

SOURCE: Reprinted with permission of Sanford Wintersberger.

with a membrane down the middle. Sound waves cause the fluid to oscillate, which in turn causes the membrane to move. From there, signals go to the brain. Very high sounds are detected by specific areas on the membrane and very low sounds by the velocity of the fluid as it moves.

The cochlea in boys is longer, and consequently boys have longer cochlear response times (Don, Ponton, Eggermont, & Masuda, 1993; McFadden, 1998). The effect of that longer response time is that it takes fractionally longer for boys to hear a sound than it does girls.

Girls' ears are more sensitive. They can hear softer sounds better than can boys (McFadden, 1998). Conversely, boys have much more tolerance for noise than do girls (Velle, 1987). Girls can hear higher sounds better than boys and their hearing is sharper (Corso, 1959). However, boys are better at sound localization. You figure out where the source of a sound is by noticing the difference in the time it takes the sound to arrive in one ear from the time it takes to arrive in the other ear. One suggestion for the reason boys are better at this skill is that male heads are bigger and so the difference in arrival times is greater, giving better information as to the source of the sound (McFadden, 1998).

Men have more profound and earlier hearing loss than do women. In addition, their losses are more likely to be in the higher frequencies, for higher pitched sounds (Nemes, 1999). This finding is complicated by the possibility that men are more likely to be exposed to louder sounds at work than are women, and it is well known that constant exposure to loud sounds leads to hearing loss. It is believed that the early male hearing loss would happen even if males were not subjected to louder sounds, but it is difficult to demonstrate that connection.

The eye. The most obvious sex difference in the structure of the eye is that the retina is thicker in men than in women. Additionally, while women have better hearing, men have better vision.

The retina is a complex organ composed not only of the rod and cone cells that react to light but also of ganglion cells that collect information from the rods and cones. The smaller or P cells, which are responsive to the longer light waves of red, pink, and orange, are more common in women, and the larger or M cells that are responsive to the shorter light waves of blue and green are more common in men. This causes the difference in retinal thickness (Sax, 2005).

Men have better visual acuity than do women (Velle, 1987). That means that men see both stationary objects and objects in motion more clearly than women do.

Color blindness is much more common in men than in women. Color blindness is a genetic trait found on the X chromosome of the sex chromosomes. Boys only need to get an affected gene from their mothers, whereas girls would need to get an affected gene from a colorblind father as well. The effect of this on boys in an academic setting will be discussed in the following chapter.

Women appear to have a higher tolerance for light, men preferring only about a half as much light as women (McGuinness, 1976). This may explain why boys prefer to watch TV in the dark. Trying to keep a balance between providing enough light for girls and lowering the light levels for boys is difficult, but if the boys complain of chronic headaches or frequently shade their eyes with their hand when they work, you may want to adjust the light levels.

Skin sensitivity. The senses included here are those of pain and tolerance for heat and cold.

Boys have a higher tolerance for pain than do girls (Fearon, McGrath, & Achat, 1996; Velle, 1987). Confounding this is the fact that boys in Western culture are taught not to show pain, but to be "big boys" and tough it out. Combine a higher pain tolerance with a predisposition to ignore pain and boys may be less aware that they have been injured and/or may not alert someone else to an injury.

If my students are any indicators, boys have a greater tolerance for cold. Some schools have a rule prohibiting the wearing of shorts in the winter months, otherwise some boys would wear them to class in all weather. Research comparing men and women on how long they could keep their hands in ice water found that men had a greater tolerance for cold than did women and reported less discomfort (Jackson, Iezzi, Gunderson, & Nagasaka, 2002).

Taste and smell. These senses are related to each other because most of what you taste you actually smell. The tongue only detects sweet, sour, bitter, salty, and savory tastes. What you experience as taste is a combination of those senses and the odor of the food, which is detected by your olfactory sensors in the nose.

For both taste and smell, women are more sensitive than are men (Velle, 1987). I'm not sure what this says about the vast numbers of male chefs, but it is probably one factor in the difficulty some parents have in getting boys to wear clean clothes. At all of the boys' boarding schools where I used to teach, dorms smell of dirty sneakers and athletic shirts and the boys don't seem to be bothered by the smell. True, we get used to sensory information through the process called adaptation. An example would occur when you have the radio going in your car as you travel. You increase the sound gradually because you become less sensitive to the sound, but if you stop the car, you will be surprised at how loud the radio is when you start the car again. Yet even when the boys have been away from the school for a while and return, they don't seem to notice the locker-room odor in the dorms. Girls attend the schools in the summer, and within a week of girls moving into a dorm the place smells noticeably better. This is not due to the application of perfume; girls care about how a place smells. The same does not seem to apply to how neatly they keep their rooms, but that is another issue altogether.

Women are more accurate in identifying tastes and smells (Velle, 1987). Every summer, the kitchen staff has to contend with the girls who complain about the way the food smells and tastes. The boys are usually baffled by this. It is not that the boys are not picky eaters—many are. But their objections usually involve foods they are not used to or foods with a certain texture that they don't like. Rarely do they complain that something smells bad although they might be reluctant to try something that looks unfamiliar (Kubberod, Ueland, Tronstad, & Risvik, 2002; Nordin, Broman, Garvill, & Nyroos, 2004).

COGNITIVE SKILLS

Cognition is the term used to describe all mental processes. It takes place in the brain, but there is controversy as to the source of cognitive differences in males and females. It is difficult to determine whether these differences are the result of differences in structure or function of the brain or are a product of society, in which case the reason that boys and girls think differently is because society says they should think a certain way. This is the nature versus nurture controversy and while there are many cognitive differences that have been identified, we are still not sure of the genesis of most of them. We don't know if they even exist or if differences are found because the researchers are predisposed to find them. Should that make a difference to teachers? Probably not. Whether boys and girls think differently because their brains are wired differently or because of societal expectations, they enter the classroom thinking differently and teachers have to cope with the differences. What we don't want to do is to exacerbate cognitive stereotypes so that boys are convinced that they can't read or girls are convinced they can't do math. What we hope to do is to understand where problems may lie and learn how to help our students overcome or at the very least cope with them.

Accepted Differences

Verbal Skills

As we have already discussed, there is a "female advantage" in verbal fluency. In response to a challenge to produce as many words beginning with a certain letter as possible in one minute, girls will do better, and will generate more synonyms when asked to do so as well (Halpern, 2000). Toddler girls may have vocabularies two times larger than those of boys of the same age (Morisset, Barnard, & Booth, 1995), but that difference does not exist in adults. Girls begin to talk before boys do and their speech is clearer, sooner. Most of girls' verbal advantage seems to be related to this early ability to use words to communicate (Kimura, 2000). Girls have the edge in spelling, although if you look at the national spelling bee, the winner is frequently a boy—probably driven by boys' attraction to competition. When memory involves words, experiences, or places, women have better recall than do men (Halpern, 2000; Kimura, 2000). It may be this early facility with words that feeds the stereotype that girls have better verbal skills, but the stereotype exists and boys will tell you that "reading is for girls" or, as the title of one book puts it, "Reading Don't Fix No Chevys" (Smith & Wilhelm, 2002).

Verbal analogies show a male advantage (Halpern, 2000). Do you remember those questions on the SAT?

Stress is to relaxation as knit is to (pick one)

   A. Crochet
   B. Unravel
   C. Sew
   D. Tangle

No one seems to have much idea as to why men are better at analogies, but one explanation lies in the information on structural differences. The belief is that women's greater neural connectivity promotes their ruminative cognitive style, leading them to think over every possibility for each answer, have a hard time making choices, and change their answers often. Men, with their more direct connections, look for the answer and move on. The girls I have taught concur with this explanation.

However, it is usually males who are diagnosed with verbal learning disabilities. Not only are men not as verbally fluent as women, but far more men than women are dysfluent (stutter). In addition, far more boys than girls are identified with dyslexia, although there is some indication that there are many girls who are unidentified (Halpern, 2000; Shaywitz, Shaywitz, Fletcher, & Escobar, 1990). Girls do much better on tests of writing skills, but the paradox is that those employed in jobs requiring writing, such as journalists or lawyers, are predominately male (Halpern, 2000). That is changing, however, as more and more women enter law and journalism schools.

One verbal skill that seems to show no male or female advantage, at least for adults, is verbal intelligence: the ability to understand and use language. In addition, adults show no difference in vocabulary knowledge (Kimura, 2000). For most areas, it appears as if by adulthood men catch up to women, although women will continue to have the edge in spelling and fluency. The problem is that by the time men have caught up to women in verbal skills, many have never acquired the habit of reading and continue to believe that their verbal skills are not at the same level as those of women.

Figure 1.3   Spatial Perception

Mental Rotation

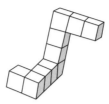

Select the two drawings below which are the same as the drawing above

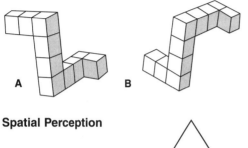

A   B   C   D

Spatial Perception

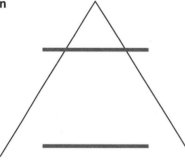

Which line is longer? Measure to be sure.

Spatial Visualization

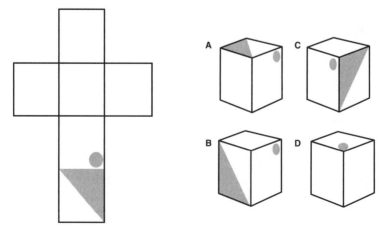

Which box would be made by folding figure on the left?

Spatial Relations

The area cited as having the strongest male advantage is that of spatial skills. There are several skills in this area, including mental rotation, spatial perception, and spatial visualization. Mental rotation is the ability to see dimensional objects in your mind and to match the original object with a picture of a rotated view of the same object. Spatial perception is the ability to locate items in space while ignoring distracting information. Spatial visualization is the ability to analyze mental manipulations of visual information requiring several steps to complete (Linn & Petersen, 1985). Males are clearly better than females at mental rotation, slightly better at spatial perception, and there seems to be no difference in spatial visualization. Males also excel at spatiotemporal tasks, where visual displays are moving—think computer games (Halpern, 2000).

Remember the study that showed that 3- and 6-month old girls had more responsive left cerebral hemispheres and boys had more responsive right hemispheres (Shucard & Shucard, 1990)? While girls use parts of both left and right language centers and boys only use their left, on spatial tasks it was found that women use only the right side while men also had some left-hemisphere involvement (Gur et al., 2000). It is thought that spatial skills involve the right hemisphere, so while the girls are gaining a verbal advantage with their more mature left hemispheres, the boys are gaining spatial-skill advantages with their more mature right hemispheres. This may also have some connection with the fact that far more males are left-handed (Halpern, 2000). If the right cerebral hemisphere is more mature and the right side of the brain is in charge of the left side of the body, then it makes sense that the left side of the body will be preferred.

Because of these spatial skills, it is not surprising that men are better at targeting or propelling an object at a specified place. One consideration is that we encourage boys to throw balls or other objects and they may simply have more practice at the skill. Even taking that into account, there is doubt that most boys are more likely to be able to hit a target with some projectile than are most girls. Boys prefer to look at moving objects, and they are also better at hitting moving targets (Halpern, 2000).

One task involving vision has a clear female advantage and that is perceptual speed. This skill involves matching objects, pictures, or designs, and has been tested using worksheets whose directions read, "On each line, circle the two pictures that are the same," or "cross out all of the words in this list that start with the letter A" (Kimura, 2000). Boys can do the problems, girls are just faster. One area in school where this skill comes in handy is in proofreading; girls are better at finding errors than are boys, and the result is that boys are less likely to check their work—it is harder for them to see the mistakes they make.

Developmental Differences

In general, girls develop earlier than boys and as you have already seen, this developmental difference extends to the brain as well as to the body. This developmental advantage begins soon after birth and continues until late adolescence or even later. If readiness to read, write, and calculate is the mark of the good student, girls are more ready for those tasks than are boys of the same age. Girls start to talk before boys (Roulstone, Loader, Northstone, Beveridge, & Team, 2002), they develop fine motor skills before boys (Berk, 1997), and they develop their hippocampi before boys—remember that the hippocampus is connected with mathematical calculations, basic arithmetic, vocabulary, and reading (Yurgelun-Todd et al., 2003). Upon entrance to school, the average girl simply is cognitively more ready for school tasks than the average boy of the same chronological age.

The areas showing the most obvious developmental differences are physical and sexual development. Girls entering puberty early may complete that phase of development before late-starting boys even begin (Berk, 1997). In an eighth-grade classroom, there may be girls who have attained their adult height and boys who will not begin their growth spurt for another year or so. These boys tend to be shorter than girls whose height they will exceed in five years or so. We will cover the problems inherent in these differences in depth in Chapter 6.

New Findings

Responses to Stress

You may remember from the last biology class you took about the stress response called "fight or flight." This is the body's response to a perceived threat, and the response is the same whether it is a threat to life and limb, such as a car accident, or whether it is a threat to one's self-esteem, such as a final exam. The theory is that our ancestors who responded in this way were ready for emergencies and survived to pass this response on to us.

Somewhat recently, the theory has been proposed that females do not react to stress with the typical fight-or-flight response. Instead, they produce behaviors designed to protect themselves, their offspring, and their social support group. This response has been named the tend-and-befriend response (Taylor et al., 2000). Theoretically, females under stress turn to each other for support and defend each other from perceived threats, and this social support helps girls manage their response to stress.

Under stress, males are more likely to stand and defend themselves or to flee the situation. The problem in the classroom is that the male response may escalate in the heat of the moment, with a small disagreement becoming a major battle, but usually only involving that student. Girls under stress may enlist the support of friends, so that what started as a discussion between teacher and student may wind up involving several girls defending their friend against the teacher. For the teacher, the difference is in magnitude of response. The male response may seem extreme, especially to a female teacher who may feel threatened by an angry middle- or high-school student defending his position. The female response may overwhelm a male teacher who is baffled as to how so many people can become involved in his discussion with one student. The more that teachers become familiar with how students are likely to react, the more probable it is that they will be able to deal appropriately with the student stress response. Methods to help children deal with academic stress and test anxiety will be covered in Chapter 4.

Brain-Based Learning

In the past decade, there has been a trend in education to develop teaching strategies based on what we know about brain function. This makes a great deal of sense since it is the brain that is doing the learning. If you are not familiar with work in this area you may want to become somewhat familiar with the main points before you continue. The reason is that what follows focuses only on sex and gender differences in the brain as they affect learning for the male brain. The information contained here is designed to be integrated into a larger instructional plan designed around brain-based learning. You will find some materials listed in Chapter 11.

2

Sensory Differences

Zits Comic Strip

SOURCE: © Zits Partnership. King Features Syndicate. Reprinted with permission.

All faculty at the boys' school where I taught were required to teach four classes, supervise a dorm, and coach two seasons a year. There was no need for another tennis coach and my other sport was field hockey, so I coached costumes and make-up for our elaborate drama productions. I spent a good deal of time trying to get the look that the director wanted. For a production of A Comedy of Errors, *the director had asked that the two sets of twins be costumed not identically, but so that it was conceivable that one could be mistaken for his brother. I decided that color was the best way to accomplish this and the director agreed. He didn't care what the colors were, just that there was a color similarity. He didn't want it obvious, but when the mistaken identities get solved, he wanted it plausible that the twins could have been mistaken for each other. I worked hard with several costume supply houses and local college drama departments to get costumes that were of the same period and of the two color schemes. At the first dress rehearsal, I was appalled to note that the lights turned one of the Dromios' (the servant twins) first-act tunic from the rust that was their theme, to red. I apologized to the director and promised him that I would get a tunic of the right color by the next night. He had no clue what I was talking about. Once I pointed out the difference, the director could see that the costume was not the right color, but neither he nor the actor considered the difference to be as great as I did. When I got a different tunic the next night, the director and actor agreed that it was the right color, but they were not bothered by the original costume.*

◆◆◆

We have no idea of how others experience the world, and we assume that everyone sees, hears, feels, tastes, and smells as we do. My brother and my son are red-green color-blind and they have problems discriminating between red and green traffic lights and deciding whether a shirt is pink or white. I know that they do not see what I see, and I still have trouble adjusting my expectations to fit their reality. The drama director is not color-blind, but he does not see the differences in colors that I do, or at the very least, the differences in color do not matter as much to him as they do to me.

The drama director is not the only male I know who cares less about color than I do. While I have run into other men who are very attuned to color, the stereotype is that men don't bother much about subtle color differences and my experience bears that out. The color combinations that the boys in my classes would come up with were sometimes rather startling—the day before Christmas vacation, one young man turned up in a pair of grass-green pants and a maroon shirt proudly announcing that he was dressed in red and green for the season. This lack of sensitivity to color differences shows up in other sensory systems as well. Because I have lived in a predominately male environment for most of my life, I am always surprised when I see children complaining that they are hurt or crying over a skinned knee. I have had students come to class even though they had broken their collarbones in a football game the day before and had them resist being sent to the infirmary because they slipped on the ice and hit their heads. I have come to the understanding that aside from the fact that boys have been taught to be stoic about pain, they really don't feel the same level of pain that I would with their injuries. Male and female sensory systems are different and they are different at birth, indicating that there is a neurobiological basis for the difference.

The differences between how girls and boys experience the world are fairly well known—some of the data on hearing differences are almost fifty years old—but only recently have educators begun to apply these differences to how they teach. Aside from having an effect on his life, the way that a boy's sensory systems work has an impact on the classroom. For example, I learned that if I didn't speak up, the boys wouldn't hear me. And, even though they looked as if they did, the punches the boys gave each other in the shoulder really didn't hurt. Vision, hearing, and touch are very important for learning, as they are major sources for information presented in the classroom. There aren't a lot of educational applications for differences in smell or taste. You should be aware that women do have more acute senses of smell than men and that the boys you teach are not likely to react as strongly to odors as girls may. There are similar responses to taste, with girls being more sensitive (Sax, 2006; Velle, 1987).

VISION

Color

There are a number of factors involved in gender differences in vision, and they do affect a child's classroom performance. Boys are more likely to be color-blind. Red/green is the most common kind of color blindness, and children with this disorder cannot tell the difference between white, pink, and pale green. Children with the rarer form, blue/yellow, will have trouble discriminating among white, pale blue, and pale yellow. It is not that the child does not see the colors, but that he cannot tell the difference among them. There is variability in this disorder. Some boys cannot tell the difference between the colors at all, while others have trouble only if the shades are similar, such as dark green and dark red looking like different shades of brown.

Not only may boys be color-blind, but they don't use color in the same way that girls do. Girls will put more color in their work than do boys (Iijima, Arisaka, Minamoto, & Arai, 2001) and are more likely to use colors to organize their work. Boys do not seem to be as aware of colors as are girls and are slower to name colors, but there is no information on whether or not girls see more colors than do boys (Kimura, 2000). The only class I taught where this was a major issue for my students was biology. For example, identification of wildflowers is partially based on color differences, and some non-color-blind students had trouble discerning between blue and lavender or between gold and yellow.

Pink v. Blue: Stereotype or Biology?

Go into any toy department and you will find the pink aisle for girls' toys and the blue aisle for boys' toys. Is this the result of social stereotyping or is there some other explanation? Recent research has found that the visual pathways in the brain do not respond in the same way for boys and girls.

The pathways more active in girls respond to warmer colors such as pink and red and respond to the shape and form of objects. The pathways more active in boys respond to cooler colors such as blue and green and respond to motion (Alexander, 2003).Toy selection is certainly influenced by this difference in responsiveness to color and to objects. Other areas that may be affected include

- *Highlighters.* Boys should use blue and green highlighters and stay away from pink ones. It is not that they don't see the pink (although if they are color-blind they won't), but pink won't necessarily attract their attention. The yellow highlighters are neutral and will attract anyone's attention, but make sure that if you have a blue/yellow color-blind student that he can see that yellow.
- *Art projects.* Boys are likely to select fewer colors and those colors are likely to be darker than colors selected by girls. In addition, the subject matter may be different, as boys like to draw objects in motion and scary subjects. It is common to find drawings of monsters in boys' books, and the gorier the better!
- *Organization.* Use primary colors to organize materials in your classroom. There will be no confusion about which color bin or sheet you are referring to if the colors are simple. If you run out of colors to use, try using stripes—you can use colored tape placed across another color to create the pattern.

Interestingly, the kinds of fluorescent lights preferred by boys and girls reflect this difference in color vision. Girls' ability to solve problems is greater in the presence of 3000K lights, which are described as a warm light—slightly pink. Boys' problem solving ability was enhanced in 4000K lights, which are cool—slightly blue. Similar results for long-term recall and mood under the two types of light were found for girls and boys (Knez, 1995).

On the other hand, boys see things in motion very well, and this may be part of the reason that they are attracted to television and video games particularly when cars are involved (Lutchmaya & Baron-Cohen, 2002). Look at video games made for boys: the colors are not bright and motion is more important than is a detailed picture

(Dwyer & Moore, 2001). Additionally, because of their lack of concern with color, boys can visually separate an object from its background more easily and ignore such characteristics as color (Maccoby & Jacklin, 1974). When I took my biology students outdoors to look for insects, I knew that they could always find bugs faster than I could. The boys were attracted by the motion of the insect and not as fooled by the camouflage as I was.

Applications for Your Classroom

- Use primary colors for organizational purposes in the classroom. The difference between a pink and a salmon piece of paper will be lost on most boys.
- Children may be overwhelmed by too many colors, and the use of simpler color coding will reduce confusion about which color is being referred to.
- If you teach in a coed situation, see if the maintenance staff can get some of both types of bulbs (3000K and 4000K). If your school has single-sex classes, try to designate certain rooms for boys and other ones for girls using the appropriate light bulbs.
- Try to move around a bit when you are talking. If you stand too still, boys are likely to shift their focus to what is moving, such as a classmate's feet or the bird outside the window. That does not mean that you should jog back and forth, just provide some visual interest to attract their attention.
- Use visual cues, especially with motion, to attract boys' attention—for instance, turning the lights on and off or raising your hand for quiet. These cues need to be very obvious, as it may be difficult for students to recognize that you have your hand up for quiet if three of their fellow classmates have their hands up trying to ask you a question. One teacher waved a small flag when she wanted everyone's attention.

CAUTION

★ The color-blind child may have trouble with color-coded signals and will need help in learning to compensate. The whole class will benefit from learning that stop signs are octagonal no matter what their color and that the red light is the one at the top. It is also a great opportunity for students to learn that not everyone experiences the world as they do.

Maps and puzzles in which color is used to delineate areas may present difficulties for many of the boys, not only those with color blindness. Learning to see differences in patterns or learning to use other visual cues will help all students.

Too little motion in the classroom may result in attention problems. If a book is dropped or someone raises a hand, some children may pay closer attention to the motion than to the message. Teach the boys how to refocus by using cues such as tapping the page they are reading to attract their own attention or reminding themselves of the task at hand to acknowledge the shift in attention and direct themselves back to their work.

Attention Getters

Loss of attention is not necessarily reserved only for children with attentional problems. All students will benefit from learning techniques to help maintain attention or to return attention to the task at hand. These suggestions will be particularly useful for older students as they become responsible for their own learning.

Tapping the page. If a student's attention is wavering, he can help maintain his attention by following the text with his finger or by tapping his finger on the page. This works because it uses the boy's affinity for movement.

Positive self-talk. Children who frequently lose attention may reprimand themselves and eventually believe that they cannot maintain attention. Make sure that children know that shifting attention is normal for all of us and that, when they do lose focus, they should simply acknowledge their loss of attention and get back to work.

Shifting tasks. The child who has a hard time reading what he thinks are long passages of material (whether they are really long or not is not the issue) will report that his eyes pass over the page, but that after several paragraphs he is not retaining much. Have this child shift to another task. This works particularly well for homework, and I recommend that the student read until his attention wanders—if that is a paragraph, so be it. Then he should move to another subject, preferably a more active one such as math. He should do several problems and then return to reading. These short bursts of attention are much more effective than trying to slog through a reading assignment all at once.

Alarm. One of the techniques used with children who have serious attentional problems is to set a timer to go off every so often and, when it does, the child is to note whether or not he is paying attention. The alarm may be a bit intrusive and you can use a small hourglass instead. Over time, the interval is lengthened, and the child learns to extend the amount of time during which he can pay attention. The intervals at first may be as short as 15 seconds, but if the child does not have serious problems, set a kitchen timer for 3 minutes. Eventually elongate the time by 10 or 15 seconds every few days until the child can pay attention for 10 minutes.

Gazing Differences

Another area of vision disparity between girls and boys involves gazing differences. In one experiment, one-day-old infants were given two different things to look at. One was a woman's face and the other was a mobile. Observers who could not see the targets and who did not know the sex of the children judged at which stimulus the infants looked the longest. It was agreed that the girls looked more at the woman's face and the boys looked more at the hanging object (Connellan, Baron-Cohen, Wheelwright, Batki, & Ahuluwalia, 2000). Since the children in this study were only a day old, it can be surmised that what these girls and boys chose to look at was due to some brain function that they came into the world with and not a behavior they had learned. In another experiment, slightly older children (one year old) were presented with videos of faces moving or of cars moving; the girls looked longer at the faces and the boys longer at the cars (Lutchmaya & Baron-Cohen, 2002). This is not news to parents of toddler boys, as the boys will grab almost any object and run it across a surface making motor noises. I've had middle-school students run a pencil across their desk as if it were a car (usually without audible motor noises), and older boys will often draw cars when they doodle. One advantage of this fascination is that if I talk about cars or use a car metaphor, I can usually get their attention.

While the boys are looking at cars, the baby girls are more likely to look at faces. They are good at reading facial expressions, an advantage that continues through adolescence (McClure, 2000). According to this study, girls are also better at nonverbal processing. What that means is that they are better able to blend information from facial expression, tone and inflection of voice, and body language with the words that are said, in order to interpret what the person means. In a classroom, girls can perceive nonverbal cues from the teacher about being quiet and staying in their seats, while boys may have more difficulty with this. While this reaction is based on sensory perception, the problem of reading faces will be addressed more fully in Chapter 6 on emotional differences.

Applications for Your Classroom

- Use direct statements when giving students information on their progress. You may know at which behavior you are smiling, but the student may misread your facial expression or miss seeing your smile or frown altogether. The boy who has just turned in a messy paper may think you don't like the paper if you frown at the mess. You need to be specific: "Your paper is great, but let us see if we can figure out a way for you to turn in neater work."
- Develop unambiguous signals to indicate approval, disapproval, and other elements of classroom management. The thumbs-up and "high five" are hand signals most children associate with doing a good job.

CAUTION

- ★ Any motion in the classroom is likely to attract attention. This can be a problem if the students are working at different tasks. Make sure that there is enough space between the various groups. You may need to arrange seating so that the other groups are less noticeable.
- ★ Some boys find it hard to sit for any length of time with all four legs of the chair on the floor. If nothing else is moving, they will, and that may mean leaning back in their chairs. Some boys' schools are equipping study areas with chairs that have a small runner projecting from the back legs, allowing the students to rock just a bit and still stay safe. It is a good compromise.

HEARING

Boys have the reputation of being loud and not listening. One reason boys have this reputation is that they have more trouble than girls do hearing higher-pitched sounds and softer sounds (Corso,

1959; McFadden, 1998; Velle, 1987). Boys are more attuned to louder and lower sounds. This may explain why adolescent males seem to play music loudly and be oblivious to the effect the noise has on the rest of the world. Boys' schools are taking notice of this finding and discovering that when teachers make an effort to ensure that all students are paying attention before directions are given, compliance is much improved. Sometimes boys just don't hear an adult asking for quiet if the adult has a soft voice.

The shape of the inner ear is not the same for boys and girls. As we have seen in the previous chapter, the female cochlea responds more quickly to sound than does the male cochlea (Don et al., 1993). That means that boys are likely to respond to aural information or questions just a bit slower than girls will. Because boys don't hear soft or high sounds very well and because they don't respond to sounds as rapidly as do girls, boys may have trouble with auditory sources of information. With the advent of campus e-mail, most schools send important messages to all students' cyber-mailboxes as well as making announcements at school assemblies. Most boys will get the message from an announcement, but some will not, and it is wise to have the information presented in two ways. Elementary schools will send notes home for the parents to read or have the parents on an e-mail message system to make sure that everyone gets all information.

If the child has a hard time hearing the teacher, he may get in the habit of not paying attention. Some research has shown that recurring ear infections in small children may affect a child's ability to hear and to acquire language (Feagans, Kipp, & Blood, 1994); boys are more likely to have such infections (Paradise et al., 1997). If a boy is not responding to spoken directions, the reason may be that he has attentional difficulties, but it may also be due to the effects of ear infections. We have all had the experience of having our ears stopped up when we drive in the mountains, are on an airplane, or have a very bad cold. We don't hear everything that is said to us and it can be frustrating. All students will be helped if the teacher makes an effort to get the boy's attention before speaking to him. Asking the class for attention and waiting to speak until all children are facing you is not enough to guarantee a boy's focus. With younger boys, I find that it may be easier to deal with small groups, as your physical closeness will improve the chances that the boy is attending. In larger groups, the boys in the back are frequently there because they find that it is not obvious to the teacher that they are not paying attention.

Applications for Your Classroom

- In your attempt to make sure that the boys in your class hear you, don't yell. Children quickly learn to tune out yelling.
- Establish classroom rules of conversation so that each child learns acceptable voice levels, turn taking, and courtesy. Acquiring an "inside voice" is useful for all children, but particularly for young boys who tend to speak loudly.
- Boys are likely to use speech to show how much they know (Baron-Cohen, 2003). Learning conversational turn taking and learning not to dominate classroom discussions will help them later.
- When you speak, make sure that you use clear pronunciation and face the children when you speak, so that what you say is unambiguous. These practices will increase the chance that boys will get your message. Try not to talk while you are facing the blackboard. Use an overhead projector or a handheld smart board so that you can write information for children to see, while allowing them to see you as you speak.
- Move the boys who do not appear to be paying attention to the front of the room. If the problem is attention, being at the front will reduce distractions, but if the problem is that the child does not hear, putting him in the front will ensure that he has a better chance to hear the teacher.
- Pay attention to how much time you give a child to answer a question. Most teachers will answer the question or give it to another child more quickly than they know. Boys need time for the question to register and for them to find the words. Ask the question, then wait; understand that staring at the floor or desk is normal and does not necessarily indicate that the student does not know the answer. You may get uncomfortable when the silence goes on too long. One strategy is to wait for a full 30 seconds for a response, then ask the student if he would like to "phone a friend" or ask a friend for help in answering. The second student should not supply the answer, but only help the original student.
- When it is important for you to get everyone's attention, make a big deal of it. Call it your "State of the Classroom" address, or hold a "press conference" encouraging the boys to ask questions. They will be amused and that will help get the point across, but don't do this too often—it is the novelty that makes this work.

CAUTION

★ Make sure that all children are looking at you before you speak to them, particularly if you are reprimanding them. Boys resent being disciplined for something they did not hear, and will think the teacher does not like them (Neall, 2002).

★ Boys may learn to dominate conversations. Listening to what others have to say is one of the keys to learning. After a student answers a question and before you acknowledge whether the answer is right or wrong, ask another student whether he thinks the original answer is correct or if he, the second student, would change the answer in any way. This works in two ways. First, the second student has to listen to what the first student says or he will not be able to evaluate the original answer. Second, this helps students understand that there is usually more than one way to respond to a question.

★ If the primary way that material is presented is lecture, some boys may not get the information. This can be a problem when giving homework assignments. Make sure that assignments, both short and long term, are either written on a portion of the white- or blackboard or posted in a prominent place in the classroom. For self-contained classrooms or long class periods, you might write a daily agenda on the whiteboard/blackboard as well. This will help the disorganized student keep on track.

TOUCH

The stereotype is that men do not touch each other. Watch any group of boys and you will see that the stereotype is not true; they are constantly touching each other. The point is that the touching takes the form of wrestling, punching, pushing, and other activities not suited to the classroom. Some touching involves elaborate rituals such as the handshakes now popular among young men. The complaint heard from many teachers, particularly those who teach in the younger grades, is that the boys fight. But if you ask them, they will tell you they are just playing.

The observation from teachers is that boys have to touch to learn and that means they touch everything in the classroom. The way that boys learn best is to manipulate their environment (Grossman & Grossman, 1994). You will recall from the description of my ninth-grade science class how the boys did the lab exercise before they learned about the topic. I now know that boys do not learn best by traditional instruction, at least not until they have an active involvement with the material under study. They may not be as sensitive to touch as girls, but touch is essential for boys to learn.

As with other senses, girls have greater sensitivity to touch than do boys (Velle, 1987). In addition, boys have higher pain thresholds than do girls and do not report a stimulus as being as painful as girls might (Lamberg, 1998). The stereotype is that men "tough it out" and don't cry, while boys try hard to "be a big boy." Because boys don't feel pain as sharply as girls might and because they are taught to hide their response to pain, boys may not alert a teacher to an injury. If a boy does not complain of pain until it is very bad, by the time he does complain the condition may be very serious. One student in a science class got a sliver of glass from a broken test tube in his finger and I found out several days later when the nurse told me. She only knew because the boy sprained the same finger in a soccer game and she found the glass when she was splinting the finger. By that time, the finger had gotten rather inflamed, but the boy claimed that it didn't hurt very much.

Applications for Your Classroom

- Get as much space as you can between desks even if that means reducing your own space. The idea is to reduce the temptation to touch each other.
- Allow for a certain amount of rough-and-tumble play and provide a safe environment. Make sure that younger boys know that they may only engage in rough-and-tumble play during free time, that it must be on the mat provided, that no more than two may wrestle at a time, and that there should be a signal if one of the participants wants to stop. Older boys will need to be supervised by your athletic staff to make sure that they are safe. There is some indication that boys who are not allowed to wrestle or roughhouse when young may be more inclined to do so when they are older, with unfortunate results (Sax, 2005).
- Provide learning opportunities that begin with manipulatives. This is easy in science and math, but will work in other subjects as well. Boys love to make maps and can make a map of a historic area, of a famous battle, or of a place in a story they are reading. Even writing is a physical activity and most boys

are more than willing to write if that gives them access to a computer.

- Teach boys how to identify serious injuries and point out the reasons why they should seek medical attention before the injury becomes more serious. This is particularly important for concussions, as even mild ones will cause some disruptions in memory for a week or so. Teach the consequences of unattended injuries. Hemingway's *The Snows of Kilimanjaro* has a wonderful discussion of gangrene that boys usually find gross—and therefore fascinating.

CAUTION

★ Some boys do not like rough-and-tumble play and may be teased if they refuse to join in. Others may be all too eager to engage in these activities and coerce other children to participate. Invite older boys to help these children learn to set their own limits. Members of a wrestling team can help boys learn to play fairly, and the boys who do not choose to participate in such activities may be helped by older students who enjoy individual sports such as swimming or track.

★ If athletics are important to a boy, he may hide injuries from his coach because he does not want to have to sit out for a while. A few boys may not even be aware that they are injured, particularly for mild concussions. The athletic department should have an education program to help boys learn to identify injuries and learn the long-term consequences of ignoring injuries.

Concussions

Because of their impulsivity and activity, it is not uncommon for boys to receive a concussion. Teachers should be notified when a student has a head injury, as the student's ability to function in class may be seriously affected.

Teachers need to be aware when a student has suffered a concussion for several reasons.

- Concussions may result in memory loss for events just before or just after the blow occurred.

(Continued)

Concussions (Continued)

- Even the most minor blow may cause damage to short-term memory for a week or so. It is not uncommon for boys not to report or even not to be aware of such injuries.
- Even if memory is not affected, persistent headaches, stiff neck, sleep disorders, and other subsequent symptoms may make study more difficult.
- More serious injuries may result in memory problems for several months.

One source estimates that in high-school football alone, as many as 20 percent of the players will receive concussions and the total number of concussions may be as many as 250,000 a year (Harmon, 1999). However, children receive head injuries on the playground, in class, and many other places as well as on the playing field. Every head injury needs to be taken seriously and, if occurring in an athletic setting, needs to be evaluated by a certified trainer or a physician (Kelly, 2001). A recent study of minor head injuries in high-school athletes revealed that even following "dings," athletes suffered impaired memory for up to six days following the injury, indicating that these "minor" injuries are very serious and an athlete should not return to a game following any head injury (Lovell, Collins, Iverson, Johnston, & Bradley, 2004).

Another problem is called the "second-impact" syndrome and is the subject of a great deal of interest. The syndrome may occur if a student receives another head injury before having recovered from the first serious injury. Even a minor second blow has resulted in death (Harmon, 1999). For this reason, if a boy has been refused permission to return to play in organized competition, he should be careful and not, for example, be taking headers in a pick-up soccer game at recess. One study found that high-school athletes with three or more prior concussions were more likely to suffer loss of consciousness during a subsequent athletic injury as well as suffering loss of memory and confusion (Collins et al., 2002). A study of professional athletes found that those with multiple concussions were more likely to be diagnosed with clinical depression (Bailes, Guskiewicz, & Marshall, 2003).

Concussions are beginning to be recognized as a serious cause of long-term head injury. Classroom teachers of boys need to be alert to the symptoms and to be supportive of the school's and the medical community's efforts to restrain those with head injuries from further damaging themselves.

LEARNING MODALITIES

Information has to come in through our senses before we can learn. If one or another of our senses is less or more sensitive, that will affect how well we acquire information through that modality. Most of us are pretty balanced, but we do have preferences as to which source of information registers best with us. When children and their teachers are aware of individual learning strengths and weaknesses, accommodations can be made to help children compensate with their strengths.

Auditory Learning

For the most part, boys are not good auditory learners. Most find it hard to pay attention when they are presented aurally with large amounts of material. Go into any large lecture hall in college and most of the students will be alert and taking notes. However, you will see students asleep, looking out of the window, doodling, daydreaming, and not paying attention; most of those students will be boys. Here are some strategies to address this problem:

- Teach boys to take verbatim notes. Writing gives them something active to do and they are more likely to pay attention. Later, they should transcribe their notes into a more compact form. Writing twice will help.
- Encourage boys to tape lectures and later transcribe the notes. The problem is that since the student is going to depend on the tape recorder, he may not pay attention in class. However it does give him the ability to play the lecture several times.
- Provide lecture notes online so that students can incorporate them into their own notes, or you can provide a copy of your lecture notes before the lecture. Some teachers like their students to have the notes before the lecture, some prefer to make sure the student gets the notes later.

Kinesthetic Learning

Most boys learn well through hands-on activities. If boys are able to manipulate the materials, they are much more likely to acquire knowledge. One of the reasons that math and science are easier for boys is that these disciplines lend themselves to hands-on learning. If this is a strength, there are several practices that students can apply to other disciplines to make studying them more kinesthetic. You will find many more examples in Chapter 9.

- Have students outline a chapter before the class when it will be discussed. Then, in class, have the student annotate the outline from class notes. Since he wrote the outline, he is now familiar with the material, and annotating it will provide another level of manipulation.
- Have students act out portions of plays or historical events. Each student should become an expert on his character and this will help the student understand how the person fits into the story.
- Have students keep interactive notebooks where one side is text and the other side includes visuals created by the students. Students take notes, cut out or draw pictures, paste in information from other sources, and arrange the material so that it suits their learning needs. Using binders will provide space for including material provided by the teacher. These work for all modes of learning because they can be individualized to each student.

Visual Learning

Boys tend to acquire information easily through visual methods, particularly if the information involves pictures and graphs rather than words. Visual/verbal learning is distinctly different from visual/iconic learning and boys are better at the iconic style. I have had many boys come up after a test to tell me they couldn't remember some fact, but they knew that it was on the left-hand page at the bottom and there was a picture they could recall there as well.

- Teach boys to outline their notes, especially using mind maps or other nonlinear forms of arranging information. The visual learner finds it easier to remember material if it is arranged in a graphic way. This also applies to making time lines and family trees in history or a storyboard for a novel.
- Some boys will underline or highlight most assigned reading material. Teach the students underlining or highlighting techniques so that when they go back for review, the most salient material stands out.

- Diagramming sentences is a classic method to teach the fine points of grammar, particularly for the iconic learner. This method can also be extended to helping students understand the structure of a paragraph or an essay and has the advantage of being a kinesthetic experience as well as providing a visual learning opportunity.

SENSORY DIFFERENCES AND LEARNING

Boys have good vision for objects, specifically objects in motion. Boys hear less well and less quickly. Boys are not particularly sensitive to touch or pain, which is why their play may be a bit rough, but touch is a major source of information. The teacher who utilizes this information will offer a learning environment that

- Provides enough visual stimulation to keep boys attentive, but not so much that it interferes with the learning process
- Provides prompts and cues for information that is presented aurally and helps boys learn to compensate for learning weaknesses in this area
- Provides manipulative learning opportunities and helps boys learn to adapt study practices into hands-on experiences

3

Physical Differences

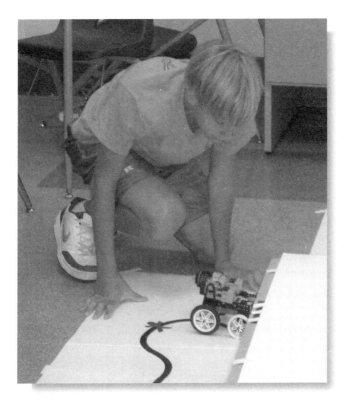

Boys don't drop things into a trash can if they can possibly help it. Instead, they will take aim and throw the object at the trash can as if they were taking a free throw with a basketball. This inclination is also seen in their need to direct all sorts of objects at targets, including developing alternative golf courses for "tolf" or Frisbee. Every spring at the boys' schools where I taught, as soon as the mild weather appeared, so did pieces of tape on trees, stop signs, and other permanent fixtures around the campus. These represented the "holes" of alternative golf courses. The designers of these courses had even decided what was par for that hole and that particular form of play, and informal contests were held for the school championship. Some boys preferred to hit tennis balls with golf clubs—tolf—and others threw Frisbees at the targets. What fascinated me about this was that most of these boys were already playing conventional golf, lacrosse, baseball, or tennis on school teams. They simply could not get enough target practice.

When boys in cartoons such as *Dennis the Menace* and *Family Circus* get into trouble for throwing things at people, the cartoonist is referring to the targeting ability common to boys. Boys do not specifically choose people as targets, but they like to throw and people make great targets because they move and because they react when they are hit. In class, if a boy asks to borrow a pencil, the donor will toss it to him even if the boys are sitting at adjoining desks. Not only do the boys like to throw things, they seem to enjoy games involving propelling their bodies and/or objects forward (Beneson, Liroff, Pascal, & Della Cioppa, 1997), which may put them in harm's way. Because boys like to propel objects as well as themselves, their activity levels may make them more visible and catch the teacher's attention.

Targeting is simply one of many physical skills that show a difference between boys and girls. Most courses in development will mention that there may be a noticeable difference in physical development between girls and boys, but may not connect that difference to the child's classroom performance. In seventh grade, for example, there may be girls who have almost completed pubertal development and boys who have yet to begin. That difference in physical development mirrors a difference in emotional and cognitive development, meaning that children of the same age in the same classroom may have entirely different ways of thinking. The difference is most obvious between early-developing girls who are thinking about boys and dating and late-developing boys who are still playing with Legos. The teacher who understands those differences, and differentiates instruction, will ensure that all students are learning.

If you pay attention to the physical interests and capabilities of children, sex differences are noticeable when children are babies. Boys and girls have different activity levels, different muscular abilities, and different growth patterns. These differences have a tremendous impact on the classroom, especially since a child has no control over whether he is the biggest, the clumsiest, the smallest, the fastest, or even the most accurate in throwing a ball.

ACTIVITY LEVELS

The activity level of boys is the stuff of legend. Most people who work with very young children have stories of boys who climbed on roofs, dug enormous holes to the center of the earth, or ran at top speed around the school building five times and asked to do it again. In fact, the activity level of boys and girls up to age 2 shows little difference and is related more to the amount of space available for movement than to sex. Boys are more likely to be encouraged to be physically active, and the high activity level we associate with boys may be partially the result of their response to the expectation by adults that they will be very active (Maccoby, 1998).

Starting around ages 2 to 4 and lasting at least until age 10 and perhaps later, boys may be more active than girls as a result of higher basic metabolism (Goran et al., 1998; Maccoby, 1998). In addition, some of what is generally seen as activity on the part of boys is actually the result of aggression, and we have long known that boys show more aggression than do girls (Halpern, 2000; Maccoby & Jacklin, 1974). It is the aggressive and competitive nature of boys that creates problems in the schoolroom, but giving them plenty of opportunity to be active will allow them to use their energy positively (Neall, 2002). A key for teachers of boys is learning to redirect the boundless enthusiasm that boys have for some parts of school and keep them on task for parts they like less. Sports metaphors abound for teaching almost every subject, from vocabulary relay races to mathematic Olympics. As a science teacher, I make good use of gory topics such as blood-typing and explosive experiences such as water-propelled rockets to tap my students' interests in these areas.

On the other hand, don't forget the boys whose behavior appears less active, who may feel out of place with their same-sex peers and may be subjected to teasing. When working with boys, it is easy to assume that all boys are active and take risks; we may forget that some boys are not that way. Within each gender, a wide variety of behaviors is considered normal. For example, my auditory skills are much more like those of a boy and I have to be careful to take good notes in class as I have a hard time remembering what I hear. Just because one of my skills is not typically feminine does not mean that all of my skills are not like those of most girls. The same differences will be true for most boys. Remember, the information included here describes what is typical for most boys, but not necessarily for all, and some of the suggestions will help the girls in your classes.

Applications for Your Classroom

- Incorporate movement into daily classroom lessons by having areas of the classroom designated for different activities, such as the science center, the reading nook, and the art area. All children need to move frequently, and being able to go to different sites in the classroom helps the fidgety boy.
- Teachers of boys recommend letting boys through the second grade stand in class if they would like to. This uses the fight-or-flight response described in Chapter 1, and research has shown that boys may actually learn better standing than sitting (Sax, 2006). In addition, they are much less fidgety and you will find that they can pay attention much better.
- Provide active and less active choices for completion of projects. Some children may be more comfortable sitting quietly and working alone or with another child to draw a picture or make a poster. Other children would rather make a model or draw one on the computer using animation techniques. This will give the boy who is happier sitting quietly a choice.
- Provide regular unstructured outdoor activity time for all children. Very small children need several, shorter recess periods per day and boys who have been encouraged to be active need vigorous exercise to be able to manage a more controlled classroom environment.
- Structure activities to include all children, so that the inactive, easily distracted, and physically challenged have the chance to be engaged in physical activities. This is particularly true for boys who have poor hand-eye coordination and cannot catch or hit a ball. One boy with hand-eye coordination problems was

very good at tap dancing, and his classmates were astounded to discover how that skill helped him succeed in soccer.

- For young children, use language-based, cooperative games such as Simon Says, Duck-Duck-Goose, and The Farmer in the Dell. Another game is to have the students stand in a circle. One child says a word and throws a sponge ball to another child in the circle. When that child catches the ball, he then has to say a word that rhymes with the first word. If he can't think of one, he is out. Using physical activities, especially those involving propulsion, will engage boys in learning areas that stereotypes suggest they may be less interested in. In Chapter 9, we will see how tying language to action will help boys acquire language skills.

CAUTION

★ No matter how well you structure the activity, there will be some boys who will find it difficult to moderate their behavior. Don't be surprised, plan for it. Be very clear about what behavior is not acceptable and what the consequences will be for unacceptable behavior.

★ Not all boys are active, and those who are quieter may be subjected to teasing or bullying. This can be a great opportunity for younger students to practice social skills with fellow classmates and for older students to examine how society deals with those who are different.

GROSS MOTOR DEVELOPMENT V. FINE MOTOR DEVELOPMENT

Boys develop gross motor skills before they work on fine motor skills. They are much happier running, jumping, throwing, shoving, and so forth, and may have trouble with learning to tie their shoelaces or buttoning small buttons. Some believe that this difference is created by social expectations and that boys can succeed at tasks requiring fine motor skills as long as the tasks are tailored to their interests (Berk, 1997). Another consideration is that boys are more comfortable using their gross motor skills because their activity level makes the control necessary for fine motor work difficult. Boys need to work on their fine motor skills, but if these are tried too early, failure may lead to ridicule and reluctance to try again. Even among boys, there may be wide differences in rates of mastery.

Applications for Your Classroom

- Break skills into smaller bits and have all children involved. Hopping repeatedly is hard because it is difficult to coordinate the feet, but hopping once is not so difficult. The boys will think it is funny to hop once, but missing one hop is not as noticeable as being unable to hop across the room. Some boys may have problems with the skill, others may have problems with control. All students have advantages and disadvantages, so any failure is not as obvious. This works equally well with more advanced skills such as catching a ball or coloring within the lines.
- If a skill is easy for some children and hard for others, don't make the next step harder, make it more interesting until all have mastered the skill. Boys may prefer to color geometric designs. Start with large, easy-to-manage designs that are easier to work with than the little spaces that occur in pictures. As boys get better at the skill, give them more colors to work with until everyone is ready to move on to harder designs. This gives all students adequate practice and time to master the skill.

CAUTION

- ★ Some boys may not be interested in trying activities involving fine muscles. One way to help them is to provide larger manipulatives. While they may have trouble tying a shoelace, they may have better success with yarn. Have all children make red yarn bows for Christmas decorations for the classroom. Even boys over three years old may be more comfortable with Duplo blocks than with Lego blocks for a while, so make sure there is a variety of sizes available.
- ★ Boys may look at small motor skills as not masculine. Invite fathers whose jobs involve these skills in to demonstrate and to serve as role models. The boys may be surprised at the fine motor skills involved in repairing cars, wiring a house, or performing microsurgery.
- ★ In early elementary school, you can make fine motor activities (art, using scissors, writing) more appealing by encouraging

choices that boys might find more interesting. One teacher had her students measure out the length of a blue whale along the corridor outside their classroom. On the wall, the students made signs and posted them showing the location of the head, the blow hole, the flukes, and so forth. Then each child made a collage from pictures of whales, other sea creatures, and even small shells that the teacher collected for them during the summer.

TARGETING

Considering their activity levels, the need to exercise the large muscle groups, and their targeting skills, it is easy to see why many boys become interested in sports. They are already wrestling and throwing projectiles, so they might as well engage in those behaviors in a socially approved activity. Sports can become a major center of many boys' lives in middle school because of their need for peer approval, competitive activities, and social structure, but don't forget that there are boys for whom sports can be a real irritant. They should not be made to think that they are weird or different because they do not like sports.

Applications for Your Classroom

- If the boys are going to throw paper wads at the trash can instead of dropping the paper in, get one of the trash can tops that look like a basketball backboard and net. I've never done that, but I have many colleagues (all men) who have. You can have a small wipe board over the trash can. Each time a boy misses the can, he has to write his name on the board as he picks up the paper. Once he has missed three times in whatever period you think appropriate, he is "out" and has to drop waste paper into the can for the next "half" or class period.
- There are many excellent lab exercises for physical science and physics that make use of targeting skills in ways boys

(Continued)

(Continued)

will find fun and engaging. My son still remembers the tre-buchet that he and several of his classmates built for a European history class. Not only did they have to research the design and construction, they had to produce scale draw-ings, build the machine out of scrap lumber, and successfully fling a five-pound weight at a target. Even though the machine broke the second time they used it (there is an inherent flaw in the design of trebuchets, which is why cata-pults were developed), the information acquired and the skills developed stick with him today.

CAUTION

★ The boy with poor targeting skills or lack of interest in target-ing may be treated with some disrespect by his classmates. Protecting him will not help. The solution is to help him find his own strengths. Older boys who have similar skill deficits may work well as role models.

★ The boy with very good targeting skills may become over-involved with throwing things to the detriment of nearby windows, automobiles, and humans. Help this student find proper outlets for his skills and encourage practice to improve his aim. You can also provide missiles that are less likely to produce damage, such as foam balls. Establish appropriate limits early for such behavior. Once the boys know the limits, it will be much easier to make sure that tar-geting skills are used in appropriate locations.

HANDEDNESS AND DEXTERITY

Most boys do not develop dexterity early and are less likely to choose activites that involve small pieces, such as doing puzzles, and/or require control, such as coloring neatly. There is a concern that the difference in dexterity between boys and girls is an artifi-cial one created by social pressure and by a difference in hand size. The standard test of dexterity is to move pegs rapidly on a peg-board. In one study, men and women were given tweezers to move small pegs. No difference in speed was found, demonstrating that the difference in dexterity is an artifact of the test and not a difference in ability (Peters & Campagnaro, 1996). Other studies found that even when finger size was accounted for, women were more dexterous than men (Hall & Kimura, 1995). This is another case where research does not agree, but for the teacher it should not create any problems. If boys believe that they are not dexterous, whether their belief is based on social stigma or physical limitations will not change their behavior or their attitudes. The real problem will be for the boy who is dexterous, as his peers may see his ability as not masculine.

Young children may not have determined which hand they find more comfortable to use and, at the beginning, may write with either hand. This is particularly true for children who will be left-handed, as they will use their right hand in imitation of the teacher and their peers, but use their left for tasks that are not school related. Boys are more likely than girls to be left-handed, or to show no consistent preference for either hand (de Agostini, Paré, Goudot, & Dellatolas, 1992). Most of these children with inconsistent hand choice will eventually settle on writing with their right hand, simply because most people use their right hands (Berk, 1997).

Handwriting becomes a major issue in elementary school because it involves several different skills. The child has to be dexterous enough to hold a pencil in an appropriate grip, and not all can do it correctly at first. Children at this age have been using crayons and markers for some time, but a proper grip is not necessary to be effective with them. Some children may have a lot of trouble in grasping pencils in a way that will not tire them out. Part of this may be due to their incomplete mastery of fine motor skills and part may be due to dysgraphia, a description of which can be found in Chapter 5. Some states do not identify dysgraphia as a learning disability. If this is the case in your state, you can use the suggestions you will find in Chapter 5 to help these students.

Boys may also not expect to have good handwriting. Boys believe that girls' handwriting is neater, smaller, and looks like the result of greater effort. Girls believe that boys' handwriting is messier, larger, and has more spelling errors (Hartley, 1991). Children are likely to live up to expectations, and boys may think that bad handwriting is normal for them. Research shows that children with bad handwriting also have poor writing skills. When students received handwriting instruction, the quality of their writing improved (Graham, Berninger, Weintraub, & Schafer, 1998; Hartley, 1991). So practice is necessary.

- The old-fashioned writing exercises—for example, making loops and circles over and over—may seem boring, so make a game of it. These exercises will help develop handwriting fluency.
- Have all children use their hands to practice writing in the air. This way they can get the shape of letters using their gross motor groups. Use hand flexibility exercises to loosen up hands and arms before working with handwriting. These can be a lot of fun and will help students gain fine motor control. Use balls designed for rehabilitation of the hand to help boys develop muscle strength and control.
- For all students, include daily handwriting practice where neatness counts. Include handwriting in rubrics for other subjects, like social studies. Good handwriting on a paragraph assignment should count for a few points, but not so many that a student's overall grade could be hurt. Boys need to see that there is an advantage to trying to be neat. It is important to grade on improvement, not comparison to other students. You will find a sample rubric in Chapter 11.
- To teach a left-hander to write, sit in front of the child and have the child mirror what you do. Some left-handed children insist on turning their hands around so that their left hand is on the right side of the pencil. This is tiring, and helping children get a proper grip from the beginning will be a great help in the future.
- Send children to the black- or whiteboard to do work. Writing on those surfaces requires larger muscle groups, and restless boys benefit from getting out of their seats. Mastering the skill with large muscles will help boys master the same skill with fine muscles.

CAUTION

★ Boys may believe that they are entitled to bad handwriting or that good handwriting is not masculine. If the expectation is that all children have the same level of neatness, the child who is unable to reach that goal may simply stop trying and the teacher may stop expecting neatness. Make sure that each child understands what level of work you expect, and continue to provide practice and encouragement to improve.

★ Boys may avoid writing exercises. Boys from boys' schools like writing more and end up majoring in subjects requiring writing more than boys from coed schools (James & Richards, 2003). When boys are not embarrassed by the way their papers look, they are likely to write more. I had a student in a ninth-grade science class turn in a lab report and apologize for the messiness. The paper looked pretty typical for a fourteen-year-old boy and so I told him, "this is messy for girls but not for boys." He gave me a brilliant smile. His next lab report was no neater, but it was longer.

★ Left-handed boys are likely to have more trouble mastering handwriting because they have the additional problem of handedness. My young left-handed students who have trouble writing have difficulty completing their written school-work. Giving them extra time may help as well.

★ Do not require a child to use only one hand if he seems to do equally well with both. Forcing the child to choose too early may confuse him.

★ Do not let children get the impression that it is somehow wrong to be left-handed. True, most of the world is right-handed, and the teacher needs to help the left-handed child learn to manage schoolwork. Many left-handed people are successful in a wide variety of fields, and learning about them will help all children appreciate the benefits of doing things a different way.

GROWTH PATTERNS

We have already noted that toddlers do not look much different in size, but once students get near the onset of puberty, growth difference are very apparent. If the only pubertal difference were height, it would still create problems for boys in a culture where men are supposed to be physically larger and stronger than women. Height difference is simply one indication of the huge differences between girls and boys in middle school. For girls, the average age for onset of the height spurt is 10, and the average age at which they reach their adult height is 13. Contrast that with the statistics for boys, for whom the average height spurt begins at 12½ and adult height is reached at 15½ (Berk, 1997; Faust, 1977). Girls have almost finished their growth before the boys begin. The age at which children enter puberty has tremendous impact on their success in school; late-maturing girls and early-maturing boys are the most successful (Caspi, 1995; Dubas, Graber, & Petersen, 1991). Emotional problems associated with pubertal development will be addressed in Chapter 6.

Applications for Your Classroom

- Be careful about making the height differences between boys and girls too obvious. Middle-school dances are particularly risky situations, as shorter boys may refuse to participate because they are afraid of being rejected by the taller girls. Parties where games are the central activity may be more successful at this stage. For example, invite students to a card party and have available a lot of board games and cards. Give them time limits and make children change games every so often. Poker is very popular and has the advantage of giving children practice in dealing with probabilities. They can bet with chips and turn in their winnings for pencils, pizza, or a homework pass.
- Encourage physical activities where height is not a major factor. Soccer is popular because even though the taller boy may be able to cover more ground with his longer legs, the shorter boy may be able to change directions more rapidly, essential in good defense. Although we usually think of basketball players as being very tall, some successful professional players have been less than six feet. The boy with good basketball skills but modest height may benefit from learning about those players and about coaches as well.

CAUTION

- ★ Boys who are physically large for their age may actually not be very strong. Do what you can to help these boys remain in activities that are appropriate for their age and not for their size. Few ninth-grade boys have the physical stamina and strength to play varsity level football and basketball. Remind the boys that professional football players are not drafted out of high school and the few basketball players who were drafted early have generally not done well the first years of their professional careers.
- ★ Boys who are physically small for their age may engage in risky behaviors to prove themselves. If you believe that you know of such a case, alert the school counselor and/or the

boy's coach so that they may guide the boy into physical endeavors that are difficult but appropriate.

★ Physical development has a great deal more to do with the classroom than just which size of desk is provided. While boys are going through their growth spurts, they frequently become clumsy. We know that it takes a while for our brains to adjust to our body sizes as we grow and boys undergoing rapid height changes may take a while before they can move smoothly. The amount of glass breakage in my ninth-grade science class is testament to the fact that boys will stumble over their feet just walking across the room. In my classes, we call it "tripping on a pile of air," but the boys are comforted by the knowledge that the seniors don't do that and they will grow out of it also.

PHYSICAL DIFFERENCES AND LEARNING

Boys are slower to mature physically. They develop gross motor skills before fine motor skills, may be less dexterous, and are more likely to be left-handed, but they have good targeting skills. The later maturation of the brains and nervous systems of boys, together with lowered hearing responsiveness, may make them likelier to be identified with attentional problems. The teacher who utilizes this information will offer a learning environment that

- Provides instruction in active learning strategies, and structures class exercises so that students are offered a variety of approaches
- Provides opportunities for activities where more active boys can get plenty of exercise, while less active boys will still feel comfortable participating
- Provides practice in developing fine motor skills, especially with respect to handwriting, and ensures that all students are familiar with the level of proficiency expected of them

4

Cognitive Differences

SOURCE: Photographer Daniel Grogan, Grogan Photography. Used with permission.

In our area, one of the broadcasting stations sponsors an academic tournament each year pitting the best students from each school against each other in answering questions on a wide variety of subjects. One year we had a particularly skilled group composed of a math whiz, a musician with lots of knowledge about a wide variety of the arts, a science geek, and a history enthusiast. The whole school got academic tournament fever and an intramural competition sprang up with both student and faculty teams. At the end of the season, our team won for our area and was set to compete with winners from adjoining areas for the championship. To prepare for the final competition, the "varsity" team was going to compete publicly against the winner of the intramural competition. Much to the boys' surprise, the intramural winners were the team composed of four female faculty including two English teachers, the school librarian, and a science teacher (me). The whole school turned out, as the boys' reputation was on the line. We faculty could not beat the boys to the buzzer—we simply were not that quick—but our larger knowledge of academic trivia and one teacher's ability to spell any word kept us in the game. Finally we lost (but not by much), because we lacked knowledge in physics and sports. What was fascinating was the feeling of the boys that they were going to win because men are supposed to be masters of trivia.

◆◆◆

If you have taught boys, you know that frequently they will begin a conversation with, "Did you know that . . . ?" Boys are walking compendia of information on whatever topic they are interested in. Not infrequently the topic is sports, and most boys (and men) can have long discussions of the relative merits of one team over another or of the lifetime records of one player. Other boys can speak knowledgeably of cars, types and habitats of dinosaurs, minutiae of military history, and the like. While girls get better grades in school, boys consistently show that they can report more facts (Ackerman, Bowen, Beier, & Kanfer, 2001; Evans, Schweingruber, & Stevenson, 2002; Wilberg & Lynn, 1999).

Up to this point, all the differences we have discussed have some tie to physical differences between the sexes or to differences in the brains of males and females. Now, we move into the area of gender differences. Previously we explored the female verbal advantage, which is probably brain based. It would seem logical that girls would be better at recalling verbal information, but no, boys are clearly better at fact recall. What is more interesting is that this seems to be true across cultures, as the studies cited above found that males in all twenty-nine countries where the research was conducted had better recall of factual knowledge in various subjects. Still, there is no evidence to determine whether this is due to cultural expectations or to differences in brain function.

If we are not sure of the genesis of these cognitive differences between boys and girls, what is the best way for teachers to deal with these issues? Should we simply accept these differences as inevitable? Or should we assume that these differences are learned—and therefore, as teachers, we can and should help children learn more egalitarian behavior? Don't forget that some of the gender differences have connections to sex differences. For example, in elementary school, most boys do not make the same progress in reading as their female age-mates, probably due to differential rates of brain maturity. Boys may get the impression that this is a permanent state. Consequently, early in school, many boys decide that reading is not for them and, if they find nothing later in school to change their minds, never acquire the habit of reading. What started out as a sex difference becomes a gender difference because of the early advantage that girls have in reading. True, many boys have trouble in the beginning stages of acquiring fluent reading abilities, but many men are very capable readers—they catch up. Whether or not we believe that cognitive differences between males and females are due to nature or nurture, the important point is to keep boys in the game and excited about school.

VERBAL AND LANGUAGE SKILLS

The female advantage in verbal fluency has been extensively covered in Chapter 1, but that chapter simply outlined sex differences and offered no suggestions to help boys cope with their disadvantages in this area. One of the most important points to be aware of is that there are many different facets to verbal skills. As we have already mentioned, girls are better at some skills, boys are better at others, and for some skills there is no discernible difference.

Knowledge Recall and Memory

As we have already seen, boys are better at remembering geography facts (Henrie, Aron, Nelson, & Poole, 1997), facts in science (Halpern, 2000), and facts in general knowledge (Ackerman et al., 2001; Lynn & Irwing, 2002). This superiority is evident in both verbal and written tests of information. The majority of students who are members of academic teams are males, as are the majority of Jeopardy winners and winners of the National Geography Bee. The overabundance of men in those competitive areas is partially a result of males' competitive nature and quicker reaction times with the buzzer, but it is also a result of their ability to recall disconnected facts.

Just because boys remember facts does not mean their memories are better overall. On other kinds of memory tasks girls are better, especially if the task involves words; they also do better in recalling objects they have seen as well as the position of those objects (Halpern, 2000; Kimura, 2000). That is very interesting considering that boys are better at mental tasks that involve spatial relationships. One theory is that girls give names to objects or to their locations, and they are actually remembering the names. Girls are better at episodic memory, at remembering the details of events, and they remember events from earlier in their lives than do boys (Davis, 1999; Herlitz, Airaksien, & Nordstrom, 1999). One theory for the development of these different types of memory is based on the hunter-gatherer model. Women needed to remember where berries were last year and how to get to that place, whereas men needed to know how best to hunt a particular animal, but since the animals changed places they did not need to remember where they found that animal the last time they got one (Geary, 1998).

As school success depends more and more on competence on tests, girls begin to move to the head of the class because of their ability to remember what the teacher says, what they read, and events in class. Boys may be able to recall the facts of a story, but find it harder to describe the theme of a novel or the social implications of the Revolutionary War. Not infrequently a teacher may believe that a boy did not read the assignment, since he can't answer questions that another member of the class finds easy. The boy becomes frustrated when factual recall is not the skill demanded. I've had students tell me that the reason they like science and math is that those courses tend to be fact based and that, while they like to read and write, they don't understand what the English or social studies teacher is asking them about reading assignments.

Applications for Your Classroom

- Each child should have a book in which to write down assignments. Make sure that you post all assignments either on the black-/whiteboard or on the bulletin board. Some younger boys may need to have their parents check their assignment books every day and sign off on them. For long-term assignments, have interim goals or checks to make sure that students are working consistently.
- When you are quizzing the class on material they have learned, assign each child a number and pull numbers randomly out of

a hat to see who gets the next question. This will help prevent the problem of some boys monopolizing class time and others hiding in the back.

- Give boys practice in finding the "forest" instead of the "trees." Give the students a paragraph and have them find all the verbs in the passage. Have the students examine the verbs to see how the writer uses them to convey the meaning of the paragraph. Then have them write a different paragraph using the same verbs in the same order, but with a different story and outcome. In biology, have the class describe the function of a cell in the liver and a cell in the lung. Then ask them to write essays showing how those cells depend on each other for survival.

- Read a paragraph about some incident to the students and then have them write down what they remember from the passage. Younger children might draw a picture about the story. This exercise helps with both memory and attention.

- When a student shares factoids with the class, make sure that he knows the source and can check it. This will help him learn to recognize urban myths.

- Require all students to memorize poems, short pieces from literature, or famous speeches. You can have a speech day, when all students stand in front of the class and recite. Fear of speaking before others is the most common phobia of Americans, and one way to help children learn to face that fear is to have them recite before a small, well-known group like their classmates. Memory is like any skill and it benefits from practice.

- Help boys develop ways to read and study with pencils in their hands. Most boys have little trouble with math—not because they inherently like math, but because they have problems to do and the act of writing helps keep them focused. Underlining and highlighting are not active learning techniques unless they are done actively. Have the student stop at the end of each paragraph in a text, lift his eyes from the page and ask himself what the essential part or the key information was in that paragraph. Then have him underline, highlight, or write in the margin just the words involved with that information and not the entire sentence where that information can be found. The idea is that when the student reviews, those terms will jump off the page and he should then be able to ask himself what those words

(Continued)

(Continued)

mean or why they are important. If your students are not allowed to write in their books, use sticky notes.

- Play memory games such as Concentration to help children expand their memory capacity.

CAUTION

★ Boys may begin to believe that knowing lots of facts is the same as understanding the material. This usually becomes a problem around middle school, when knowing why or how something happened may be more important than knowing what happened. Once a child can recite a fact, ask him how he knows that fact or where that fact fits in the larger picture.

★ The boy who thinks that he never gets a chance to answer believes that the teacher does not like him, and will not work for that teacher. The best way is to devise a system that all students agree is fair for calling on students.

★ In coed classes, it is well established that teachers call on boys more than girls (Sadker & Sadker, 1994). Attempts at correcting behavior account for some of the disparity, but many times the teacher simply calls on the boys before they blurt out the answer. Don't let yourself fall into this pattern. It may give the boys and certainly gives the girls the impression that boys are more important. In a class of all boys, this is less of a problem, partially because the boys police each other and partially because they don't need to show off.

Verbal Fluency and Reading

Boys are not as verbally fluent as girls, who can produce more words that start with a certain letter in a specific time (Halpern, 2000; Kimura, 2000). This may well be connected to the larger language center in the female brain that we referred to in Chapter 1. Girls begin speaking before boys, speak more clearly, and speak more often to adults. Advantages in the areas of spelling and grammar will continue into adulthood for girls (Kimura, 2000). Most important, all of these skills combine to help girls become better readers, an edge they keep through high school (Hall & Coles, 1997; Pottorff, Phelps-Zientarski, & Skovera, 1996). The foundation for a lifelong habit of reading is laid in elementary school, and boys seem to be getting the idea that reading is for girls (Langerman, 1990; Scieszka, 2003; Smith & Wilhelm, 2002).

One of the problems at this age is that many of the books are written for girls, and boys won't read them. One man, reporting on a student of his acquaintance who attended an elite private school in the United States, described the problem the boy was having in his third-grade reading group. The upper-level group, with eight girls and four boys, was reading *My Hundred Dresses*, a book about a poor girl who claims to have many dresses, but all the dresses are pictures. The boy's previous enthusiasm for reading waned because he was simply not interested in the story. The point is that care is needed to pick books that both boys and girls will enjoy (Stephen, 1998). *Reading Don't Fix No Chevys,* by Smith and Wilhelm (2002), is a thoughtful and careful examination of the problem of encouraging all sorts of boys to become active readers. Jon Scieszka, author of *The Stinky Cheese Man, Time Warp Trio,* and other books favored by young boys, has a Web site (www.guyread .com) devoted to encouraging boys to read. It contains lists of books boys will find interesting and provides a monthly newsletter. Classic adventure novels such as *Treasure Island* will appeal to some boys. A list of recommended books will be found in the Resource section at the end of the book. This list is not exhaustive, but may give teachers a place to start when looking for books that appeal to boys.

Applications for Your Classroom

- Make reading an important part of the school day.
- For younger children, read to them even if it is a book they can read. Hearing the words will help the students develop fluency.
- Have a silent reading period several times a week, when teacher and students alike take out a book of their choice and read for about fifteen minutes. DEAR—Drop Everything And Read—is quite popular in many K–6 schools. Students are allowed to find comfortable places to read (not just their desks), and afterward they discuss what they are reading.
- Have a reading competition. When students complete books not assigned for schoolwork, they can fill out a card with information about the book and a short description of their favorite character or moment in the book. The student with the most books read at the end of the year may be awarded a prize. If others in your school will participate, the competition

(Continued)

(Continued)

can be among classes and the winners can have a pizza party or similar reward. In Chapter 6, we will discuss how to use competition to get boys engaged in school.

- Boys will be more willing to read if the book is one they are interested in. Research shows that boys prefer books that are about real events (or seem as if they were) or scary or violent events (Collins-Standley, Gan, Yu, & Zillman, 1996; Langerman, 1990; Murphy, 2001). The success of the Harry Potter series has meant that adults have tried to find clones of that genre, but boys will read lots of other books as well.

- Boys will read when they feel comfortable with the material. Boys who won't read books will read *Sports Illustrated* or *Popular Science* from cover to cover. You will also find that many boys are comfortable reading material accessed through the Internet. The best help is for boys to be read to when they are very little. This is great for all children, but boys learn to sustain attention when they are read to and they get in the habit of reading before their skills are good enough for them to read to themselves. My son was a slow reader and we read to him nightly until he was twelve. It was at that point that he found a book he was interested in (a Harry Potter, of course) and began to inhale books. One of the biggest complaints his high school made was that he read novels all the time instead of his textbooks. I believe that another factor in my son's reading improvement was that he was in an all-boys' middle school and was surrounded by male peers who were reading.

- If writing is a problem, have children do short, practical writing assignments such as thank-you notes, letters to their grandparents, or a description of their pet. They may be more willing to write if the topic is something that interests them, such as a description of their favorite car, or something they find funny, such as what might happen if they were principal for a day.

- Encourage all sorts of reading. Some boys like graphic novels, which look more like comic books. These may not be appropriate for young boys, nor will the graphic books created to go with Japanese anime.[1] If you want the students to get information from the newspaper, boys may be more interested in reading the sports page or accessing the Web site for the newspaper.

- Teach children to outline before they write. This will help keep the more verbal students from getting lost in their words and the less verbal from being overwhelmed by the task. Younger children do not need an elaborate outline; it will help them just to put down the basic themes. For example, if the class is writing about a pet, have the class decide what topics should be included: kind of animal, size, color, age, sex, where it came from, how it got its name, where it sleeps, what it eats, and so forth. Then, when they write, they will be sure to include all the information. Boys are good with facts, but they have a hard time selecting which ones are important.

- The standard points for a good newspaper story—Who, What, Where, When, and How—makes a very good way for boys to organize their writing. You can give them newspaper articles and have them look for those elements in the report.

- For elementary-and middle-school kids, the use of the graphic organizer for paragraph construction is also helpful. The most common one is the hamburger: the opening and closing sentences are the bun and the hamburger patty is the meat of the paragraph. Condiments such as tomatoes and lettuce, are the descriptions, examples, and so forth in the paragraph.

- Teach children to condense information. Using stories from the class reading, have students write one sentence describing a character, then pass the sentences to the next child and see if that child can identify the person from the sentence. The less verbal will learn to get their points across and the more verbal will learn to be more succinct.

- Have students practice retelling stories. Small children usually have trouble keeping the facts in order and not telling every detail, but with practice, they will get better.

CAUTION

★ Boys may give up on school if they cannot find ways to be successful. Boys can read and write well if they are encouraged, given reading material they are interested in and which is at their reading level, and given male role models to emulate.

★ If boys do not attain facility with verbal skills by the end of high school, they may believe that they cannot succeed in college or, if they do go to college, they may focus on courses that do not require papers or large amounts of reading. Do not let boys fall through the reading cracks.

(Continued)

(Continued)

★ Boys may pay less attention to lessons primarily oriented to reading and listening. In Chapter 3, we learned that it is hard for boys to sit still and listen. They tend to daydream or pull out the stitching of their zipper with the end of a mechanical pencil (it really happened!). Teachers concerned about attentional problems might assign a project for students to do with their hands and see whether the boys focus better. Here are some additional suggestions:

- Break up lectures by stopping and asking for a synopsis of the past ten minutes. The shift from intake of information to output will increase attention.
- Teach students to take notes or use other forms of organizers. This gives boys something active to do while listening to the lecture.
- Have all students in a math class stand at the black- or whiteboard and solve problems under the direction of the teacher, who goes around the room helping. In a coed class, some students may have performance issues, so you can have them work with partners.
- Use learning centers in the elementary classroom. This is one of the techniques of differentiated instruction; students move among stations as they complete each activity. In a class on earth science, there can be centers for each type of rock. Students go to each center, examine the rocks there, read the materials, and answer questions about that type of rock.

Verbal Strategies

We mentioned in Chapter 1 that boys are better with analogies (Halpern, 2000). You remember analogies: baseball is to bat as golf is to (pick one) glove, tee, golf club, ball. Boys quickly make the association between a baseball bat, which hits the ball in that game, and a golf club, which hits the ball in golf. Boys are able to isolate the correct answer and respond quickly. As we saw earlier, girls tend to go over answer choices several times to make sure that they are correct (Stumpf, 1998). While this tendency will reduce errors in most cases, it increases them with analogy questions because the girls try to make all answers correct before they start to eliminate them. So the girls make more errors and they are slower at it. That is why girls tend to have more trouble both on the math and the verbal sections of the older style SATs (Lowen, Rosser, & Katzman, 1988). In addition, the multiple-choice questions on standardized tests tend to use isolated bits of information, which boys are better able to deal with; girls do better on multiple-choice questions on teacher-made tests, where the material is in context (Willingham & Cole, 1997).

Although girls may have trouble with multiple-choice or analogy questions, they will go over an entire test to check their answers, whereas boys just turn the test in without checking. Part of boys' difficulty in checking their work is that they are not as quick as girls to notice differences in items on the page. Using their skills in perceptual speed, girls are able to pick out identical designs from large groups of similar designs more rapidly than boys (Kimura, 2000). As we mentioned before, this is also the reason that boys have more trouble finding errors in their work.

Boys do show a lot of reading problems, which may stem from problems in phonological processing (Majeres, 1999). Remember that boys do not hear as well as girls, and phonology deals with how sounds go together to make words. If a student confuses words such as *meet* and *met*, this may be the problem. That, along with boys' reduced ability to recall information from written sources, leads them to have difficulties, especially on tests and other written material. Combine all this with boys' reluctance to go back over an answer, as mentioned earlier, and the result is that boys frequently finish tests and other written work much more rapidly than do girls, with less positive results. The elementary-school boys, who were full of facts and information, now drift to the back of the middle-school classroom and rarely volunteer information because they cannot rely on their fact-based knowledge.

Applications for Your Classroom

- Encourage boys to be more careful in responding to questions. This is hard to do.
- Make boys work a set of math problems twice using fresh paper the second time through. Then have them compare their two sets of answers.
- Have boys include the outline for an answer to an essay question as well as the answer. The outline does not need to be elaborate, but it will help them frame an answer. They should then jot down an example for each part of the outline. After

(Continued)

(Continued)

doing that, they will be able to write an essay that is fuller and has more meat on its bones, so to speak.

- Teach a variety of ways to frame answers and have the class brainstorm different approaches. Frequently one student will have an approach that will work for a classmate.
- Teach boys how to proofread. One way that works well is to read a passage out loud, and I really mean *out loud*. When you do this, problems in grammar, sentence structure, and meaning are more obvious. This may also help draw attention to spelling errors, except in the case of homophones like *their* and *there*. (One way to teach the difference between these words is to remove the *t* at the beginning. Then the words are *heir*—who is a person—and *here*—which is a place.) Another technique that helps is to have students read each other's papers for errors.
- Work on teaching problem-solving strategies and ask children to use those strategies when they answer questions. Help them learn to identify which strategy works best with certain kinds of problems. For example, working backward works well with large projects, and using analogies may work well in science. Point out that this is a bit like learning different sports skills. Being able to swing a bat and a tennis racquet involves similar skills that are applied differently to fit the needs of the sport.

CAUTION

★ Boys may give up on subjects requiring verbal skills. Many men do not read much and their skills get rusty. Even if boys don't like to read, encourage them to read the newspaper or the news summaries on Internet news sites. Boys may enjoy finding international news Web sites, many of which are in English, and comparing how the information on a major news story is presented by U.S. news sources and by those in other countries.

★ Some children find that standardized tests become hurdles. The anxiety created by the prospect of standardized tests may prevent both boys and girls from taking the tests or from doing as well as they could. These tests are required not just for college admission, but frequently for career advancement and, due to recent federal requirements, to graduate from high school. Practice will help reduce this anxiety as the boy becomes more proficient.

Problem-Solving Strategies

Practicing different ways to solve problems is invaluable training because not all problems can be solved the same way. Most of these approaches are familiar, but we rarely examine what strategies we use unless we are unsuccessful at solving a problem.

Analogies. We have just mentioned analogy questions used on tests. This method is similar in that it involves using successful strategies from other problems to help solve the present problem. For example, when students have trouble understanding percentages, I ask them how much a $16 CD would cost if it were on sale for 20 percent off. It seems to be easier for students to understand percentages involved with money. Once the students can manage percentages and money, we can then move on to more abstract percent problems.

Working backward. This is simply a matter of knowing where you need to be and then figuring out how to get there. In teaching, we frequently first decide what we want students to know and then plan our lessons to provide that information. For students, a similar exercise would be planning the steps for a long-term project. If they know when the deadline is, they can work backward to see when they need to start. While this may seem obvious to you, there are many students who will be surprised at how well this technique works.

Means-end analysis. This business term means breaking down a problem into smaller bits, working on the smaller tasks, evaluating what is left to be done, and then reevaluating the plan of action. Students working on group projects find this approach helpful. They can break down the tasks and assign the tasks to the participants. Every day or so, the students can get together to monitor progress on the tasks and see if someone needs help or if the plan needs to be rewritten.

Trial and error. This extremely common technique will get an answer, but the process may take a lot of time. The difficulty is that as time passes, the problem may change and the student may not know that he has an answer when he gets one. If a student tries to balance a chemical equation by trial and error, simply plugging in numbers, he may never hit upon the correct solution, when he could quickly find the answer by using a formula.

Logic. Many students do not intuitively see that knowing some information will help them figure out other pieces of the same problem. If they are missing crucial data, they will simply give up because they do not understand how they can determine the data from what they already know. Many word problems assume that the student can use

(Continued)

Problem-Solving Strategies (Continued)

logic to provide necessary information to solve the problem. For example, if the problem says that the desired solution is an odd number, students may be stumped because they may not know how to be sure that the number is odd. The first step in solving problems logically is to state what you do know.

Multiplying any number by 2 will make it even.

Odd numbers are either one more or one less than even numbers.

Solution: If 2X represents an even number, then $2X + 1$ or $2X - 1$ represents an odd number.

Give boys logic puzzles on a regular basis for practice. They generally like this mental exercise and will ask for the puzzles as a treat!

PRACTICE THE SKILLS NECESSARY FOR THE SAT AND OTHER STANDARDIZED TESTS

All students can improve in test-taking skills if they work on them several times a week and learn to develop strategies to solve specific types of questions. You will find some hints on how to improve test-taking in Chapter 10.

Boys need practice in learning to review answers and in going back over questions. In math, students can work problems in a different direction—add from the bottom up instead of the top down. For objective tests, have the boys complete the test, then cover the answers with their hands and answer the questions again to see if they get the same answers. For free-response items, have them at least read over what they have written, as many boys will not do even that.

The writing portion of the new SAT may be a problem for some boys, and weekly in-class timed writing exercises will help them get used to the task. This technique can be used in every class. In math, the students can write for ten minutes on how certain math techniques can be applied to a real-life situation. In social studies, the students can write about the effect on small towns in the Midwest of the move to large corporate-run farms.

Test Anxiety

Test anxiety occurs when a student has a stress reaction to a testing situation. The stress reaction, commonly known as fight-or-flight, helps us cope with stressful or dangerous situations. The problem is that as humans, we react this way whether the situation presents a physical or an emotional danger. If your heart starts to beat rapidly and you increase your breathing rate when you are in a car accident, that is considered normal and you may be directed to sit down and take it easy. If you have the same reaction in a test, you may be told that you have test anxiety and you shouldn't be afraid of a test. The problem is that we may have learned to be afraid of tests at some point in the past and it is not easy to unlearn that reaction just because we want to.

The first step is to identify a child's reaction as text anxiety, since not all children will exhibit the same symptoms. Most of the fight-or-flight reaction is involved in providing energy to the muscles so that they can work more efficiently to fight or to flee. The energy in blood sugar is most efficiently released in the presence of oxygen and so, when a danger is detected, the body attempts to release stored sugar, increase circulation to the muscles, and increase respiration to heighten the blood oxygen level.

Bodily reaction	Reason for the reaction
Increase in heart rate and blood pressure	Gets energy to the muscles and brain
Increase in respiration	Provides more oxygen for energy
Increase in blood sugar and fats	Provides the source of energy
Increase in blood flow to muscles	Delivers sugar and oxygen to this area
Decrease in blood flow to skin	Protection from cuts
Decrease in blood flow to gut	Gut not in immediate use
Dilated pupils	Improves vision

If the stressful situation continues for some time, the individual can become exhausted. The student will then find it hard to think and/or be susceptible to infections such as colds and the flu. This may be the situation toward the end of a protracted midterm or exam period, and I have known students to fail major exams because they were so tired.

(Continued)

Test Anxiety (Continued)

The effects of these reactions can be interesting in the class. A very stressed boy may run out of a classroom or find it difficult to control his handwriting because of the pressure to use the energy now being supplied to his muscles. I have seen boys throw book bags and slam doors coming out of a test. One student had symptoms of hyperventilation—tingling hands and feet—because of rapid, shallow breathing. If the student is very stressed, blood flow to the brain will be reduced in favor of blood to muscles, thereby interfering with the ability to think. Once a student relaxes after the test, he may remember all those facts he forgot during the test.

The stress response is an automatic reaction. Once we are faced with a stressful situation, our bodies will react in this way and there is only one part of the response that we can control: our breathing. By using yoga breathing techniques or purposeful relaxation, we can reverse the stress response. The great thing is that children can employ deep-breathing techniques in the middle of a test and no one has to know what they are doing. This cannot be taught while a child is stressed, so the child needs to practice it before the testing situation. If you suspect that a child has test anxiety, check with the school counselor to see what the school policy is on management of test anxiety. Some counselors are trained to teach children relaxation techniques or may know of local professionals who are qualified. As the teacher of a test-anxious child, you can help by

- Identifying test-anxious children to parents and to the appropriate school services
- Offering alternative testing methods and sites to reduce anxiety
- Encouraging students to use relaxation techniques appropriately
- Providing a class atmosphere where students feel comfortable in coming for help

SPATIAL ABILITIES

There is general agreement that boys are better at tasks involving spatial abilities, specifically those of mental rotation (Halpern, 2000; Kimura, 2000). As discussed in Chapter 1, this skill involves being able to determine how the orientation of an imagined object will change when it is rotated or turned. One implication of this is that if a boy goes somewhere, he will be better able to find his way back by simply imagining his route in reverse. This is part of the reason that men don't ask for directions. It is easier for them to picture the turns they have made and do the opposite. In addition, men may find it easier to follow a map and to remember details from a map (Henrie et al., 1997).

Male v. Female Directions

If you have ever had friends give you directions, you know that there are two types. Men are more likely to use compass points and/or distances, while women will refer to landmarks, usually including extraneous information (MacFadden, Elias, & Saucier, 2003). Here is an example of how a man and a woman might give directions to a restaurant.

Male directions: Go three miles south on Rt. 29 and turn east at Rt. 250. The restaurant will be on the left after you go through the first light.

Female directions: Go down Rt. 29 towards the big shopping center, which will be on your right. Turn left onto Rt. 250 at the stoplight after the shopping center. There is a McDonald's on the right before you get to this intersection and you know you have gone too far if you pass a car dealership. Once you are on Rt. 250, there will be several blocks before a traffic light at Maple Street. The restaurant is on the left after you go through the light. It is in a brick building with a green awning. There is a parking lot for the restaurant just past it.

There is a lot of interest in whether spatial abilities lead to better math skills. Some claim that there is a direct relationship and cite studies to make the case (Halpern, 2000). Others, also citing studies, just as firmly state that no case can be made to connect spatial abilities and success in mathematics (Kimura, 2000). Still others find some relationship, just not quite enough to make a definitive case (Casey, Nuttall, & Pezaris, 1997; Friedman, 1995). Many math teachers believe that there is a relationship, especially with respect to geometry. This is another area where the research is contradictory, and we will probably find some connection when the right questions are asked.

Boys are better at mechanical reasoning, which means that they are good at figuring out how things work (Finegold, 1992; Halpern, 2000). This is the reason why boys are so interested in taking mechanical objects apart. Combine this interest with their skills in spatial relationships and you can understand why they are fascinated by how engines function, what is required to dam water, and how to make a better kite. Some boys will spend a lot of time trying to figure out how to make a toy or other object do something different than what it was designed for. The problem in the classroom is that the teacher may be interested in students learning how a pulley works, while a boy works on changing the configuration to see what happens when the cords are strung differently. The boy wants to investigate the mechanical aspects of the equipment and the teacher wants to move on to the rest of the lesson. You may need to consider developing ways for this boy and other interested students to expand on their understanding of the subject at another time.

Applications for Your Classroom

- Not all students will be good at using spatial information. If children are asked to draw a map and write directions based on it, those who are spatially adept will shine on the map and those who are not will probably have more success with the directions. Both types will then use their strengths to become proficient at the other skill. If appropriate, you can pair students up, with one drawing the map and the other writing the directions.
- If a book the class is reading has a description of a character going someplace, have the children make a map of the route taken and use sticky notes with quotes from the story to justify the direction or change in direction. When her class was reading *Johnny Tremain,* one teacher made a big map of the Boston area and had the boys put pins on all locations mentioned in the book. Using skills that boys are good at will help them in areas that may be more difficult, such as reading.
- Orienteering exercises are a good way to use map skills and, because the directions are written, to encourage boys to read. Younger children will be able to follow directions around their classroom or the playground, and older children will be able to follow directions in a local park. Some science museums have orienteering projects as well. Require both a written narrative and a map, and have the boys compare notes to see if they can follow another student's directions.
- Give all students manipulative materials as part of class exercises. This is easy for math and science, which is why boys traditionally like these subjects. In history, have the students make time lines or posters about important people. In language arts,

put prefixes, roots, and suffixes on cards and help the boys build new words. To help children learn parts of speech, put nouns, verbs, adjectives, and so forth on color-coded cards. Have the children draw cards at random from the appropriate groups to build sentences. The sentences may be silly, which boys love, and they will learn that parts of speech may not be interchangeable. This exercise can then move into how to diagram a sentence.

CAUTION

★ Boys, particularly younger boys, may have more trouble paying close attention to lessons that have few manipulative tasks. Books may be more interesting if students can act out parts of the story in class.

★ Some boys will view verbal tasks as difficult even before they have begun. They may find such tasks more approachable if they can visualize them as mechanical tasks, such as seeing how sentences are constructed, developing outlines and web maps of stories, and using the hamburger analogy for paragraph development. Take this metaphor to its limit: turn parts of speech into building blocks and the students into construction workers, and build sentences. This can also be used as students learn to build paragraphs: The thesis sentence becomes the foundation, and so forth.

LEARNING MODALITIES

Cognitive skills are the basis for many learning modalities. We know that some of the cognitive differences between boys and girls are based on biological/brain differences, but it is likely that experience polarizes those differences. Most boys do not have a completely male brain—no matter how that is defined—and may be somewhat embarrassed when they are young that they have good handwriting or read well. Do not point out these students as models to emulate; it will make them self-conscious.

While research has corroborated the distinction between the field dependent and field independent learning types, no work of this kind has been done for the verbal/iconic styles. However, teachers have found that thinking about learning in these ways is useful when working with students who have trouble (Barretti, 1993).

Verbal v. Iconic

Most boys have less facility with learning from the written word than do girls, and they do much better with anything they can put their hands on or manipulate. The trick is to turn a language-based course into pictures. I remember telling my dean in high school that if I could study history like I studied math I would be fine. She replied, "That's silly, of course you can't do that." Well, she was wrong.

Iconic learning involves pictures, so turn all verbal material into icons: pictures, tables, charts, time lines—any kind of graphic presentation. This works best if the student does it himself. The graphic organizer is the best example.

Teach the student to program the calendar function on his computer so that he will be reminded of upcoming assignments. Seeing the reminder pop up can be more effective than just putting it on a static calendar.

Teach boys webbing as a way of taking notes. Not only is it more interesting for them, but that style may be easier for them to review. There are several different types of software available to help students organize material in this fashion.

Field Independent v. Field Dependent

These are also known as global v. analytical styles. Males tend to be more field independent (analytical) and females more field dependent (global). In addition, children tend to be more field dependent, and as they mature, become more independent. In the classroom, this translates into the ability to separate a task or information from a larger context (Jonassen & Grabowski, 1993). For example, boys may focus on the events in a story and girls may be more interested in the outcome.

The global individual tends to see the entire picture, whereas the analytical individual tends to see all the parts but may not see how those parts are interrelated. For boys, this is one reason they gravitate toward more quantitative subjects such as science and math, where the focus is on facts. They may have more trouble with qualitative subjects such as literature and composition, where the focus is on synthesizing facts into a cohesive whole. Boys are not usually strong in this skill, and it may be difficult for them to see the larger picture.

Collaborative group projects help students understand that not everyone sees a subject in the same way they do.

One of the reasons that men have the reputation for not wanting to read directions is that they are field independent, meaning that they focus on the task at hand and may not notice auxiliary information such as directions. Some boys in the middle of a task will be surprised to learn that directions even exist. Have your students write directions for a simple task and see if others can follow them.

Insert questions into a lesson instead of just having them at the end. This will help the student stop and think about what he is learning and understand the relationship among all the parts of the lesson.

STRATEGY DEVELOPMENT

One of the largest stumbling blocks that boys have to learning is their failure to develop a wide variety of learning strategies (Connell, 1996). One of the most important things that can be done to help boys be better students is to provide them with a wide variety of strategies aimed at each student's individual learning strengths. The key is that not all students learn alike, not even all boys, and the effective teacher differentiates instruction to meet the students' academic needs. Research has shown that using a variety of learning strategies can help improve a student's academic achievement (Cassidy & Eachus, 2000; Gettinger & Seibert, 2002). However, there is little research on the effectiveness of using learning styles to develop learning strategies. Teachers have found that helping children use their learning strengths to compensate for learning weaknesses does help, if only because the child believes that it helps. Learning style assessment instruments available to all are listed in Chapter 11.

COGNITIVE DIFFERENCES AND LEARNING

Boys are more likely to run into impediments in the area of verbal skills. They are not as fluent, have trouble spelling, are more likely to be identified with dyslexia, and have more problems with reading and writing. However, boys are good at analogies and vocabulary and will catch up to girls in the areas of reading and writing if given the chance. Boys also find tasks involving spatial and mechanical skills easier and are good at remembering facts. However, they have fewer study strategies and tend to stick to the few they are used to even if they don't work. The teacher who utilizes this information will offer a learning environment that

- Provides opportunities to develop reading skills by making available reading materials that boys find interesting and by encouraging boys to read

- Provides structure to help boys through active learning opportunities
- Provides instruction and practice in a variety of study approaches based on each student's strengths and styles.

NOTE

1. Anime is short for animation and refers to graphic or animated films from Japan. The target audience for anime is primarily high-school and college-age students who would be described as geeks or gamers. Many of the films are concerned with violence and other topics not recommended for younger children.

PART II

Societal and Biological Influences

5

ADHD and Learning Disabilities

After psychology class one day, when we had been discussing behavior manage-ment, Peter asked me if he was going to have to take medicine his entire life to man-age his attentional difficulties. When I asked him what he wanted to do with his life, he replied that he had hoped to work in investments. I mentioned that I had recently visited a friend who was a stockbroker and found him sitting behind a desk. Peter's face fell. Then I went on to say that the broker was also talking to me, answering the phone, watching the information from the stock exchange crawl across the bottom of his computer monitor, and reading some material I had brought him. Peter looked up with a big smile and said, "I could do that! It's sitting still and paying attention that I can't do." I replied that was why he would proba-bly never be an accountant, but that he would have an advantage in a job requir-ing multitasking. He replied, "Yeah, what some people see as a disability is an ability in other places."

━━━━━━━━━━━━━━━━━━━━◆◆◆

If you go into any special education classroom, you will find more boys than girls. Additionally, more boys will identify themselves as learning disabled (NCES, 1997; "What the numbers say," 2000). Many of my students have either been identified with, have been assessed for, or have been told they have learning problems. Because they are boys, the most common of these learning disabilities (LD) are attentional and reading difficulties. Why, if the students are boys, are attention and reading the most frequently identified learning disabilities?

One theory about why boys are more frequently identified is that their increased activity level is difficult for teachers to manage in the classroom. The activity level in kindergarten is acceptable, but by the time the boys get into third or fourth grade they are expected to set-tle down, and many simply cannot do that (Anderson, 1997). In addi-tion, the verbal advantage for girls creates the appearance of a relative disadvantage in boys who pick up verbal skills at a slower rate than their female classmates. The boys find reading difficult and they want to move around, so they get off task and the teacher sees them as hav-ing attentional and learning problems (Bennett, Gottesman, Rock, & Cerullo, 1993; Sax, 2001).

One common belief is that gender bias is the reason that boys out-number girls among students identified as learning disabled by their teachers, even though some research indicates that boys and girls are affected at similar rates (Shaywitz, 1998; Wehmeyer & Schwartz, 2001). According to this idea, it is not that more boys are learning dis-abled, but that fewer girls are identified. On the other hand, a recent review of studies in reading disabilities found that when other factors, such as attentional issues, race, IQ, and severity of disability were taken into account, it could not explain the larger proportion of diagnosed males (Liederman, Kantrowitz, & Flannery, 2005). That report indicates that selection bias is not the cause of the larger number of diagnosed boys. Again, this is an area where the experts do not agree.

Does this mean that identification of learning issues is simply a matter of students not fitting into a feminine classroom model? Absolutely not. After all, learning disabilities affect everything a student does in and out of the classroom. Children who suffer from Attention Deficit Hyperactivity Disorder (ADHD) will have trouble finishing a chore at home as well as finishing their class work. Children with dyslexia have trouble reading even when they are motivated to read and have just as much trouble reading the sports pages as reading a textbook. Dysgraphia makes it difficult to play the piano as well as to write. Dyscalculia interferes with one's ability to quickly calculate the tip for a waitress as well as one's ability to recite the multiplication tables. You will find descriptions of these learning problems later in this chapter.

According to the Individuals with Disabilities Education Improvement Act (IDEA), the definition of a specific learning disability is "a disorder in one or more of the basic psychological processes involved in understanding or in using language, spoken or written, which disorder may manifest itself in the imperfect ability to listen, think, speak, read, write, spell, or do mathematical calculations" (Office of Special Education Programs, 2005). The problem is that a child may have a hard time in one class and not in another. How can this happen? Some classes require students to access information in one way and other classes in other ways. For example, I learn better when I can manipulate materials and see what is happening, so it is no surprise that my field is science. I never did very well in history until I learned to study that subject in a more active fashion. When I changed the way I studied the material and took notes in class, my grades improved, as did my understanding of the subject. While I may have a learning disability in the area of auditory learning, changing the way I approached learning solved my problem. On the other hand, my dysgraphia means that there are a number of tasks I have to work around because I cannot handwrite well or for long. There is no alternative to writing, and even though I can use a computer for some tasks, problems as a result of dysgraphia affect everything I do.

When a learning difficulty exists in one class but not in another, I do not refer to that problem as a disability. I know this is merely semantics, but this distinction makes a difference to boys. They can understand that ADHD, dyslexia, dysgraphia, and dyscalculia are learning disabilities. What they have a hard time with is being told that the way they learn best is wrong and that they need to change. Having said that, I know that students may well benefit from many of the accommodations for dealing with learning disabilities, which may include teaching better learning strategies. The caveat is the necessity to ensure that the learning strategies being taught make best use of the student's strength and the strategies are not simply imposed based on what works for other students.

That is the major problem with most learning skills courses I am aware of. The courses are designed to teach skills that most people have found are the best ways to manage and access information. Students who do not do those tasks well do not benefit from such courses. For example, my dysgraphia and attention issues make it impossible for me to take conventional class notes. I have learned to take verbatim notes and then type them into a class file on my computer within twenty-four hours (usually I can still recognize what I wrote within that time frame). I know that this method works for me, but probably would not work for many other people. My dysgraphic son is an auditory learner, so he pays close attention in class and writes very little. Students who need help coping with academic problems need to work with someone on an individual basis to develop strategies they can and will use, based on their strengths and weaknesses.

Disorganization is a major issue for many boys, and having them use color-coded envelopes for handouts and homework to make sure they don't lose their papers will work with many of them. But this method will not work for every child, as some simply are unable to remember which color belongs with which class or are not yet motivated to use the system. Forcing them to use the colored envelopes will only cause frustration for both student and teacher and result in the student believing that he is incapable of being a good learner. To be successful, learning strategies must be responsive to the way the student learns best.

ATTENTION—ADHD

No one expects a four-year-old child to sit quietly in his seat for a half an hour, but we do expect that behavior of a fourteen-year-old. If the fourteen-year-old cannot sit still, we view his behavior as nonstandard for his age group and look for some explanation. All too frequently the teacher's explanation is that the child suffers from ADHD, and medication is the answer. The fact is that boys, particularly pubescent boys, are likely to be more impulsive and their inability to maintain attention in the classroom may be normal behavior.

The Diagnostic and Statistical Manual, fourth edition (DSM IV), published by the American Psychiatric Association, contains descriptions and diagnoses for all mental disorders recognized by the APA. For ADHD, symptoms include

- inattention and/or failure to maintain attention
- not listening when spoken to
- disorganization and tendency to lose items
- ease of distraction
- high activity level (fidgety, leaves seat, run or climbs when not appropriate)
- difficulty in playing quietly
- impulsivity

If you compare the descriptions of boys' normal behavior and the list of ADHD symptoms, you will find a lot of behaviors in common. There is a school of thought that some boys diagnosed with attentional problems are actually normal boys (Armstrong, 1996; Hartnett, Nelson, & Rinn, 2004) who suffer from what I refer to as "wiggly boy syndrome." Because of their increased activity level, their lack of ability to hear soft sounds, their impulsivity due to immaturity, and their need to touch and handle materials, some normal boys may be identified with attentional problems. In fact, many more boys than girls are referred by teachers for a diagnosis of ADHD: around nine boys to one girl. When groups of students are tested at random, undiagnosed individuals are identified in the ratio of two or three boys to one girl. This indicates that there may be some bias in identifying ADHD in boys, primarily because of boys' disruptive behavior (Sciutto, Nolfi, & Bluhm, 2004). Nonetheless, there are still more boys than girls with this disorder.

What are some of the physical characteristics of boys affecting what happens in the classroom? We have touched on these in previous chapters.

- Boys have a higher activity level than girls. Whether this is learned behavior or reflects a biological difference does not matter; the impression is that boys appear to be more active. In a large classroom, several very active boys can be disruptive.

- Boys can be less dexterous than girls. They may appear clumsy and they may have a harder time managing writing implements. As boys enter puberty, their sudden growth spurt may make coordination more difficult as well.
- Boys are more impulsive than girls. This is courtesy of the later development of their frontal cortex. Some of this behavior may be stereotypical, but it doesn't matter what the source is: Boys tend to be impulsive.
- Boys do not hear softer sounds as well as girls, and so it may appear as if they are not paying attention to what a teacher says in class. In a large, noisy classroom, it may be very difficult for children, particularly the boys at the back, to hear.
- Boys are louder than girls, partly because they have a higher tolerance for noise. The problem here is that children with ADHD have particularly loud voices (Breznitz, 2003), and this may cause teachers to confuse loudness with ADHD.
- Boys learn by touching, so they are likely to put their hands on materials in the classroom. Impulsive boys are likely to find it difficult to keep their hands off of materials that don't belong to them or off of their classmates. This can cause disruption.

How did schools deal with very active and/or easily distractible children before the advent of the diagnosis of ADHD? Frequently, these students were labeled immature and either held back a year or shifted to a nonacademic track. In those classes, a student's inability to control his impulses was not as obvious as in an academic class, where students are expected to sit quietly, listen, and take notes. Even today, many children diagnosed with ADHD show the behavior only in a conventionally structured classroom setting. At home, on the athletic field, and in other activities these children appear to have the same capabilities for impulse control as do other children (Armstrong, 1996; Sax, 2005).

Does this mean that ADHD is simply an artifact of diagnosis—that is to say, it only exists because certain normal behaviors are labeled as nonstandard? Absolutely not. There is no question that ADHD really exists, but individuals with the disorder show the symptoms in other aspects of their lives as well as in school. The diagnosis has become popular as a way to deal with very active boys whose behavior can be disruptive and who show little interest in school (Armstrong, 1996). One explanation is that because boys do not mature at the same rate, many appear disabled when in fact they are immature. I have seen boys come to believe that they are disabled and not be motivated to acquire mature behaviors later on. They are prone to use the diagnosis of ADHD to excuse their impulsive behavior rather than trying to acquire methods to deal with the problem.

Some of the boys with a diagnosis of attentional difficulties may actually be gifted, not ADHD (Hartnett et al., 2004; Webb, 2000). Gifted children have high activity levels, attentional problems, persistence problems, and difficulty complying with rules. Not infrequently, gifted children who are bored will underachieve and be disruptive in the classroom (Baum, 1990; Hartnett et al., 2004; Lawler, 2000). Combine normal boy behavior with gifted student behavior and gifted boys may appear to fit the description of ADHD. Figure 5.1 outlines the differences between gifted children who are bored and children with ADHD. You will note that the behaviors are similar but the reasons differ.

Children need practice in learning to pay attention. Boys, with their increased activity levels, may need help in the early school years in acquiring this skill. A boy who has never been read to as a small child or engaged in activities requiring sustained attention, such as playing board games, may not be able to sit still while the teacher or librarian reads even a short book. Playing games on the computer, while absorbing, does not qualify as practice at sustained attention. In fact, increasing hours of television watching may actually hinder the development of the ability to sustain attention. Recent research indicates that children who watched a great deal of television subsequently were recognized as having attentional problems (Christakis, Zimmerman, DiGiuseppe, & McCarty, 2004). There is a chicken-and-egg quality to this argument. Is it that children who watch lots of television do not develop attentional skills, or is it that children with attentional problems choose to watch lots of television because of the movement on the screen? We don't know the answer yet. Nevertheless, this and other information has led the American Academy of Pediatrics to recommend that children under the age of two watch NO television and older children should watch no more than two hours per day.

In addition, recent research links frequent exposure to violent TV and video games with reduction in executive function—decision making—as reported by adolescents and their parents. A follow-up study examined the brains of adolescents who were identified with behavior disorders and adolescents who did not exhibit behaviors associated with conduct disorder. A functional magnetic resonance imaging (fMRI) scan was taken of each subject. The fMRI can identify which parts of the brain are working when a subject is doing a certain

Figure 5.1   Comparison of Behaviors of Gifted Students and Those With ADHD

Area	Gifted/Bored	ADHD/LD
Attention	Daydreaming because material seems irrelevant or too simple	Problems with sustaining attention
Persistence	Loss of interest once task is mastered	Attention problems interfere with completion of task
Beginning tasks	May not believe that task will assist in mastery of skill	Inability to segment tasks so only sees whole task – too hard
Completion of tasks	Too many interests – begins many, sees few to completion	Shifts back and forth between incompleted tasks
Maturity level	Intellect may develop before judgment	Impulsive and has poor delay of gratification
Confrontational	May see adults as not seeing the circumstances correctly	Argues to cover failure to pay attention or lack of understanding
Activity level	Frequently higher than average child	Frequently higher than average child
Talking problem	Prefers to talk with adults as peers may not be interested – may monopolize	Impulsivity in class – calls out frequently and answers may not be on task
Discipline	Challenges power structure as being irrelevant	Difficulty in identifying when specific rules apply
Disorganization	So many uncompleted projects make it difficult to find one to work on	Items not in immediate sight are forgotten or misplaced
Carelessness	More concerned with big concept, may ignore details	Lack of attention to details produces incomplete work
Sensitivity	Reacts negatively to criticism	Reacts negatively to criticism
Pervasiveness of problems	Do not occur in all situations	Are present in all situations, but to varying degrees
Performance levels	Generally constant speed, but level varies with interest	Speed and performance vary with ability in area

SOURCE: Howard, L. A., James, A. N. (2003). *What principals need to know about teaching: Differentiated instruction.* Alexandria, VA: National Association of Elementary School Principals.

task. The findings indicated that normal subjects who watched a great deal of violent media had frontal lobes that functioned in much the same way as did those of the subjects identified with serious behavior disorders (Kronenberger et al., 2005; Mathews et al., 2005). This research is very new, but has large implications for the link between visual information and the response of the brain.

Boys will tell me that they were diagnosed with ADHD as children, but now that they are in high school, they have "outgrown" the condition. There are probably three different explanations for this. One group will not have outgrown ADHD, but do not want to be labeled as different from their peers so they deny they have the disorder. This feeling may be complicated (or brought on) by families who are concerned that their child carries a label and will do a great deal to have the label removed.

Most of the boys I have worked with who claim to have outgrown ADHD fit in the next two groups. A second group will not have outgrown ADHD, but will have acquired learning strategies to help them compensate. A final group will have been misidentified and, as they mature, will settle down and have fewer problems with focus. If a child truly has ADHD, he will not outgrow it; however, as an adult, he may learn to manage his symptoms. I am always amused to see Edward Hollowell speak. Dr. Hollowell is the coauthor of *Driven to Distraction*, an authoritative work on ADHD, and someone with attentional problems himself. At conferences, all the other presenters will stand behind a podium to speak, but he requires a body mike so that he can walk around the dais, as he cannot stand still for long. However, having ADHD has not kept him from a distinguished career in psychology.

Most of the boys I have worked with who claim to have outgrown ADHD are academically capable. They were probably hard to manage in the classroom, and the treatments and accommodations for children with attentional issues helped get them through school. However, focusing on their problems may have masked the real issue—they were uninterested in what was going on in the classroom (Webb, 2000).

One caveat: there is a growing belief that behavior that looks like ADHD may actually be the result of classroom practices that are boosting symptoms. Most of these practices are the result of curricula driven to prepare students for mastery exams. These practices include teachers talking rather than offering interactive instructional opportunities, presentation of too much material at a time, emphasis on seat work with few opportunities for students to move around, and a classroom environment focused on acquiring information rather than exploring how the information is linked to previously learned material (Sousa, 2001). If you believe that several students in your class have ADHD, examine the pace in your class to see if you could allow for students to interact with the material. Then see how many of the identified children still exhibit symptoms.

Applications for Your Classroom

- If you have a student who has been identified with ADHD in your classroom, the best source of information on how to accommodate learning activities for this student will be his special education teacher; specific goals will be listed on his Individualized Education Plan (IEP). You will need to keep work samples and document all communications with both the special education teacher and the student's family as required by IDEA.

- All of the suggestions about making the learning process more active will help the child with attentional issues.

- Most boys can be restless especially if they are not given frequent breaks. When you change from one subject to another, have the children stand up and stretch. Everyone needs a change of pace and this will give the wiggly child a legitimate place to move.

- For a student who finds it difficult to sit still, suggest that he walk back and forth in the back of your classroom. He simply slips out of his desk when he needs to, and goes to the back of the classroom. When he is ready, he returns to his desk. Most students will be glad to have the freedom to move and you will be astonished at how well the child will be able to focus on what is going on in the classroom, especially while he is walking.

- We have used fidget toys with great success when boys need to be quiet and listen. These toys can be a large nut and bolt to screw and unscrew, or squishy balls, particularly the kind used by physical therapists for hand rehabilitation. What you are looking for is something the child can fiddle with and that won't bother his neighbors; you are trying to get away from clicking pens or drumming fingers.

- Another way to improve attention is to let children chew gum. Yes, I know chewing gum is not popular with the school maintenance staff and it is probably banned in your school, but for these children it can really help and keeps them from chewing pencils, pens, or their fingernails. After the third time that one young man came into my class with blue ink all over his face and clothing from having chewed through the top of his pen, I gave in and let him chew gum. He was not allowed to chew gum outside of class and he had to dispose of the gum properly

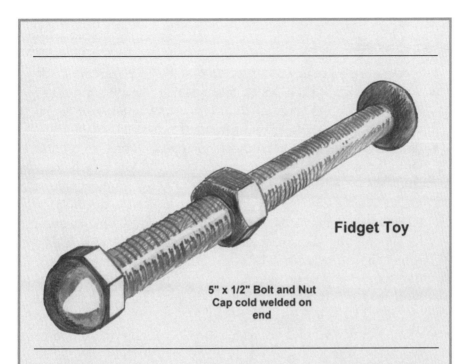

Fidget Toy

5" x 1/2" Bolt and Nut
Cap cold welded on
end

as he left. A recent report links the activity of chewing gum with an increased ability to recall words as well as an improvement in several parts of working memory (Wilkinson, Scholey, & Wesnes, 2002), so there may be a academic benefit as well. *No bubble gum!* The popping is as bad as clicking pens. Younger children may need to learn to chew regular gum with their mouths shut.

- Shift tasks frequently. This applies to homework as well as to other tasks requiring sustained attention. I write for an hour and then I play solitaire for ten minutes. The trick is that I quit playing cards after ten minutes. Some of my students find it difficult to shift from tasks that involve hands-on work (I thought they had ADHD?) to something more passive. Kitchen timers set for twenty minutes or half an hour will remind them to go back to the less active task. Older students may find that trying to read a chapter in a textbook is next to impossible, as they cannot sustain the attention necessary. Encourage them to put all their homework out and read until their mind begins to drift, then move to a more active task. The focused person will find this very distracting, but the child with attention problems will find that he can focus for short bursts as he changes tasks.

(Continued)

(Continued)

- Some schools are installing sound systems in classrooms. The teacher wears a body mike, and speakers around the classroom balance the sound so that it is at the same level for all students. This can be a great solution for the boys at the back.
- After you have identified boys who appear impulsive or inattentive, notice which classroom activities are going on when the student's impulsivity is the worst and when he is most able to wait. Not only will this provide documentation if a diagnosis of ADHD is under consideration, but it may give you information to help the child learn to control his behavior. For example, if he is most able to work quietly while on the computer, encourage the student to take notes in class on a laptop. For elementary-level students, use Alpha Smarts, which are fairly durable and can stand some bumps and drops.
- ADHD children who are academically capable will be most successful if they are extremely busy. Such students take a full academic load, compete on athletic teams, are active members of church or social service organizations, and give of their time to help others. They have no time to be disorganized, even with things happening so fast that they rarely forget their obligations. (This is my son's favorite method.)
- For students who lose their book bags or items in them, the following may be helpful:
  - Establish a rule that the book bag is to be put down in only three places: the study area, the locker, and one other place of the student's choosing. This will not prevent the student from forgetting his book bag, but it will limit the number of places he has to look when it is misplaced.
  - Every Sunday evening, the book bag is to be dumped out and all papers either thrown away, filed to be kept, or organized in packets to be returned.
- Organizational packets will help, but this requires the student to decide which one will work best for him. I like translucent colored envelopes with flaps, because I don't lose papers out of them. Some of my students don't like the flap and use translucent colored sleeves instead. Some of the sleeves come with holes punched in them and can be clipped into a binder—a bit bulky, but less likely to be lost. Pick a color for each class and have all papers go into the appropriate packet.

It can still be a mess, but it limits the number of papers the student has to rifle through to find his homework. He has to remember to put all papers into the appropriate envelope or this doesn't work. If the envelopes or sleeves don't appeal, large colored clips can be used to hold papers together. Help the student find some method to group similar papers.

- Pens, pencils, and other such equipment should be kept either in the pocket made for that purpose in the book bag or in a plastic envelope that clips into a binder. Pencil boxes not attached to something larger get lost when they are taken out and not returned to the bag. If the contents seem to walk, attach pens or pencils to colorful plastic key chains that are expandable and go around the wrist. This gives the child a quiet fiddle toy and something more obvious to see.

- If, while in the middle of one task, I thought of something else that needed to be done, I used to drop what I was doing because I was afraid I would later forget what I had just thought of. The problem was that I didn't return to the original task. I now carry a pad of paper around with me and jot down reminders so I don't have to shift too soon. Attaching a small notebook on a string to the book bag will accomplish the same purpose.

- Some students find it helpful to talk out loud when studying. This can help the student stay engaged with the task as well as providing auditory feedback. If reading silently, the student can stop at the end of a paragraph or two and talk out loud about what he has just read. This offers two ways to get the information into the brain—through the eyes and the ears—as well as giving the student a physical action to perform.

- While highlighting or underlining text gives the ADHD student something tactile to do, their textbooks not infrequently look completely highlighted or underlined. Have the student read a paragraph, then lift his eyes from the page and determine what one word or phrase—not sentence—conveys the idea in the material. He then highlights, underlines, or writes in the margin just that word or phrase. If students are not allowed to write in their books, use narrow sticky notes placed over the text and write on them. At review time, the student can put the sticky notes in order on a piece of paper to

(Continued)

(Continued)

make a review sheet. Because the student is shifting academic gears from passively reading to actively analyzing, focus is easier to maintain and memory for the material is enhanced. Boys are likely to concentrate on an example in a paragraph because it offers facts to remember. This method will help the student learn to find the concept modeled by the example.

- The ADHD student cannot put anything away until the project is totally finished. Filing papers only means that they get lost and/or forgotten. Shallow bins on his desk for each project will help corral papers and still keep them visible. Match the colors to the book bag packets. The desk will still be messy (the ADHD child usually cannot maintain a minimum level of neatness), but he will be able to locate what he needs without creating more mess. Here is another situation where you may need to have variable standards for different children.

- The desks and lockers of children with ADHD tend to be astoundingly messy. However, you can insist that all garbage (food wrappers, last week's lunch) be thrown away as soon as possible. Here is what happens. The child is in the middle of eating and something else comes along to divert him. He puts the half-eaten food down and pursues the new activity. When he has to clean up, it is simply a matter of stuffing everything in the desk or locker, so the food goes in also. It has taken me years of practice, but I no longer ignore such garbage and put it in the appropriate receptacle when I clean up. I've lost some food I wanted to finish, but I no longer have bugs. Your students can learn the same lesson.

- It is hard for the ADHD student to wait for questions to be completed, for classmates to finish their explanations, or for projects to be finished. As the child grows up, he should be made progressively more aware of occasions when he encroaches on other students' space and time. Younger students can pass an object such as a stuffed animal around the class, with only the student holding the animal allowed to speak. When selecting the object, take care to choose one that is not likely to cause problems when it is tossed, as it surely will be at some point. For older students in some boys' schools, only the student who is standing is allowed to speak, and students stand only when called on by the teacher. This method works very well in single-sex classrooms, but is less effective in coed classrooms because students do not like to appear unprepared or unable in front of a mixed group. In coed classrooms, the presence of the teacher walking around the classroom can be powerful enough to subdue the most impetuous.

CAUTION

★ Children who are quiet are not necessarily paying attention. If the child who is doodling, playing with a fidget toy, staring out the window, or engaging in some other off-task behavior can tell you what you just said, he is paying attention. It may not be your idea of attention, but it is his. The child with ADHD who is quiet is likely to be attending to something other than what is going on in class.

★ Restless children can and will bother their more focused classmates. Put the restless child up front where there are fewer distractions and a more potent teacher presence, or let him walk in the back where no one else can see him. As the child grows up, he should be taking an active role in learning to manage his attentional problems in the classroom.

★ If you have several restless children in one class, you may need to keep them away from each other. It is quite common for restless children to become more so in each other's presence. If at all possible, make sure that the restless ones are not looking at each other or working in the same groups.

★ There are lots of organizational techniques, but none are going to work until the student is motivated to do something for himself. Setting up behavioral contracts early, with short-term goals, will help the student with attentional problems learn to monitor himself effectively. The special education teacher can help you develop behavior contracts.

★ It is tempting for both teacher and parent to step in and help the ADHD child get organized, remember assignments, and find lost items. As the child grows up, gradually step back, remembering that it is better for the child if you serve as a scaffold and not as a crutch. Eventually, the student needs to build his own scaffold, seeking help when needed.

(Continued)

(Continued)

> ★ A diagnosis of ADHD is not a license to be inattentive, but the child with this problem will benefit from structure and accommodations. Each child with an IEP will have specific modifications and accommodations that the teacher will need to implement with the assistance of the special education department. The special education teacher is your best source of information about each child's particular educational needs. The problem with books about ADHD in the popular press is that the suggestions do not specifically target the child in your classroom, although you may get useful hints on how to assist him. The same applies to the suggestions you find here.

MEDICATION

When I was in elementary school, which was long before ADHD was so well known, a child who could not settle down was sent to the principal's office, lectured (frequently) by the teacher, or, in the case of several boys I knew, sent to military school. Actually the structure of military school can help the ADHD child by delineating every minute of his day. The problem in the long run is that the child does not learn to structure his life for himself.

The most popular treatments for ADHD at the moment are stimulant drugs such as methylphenidate (Ritalin, Concerta, Metadate) or amphetamines (Adderoll, Dexedrine, Desoxyn). Other drugs such as Wellbutrin have been used with less than general success. Do these drugs work? For students for whom ADHD is unquestionably the correct diagnosis, the stimulant drugs have been a great success, at least as far as teachers are concerned. However, there is growing evidence that while drug therapy may result in improved classroom behavior, it does not necessarily result in improved academic performance (McCormick, 2003; Sax, 2005). Many of my students hate taking the drugs because they dislike the way the drugs make them feel. Personality changes and interference with sleep patterns are two of the most common complaints that lead to noncompliance.

If the drugs are not universally successful, why is the rate of prescriptions increasing? A recent survey of studies of the success of drug therapy found a complex combination of factors that make it difficult to reduce the demand for such therapies (Safer, Zito, and dosReis, 2003). Schools are trying to reduce the use of drugs, but their efforts are frequently unsuccessful because of the demand by parents and educators for such treatment. The demand is also fueled by pharmaceutical advertising, managed care organizations, and physicians with little information from controlled studies specifically targeting educational outcomes for children. Most of the research on the effect of stimulant drugs has been done with adult subjects (Safer, Zito, and dosReis, 2003), a fact not well known among educators and medical professionals. As with many medical issues, we are looking for a "magic bullet" that will cure the problem.

From the beginning, there have been many suggestions as to how children can manage their attentional problems without the use of medication. The problem is that these programs require a good deal of teacher supervision, effort, and planning time, which the classroom teacher may simply be unable to provide (Blazer, 1995; Gardill, DuPaul, & Kyle, 1996; Kirby & Kirby, 1994; Stormont-Spurgin, 1997). The best solutions don't require a huge amount of effort from the teacher but do require effort from the student, with assistance from the family when appropriate. Consequently, these are likely to be more successful with students above elementary-school level.

Most important, by the time the student enters high school, he should understand that he, and he alone, is responsible for his actions. He can learn to be more responsible. If you have observed the student doing what is required in the past and he has agreed to a plan of action, do not succumb to the pleas of the student and of his family to be given "just one more chance." Point out to the student and his family that the student does a great deal without being reminded and that he has to learn how to manage his own behavior as you and his family will not always be around to mop up after him. If this seems harsh, let me assure you I know what I am talking about. I have ADHD myself and have a great many ways to make sure that I meet my obligations, do not lose important papers, and remember my appointments. My book bag is enormous, but I follow my own book bag rules and rarely lose papers. I live with wildly colored sticky notes, some on the steering wheel of my car, and I still do not make every appointment—but when I fail, it is my mistake and I take the responsibility. On the other hand, being a teacher with ADHD is an advantage, as I can pay attention to the activities in the classroom, guide the discussion so we get to the next topic, and scowl at the students in the back who are chatting with each other all at the same time!

Forgetting and "Forgetting"

Schools struggle with the proper way to deal with students who either forget to take their medication or who "forget" to take their medication. The first problem is that it is difficult to determine whether the child actually forgot or chose to forget. Younger children usually report to the school nurse and consequently their medication is monitored. It is easier for older children to fail to take their medication, as they may be on timed-release versions with medication being administered once a day.

Once you are aware that the child is not taking the medication on a regular basis, see if you can find out whether he is doing this on purpose or not. The child who does not wish to take his medicine is likely to be somewhat defensive. Offer to help him figure out ways to help him remember. Find something he does every day and connect that to the medication. Suggest that he put the pills beside his toothpaste or his orange juice; many families leave the medication on the table where the child eats his breakfast. A large chart that must be checked off each day can be put by the door.

If in spite of these methods the child is still not remembering, inquire whether or not the child feels the medicine helps. In my experience, every child who is deliberately forgetting has some issue with the medication. He may feel odd or different because he takes medication on a daily basis. Point out that other children wear glasses or test their blood sugar daily, and this is no different. Other children do not like the way the medication makes them feel, complaining that their personality is different on the medication and they feel drugged and unresponsive.

Medication Trial

The student may not believe that he needs the medication, a common complaint and one that may be true. If the student is in high school, a medication trial set up with the agreement of his parents, his physician, and the special education department may be appropriate. Some medication cannot be stopped suddenly, so make sure that the physician is involved in this. The idea is that for two weeks the boy does not take the medication, and he charts how well he does—grades, missed assignments, completed work. Then for two weeks he takes the medicine faithfully and charts again. The trick is the teachers are not to know when he is taking the medicine and when he is not. If he truly needs the medicine, it is unlikely that he is going to be able to keep his work up for two weeks when he is off of the medication; and if he doesn't, there should be no difference in his work whether he is on or off. Good behavior is not the test of success of the medication, attainment of academic goals is—this is the important point and it is why the teacher is not to know when the child is on a trial. This will give the student some tangible evidence of the effectiveness of the medication and a degree of control over what happens to him. Boys like to attribute academic improvement to effort and not to the medication (Pelham et al., 1992), and this test will address that belief. A survey of research on the treatment of ADHD with medication found that while 75 percent of those on medication reported an improvement in behavior, little current research had been done indicating any academic improvement as a result of stimulant medication (Safer, Zito, & Fine, 1996). Medication is not the only way to manage attentional problems.

Self-Medication

One other issue about medication and ADHD is that children identified with the disorder are more likely to abuse both legal and illegal substances (Biederman et al., 1997; Smith, Molina, & Pelham, 2002; Tarter et al., 2003). Some of the boys I know who have been diagnosed with attentional problems began to abuse drugs, both legal and illegal, early. And why not? After all, many of them are being made to take psychostimulants. If Ritalin and its cohorts work, why wouldn't lots of caffeine, nicotine, or cocaine—all stimulants? Alternately, boys may try to self-medicate with psychodepressants. One way of describing ADHD is that your mind is like a motor that is running all the time, so psychodepressants help slow down the brain. The easiest of these to obtain is alcohol. While marijuana is classified as a hallucinogen, it slows down perception and helps "mellow out" the racing brain.

You might think that boys who know first-hand what effects these stimulants can have would be less likely to abuse drugs. However, there are two factors at work here. First, we have seen that impulsivity leads to risky behavior, and taking drugs is certainly risky. Just being involved in the abuse of drugs can convey a feeling of elevated arousal, part of the feeling of being "high." Second, one symptom of ADHD is poor social skills. Peer pressure influences many boys to take drugs because taking drugs helps them fit in. The problem for boys is that education about the negative effects of drugs does not negate the positive effects of peer support (Sax, 2005).

Some education can help, if you emphasize the problem and not the effects of the drugs—believe me, they know what the drugs do. Start early—before the child has a chance to abuse, before his peer group gets involved—and enlist the child as a part of the program. I tell boys diagnosed with ADHD early and often that drugs may be a problem and that they need to be on their guard. I tell them that they are going to be tempted, why they are going to be tempted, why they should not succumb, and what they can do instead of taking drugs. The high from risky behavior is the real drug, so—with family support—suggest mountaineering, debate competitions, drama, or any activity that raises adrenalin and keeps the boy busy. One reason that boys tell me they believe what I have to say is that they know I am a fellow sufferer. I abused nicotine and caffeine for years before I realized what I was doing. Authenticity helps the boys believe the message. More information on boys and drugs will be found in Chapter 6.

THE "AT RISK" STUDENT

As a boy falls behind, a frequent explanation is that the problem is caused by a learning disability. If, after testing, it is determined that the boy has a learning disability, the special education team at his school, together with the student's classroom teachers and his parents, will develop an IEP, which outlines how the child will be taught. Depending on the severity of the child's disability, the spectrum of assistance may range from being assigned to a special education classroom to inclusion in general education classes with accommodations for the specific disability. The future for students identified with learning disabilities is not positive, as they are more likely to drop out of school, to have lower educational goals, and to have behavior problems (Smart, Sanson, & Pryor, 1996). However, this is not a handbook on methods to deal with learning disabilities, as that belongs in the domain of special education.

But what about boys who fall in that gray area between being learning able and learning disabled—the students who are "at risk" for learning disability? These are students whose learning problems are either not serious enough to qualify them for special services or who may be learning disabled but are also capable enough to compensate for their learning disabilities. These students function in the average range in the classroom, but the teacher believes they could do better if they would just (pick one) pay attention, work harder, turn in their work, read the assignments, do their homework, get organized. . . .

If you teach upper-level boys and you get discouraged working with students who seem lazy, who seem like they don't care, or who simply don't try, go visit a kindergarten class. You are not going to find many lazy learners there. What happens between then and middle school? Why do the problems show up later and not affect children in the first years of school? In fact, the problems do show up in the early years, but there are several reasons why the problems do not seem as serious.

If a child has LD, his kindergarten teacher will notice it or at least suspect it. However, for children in kindergarten and the early grades, there is a wide range of expectations for academic competence because the developmental levels of these children vary more than they will later. The difference in maturity between a child who is five and a child six months older is noticeable, whereas there is likely to be little discernible difference between a child who is ten and one who is ten and a half.

My students tell me that most of them were identified with learning problems around the third or fourth grade. By this time, it is presumed that learning differences are due not to developmental differences, but to learning problems. The most likely place for a boy to have trouble is in reading. The boys have been behind the girls in reading all along, but after children are presumed to have learned to read, the focus shifts to reading for content. We notice that boys in the third and fourth grades are beginning to lag behind the girls in physical maturity, yet we do not also take into account the possibility that these boys are lagging behind the girls in the maturity of their brains. The boys are not making the progress in reading that the girls are and, in contrast, appear to have problems. Again, time will help as long as the boys don't get the idea that reading is not for them.

In addition, boys don't settle down as easily as girls do. This may not be because of attentional or learning problems, but rather maturity issues (El-Sayed, Larsson, Persson, Santosh, & Rydelius, 2003). Teachers who help boys manage their need for activity, provide more active lessons, and understand that some learning problems may be developmentally based will help these young men develop learning approaches suited for their more active learning styles.

Dyslexia

One major area of learning disabilities involves reading problems. Dyslexia refers to any trouble that a student has with understanding information from the written word. The input of information is at fault. Students identified with dyslexia need specialized instruction in order to be able to learn to read. But what about the child whose reading skills do not qualify him as dyslexic, but whose skills are not progressing at the rate of his classmates? These students are frequently slow to become fluent readers and, without some understanding from the teacher, may never persist long enough to become fluent. The boys appear slow partially because, in contrast, many of the girls are facile readers. These boys are embarrassed to read out loud in class and rarely read a book that is not assigned. Boys' competitive nature makes it difficult for them to fail publicly, and they assume that they will never get better. So they give up. I have students in high school who tell me they have never read a book all the way to the end, simply because it takes them too long to read. Part of this is a problem with brain maturity, and time and practice will solve the problem. If it has been determined that the boy does not have dyslexia, the teacher can help in two ways.

1. Make sure that the boys know that maturity is a big part of the problem. Point out that the girls are getting bigger, that they will catch up to the girls physically in high school, and that reading skills are no different.

2. Help the boys continue to develop their skills by offering them literature they are interested in, and/or developing a boys' reading group where their slower reading skills will not be so obvious (Jones & Fiorelli, 2003). Boys would rather be successful in their own group than unsuccessful in the class as a whole.

Many children identified with learning disabilities do just fine at work or in other nonacademic settings. Some identified children get the impression that they are totally disabled and unable to learn anything. I once told a boy that what he had was a learning disability, not a living disability. One of the best things you can do for these boys is to have them make a list of all of their accomplishments so they can realize what they can do. I worked with a young man whose dyslexia was so severe he could not read effectively, but he could take a computer apart and rebuild it without any directions or instruction. I pointed out that while I could read, I was illiterate about the workings of my computer and that his skill was likely to be more in demand in the future. My contention was that as long as school tests us on our ability to read and not on our ability to rebuild computers, people like me look smart, but if it were the other way around, he would be the genius.

Applications for Your Classroom

- Don't ask poor readers to read aloud. If you think this is important—and reading aloud has many benefits—ask the child to read to you alone or assign a reading volunteer to work with the student. Many schools use older students, parents, and senior citizens to help children attain reading fluency by working with them one-on-one.
- If the child is concerned that he is the only one in the class who is not reading aloud, have him practice so that he feels comfortable with the material. The rest of the class does not have to know that he has prepared the passage in advance.
- Many famous people suffer from dyslexia. Have the students find out who these people are and what they have done to compensate.
- If you believe a student is not paying attention, do not ask him to read the material aloud. Use other ways to find out if the student is not paying attention than by putting him on the spot.
- One method to help the poor reader is to use transparent rulers under the line being read. It gives the child a frame of reference and seems to help him keep his eyes on the appropriate line. You may also find reading guides that look like small rulers, but they are clear in the middle so the child can slide the guide, uncovering the text as he reads.

CAUTION

★ Some families can be very eager to get their sons identified because they believe the accommodations made for disabilities will help all academic problems. Do what you can to help the special education department ensure that children who are identified with learning disabilities actually are disabled, and that boys who are cognitively immature are given the time to improve. Spend some time with the families to reassure them that their son is making progress and point out some ways that they can help their son at home, such as reading to him. Your documentation can serve as a baseline to help the boy and his parents see that he is making progress.

(Continued)

(Continued)

> ★ The identified boy may believe that he cannot do well without help and that school is not the place for him to succeed. You can do much to help the boy see that his learning disabilities do not affect his entire life and that there may be places where his academic disability is an advantage.

Dysgraphia

Dysgraphia is a learning disability that is frequently identified through poor handwriting, but it is actually a processing problem involving both motor and verbal skills. If dyslexia is an input problem, dysgraphia is an output problem. Symptoms include

- Immature and awkward pencil grip
- Illegible handwriting
- Inconsistencies in writing—use of both print and cursive, change of slant in the middle of a sentence, irregular sizes of letters
- Spaces in the middle of words
- Difficulties in maintaining columns and lines in written work
- Tiring when writing more than a few words
- Saying words out loud while writing
- Unfinished or omitted words
- Poor spelling
- Problems organizing thoughts on paper
- Resistance to and avoidance of writing
- Gap between comprehending what is written and what is heard

Related problems may be difficulty in playing the piano or guitar and catching balls (although most have no trouble throwing a ball), or any skill requiring both hands doing different tasks at once.

Make sure that a boy actually has dysgraphia and is not simply being sloppy. There are ways to test for dysgraphia, and your special education department should be able to help here. I cannot emphasize enough the necessity of catching this early, as research has shown that therapy instituted early can help. Some states do not identify dysgraphia as a learning disability. If this is true in your area, you can help the student by using some of the suggestions listed in the text box.

Most experts agree that early intervention with patterned and repetitive handwriting skills can alleviate the symptoms of dysgraphia (Berninger & Fuller, 1992; Graham, Harris, & Fink, 2000). These measures must start very early, around kindergarten to second grade, and most children do not have great handwriting at this age anyway. However, problems with pencil grip and inability to stay on lines may be early signs of this disorder.

Accommodations for Dysgraphia

- Provide pens and pencils with soft grips and make the diameter of the writing instrument larger. Many grips are available and you should provide a variety to fit different hands.
- Work with developing proper hand grip, do hand strengthening and coordination exercises (spreading and flexing fingers, folding one finger down at a time, touching thumb to fingers in various patterns).
- Give children balls or clay designed for hand rehabilitation, or squishy balls to help develop hand strength.
- Practice forming letters and other shapes.
- Allow extra time.
- Encourage the use of a word processor to facilitate the writing process.
- Encourage the use of the spell-check function.
- Develop writing organizational skills (outlining, first drafts).
- Turn lined paper sideways to provide columns to keep lists straight.
- Utilize different formats for written work, such as oral reports.
- For younger children, use a scribe for written work.
- Allow the student to record lectures.
- Use school-ruled paper into middle school and through the beginning of high school if necessary. The alternative, collegiate-ruled paper, is too narrow for most boys until they have mastered writing skills.
- Allow for alternative methods of writing. Even in my college classes, I have students who take their tests to the computer center to write their answers.

For more information, contact the National Center for Learning Disabilities, www.ncld.org/LDInfoZone_FactSheet_Dysgraphia.cfm

Dyscalculia

The child with dyslexia may not be able to make sense of the written word. The child with dyscalculia may not be able to make sense of numbers. The most common complaint of the child with dyscalculia is that he has trouble with mathematical calculations, but there are other related difficulties. Some of the symptoms include

- Time difficulties—understanding time, keeping track of the passage of time
- Problems with name and face retrieval
- Mental math problems—trouble with checkbooks, making change
- Difficulty with recall of numbers—reversals, omissions, additions, substitutions
- Poor retention of math facts—can do it one day, but forgets it the next
- Poor sense of direction
- Problems with sight-reading music or fingerings for an instrument
- Difficulty with athletic coordination (Newman, 2000)

Dyscalculia is not as well known as other learning disabilities, but ignoring it can lead to a lifetime of trouble. As we have seen, boys are more likely than girls to suffer from dyslexia, but boys and girls suffer equally from dyscalculia. The problems with dyscalculia are similar to those with dyslexia, but involve numbers instead of letters. Children with dyscalculia will copy a number down wrong, will reverse digits as they move from one part of a problem to another, will not see operational signs or directions, or will not know which mathematical operation is necessary to successfully negotiate a problem. There seem to be several different types of dyscalculia; some students will have trouble understanding what a number represents, while others will be unable to estimate an answer (Vaidya, 2004).

Applications for Your Classroom

- Many children, and those with dyscalculia particularly, will benefit from doing math on ruled paper turned sideways to keep columns straight. Graph paper can be very confusing to students and they may have trouble following the appropriate group of squares.

- Children with dyscalculia may benefit from using a graphing calculator, as the screen allows the user to see what was keyed in. Teach these children to do their work in two directions. If they have a problem involving long multiplication, they should do the problem as written first, then flip the numbers and do it again.
- If the child has no trouble with language, approach the study of math as if it were a foreign language. Dyscalculics (people with dyscalculia) may have trouble understanding that several different terms, such as "multiplied by" and "times," can refer to the same operation (Vaidya, 2004). Have each student compile a math dictionary in his notebook by putting down terms, giving a definition and an example.
- Start early in school—preschool or kindergarten—exposing all students to the study of patterns and sequences. Knowing that you have to do A before you do B will help the dyscalculic learn the steps of a problem.

CAUTION

★ These students can have total meltdowns in the middle of math tests. I have had students throw their papers on my desk telling me they can't do math. Others refuse to do any problems involving more than one step. Early identification of the difficulty and engaging the student in proactive remediation will help a great deal.

★ Boys with dyscalculia will deny that they have problems and prefer to let you think they have not studied the lesson. After all, girls are supposed to have trouble with math, not boys. Finding an older student or adult with the problem may help but can be hard, as dyscalculia is seriously under-identified. Education about the condition is the other major way to deal with denial. Here are some suggestions from the www.dyscalculia.org Web site:
  - Give the student lots of scratch paper to allow plenty of space to figure out problems.
  - Watch the student carefully as he solves problems, having him tell you out loud what he is doing. You may be able to catch incorrect strategies or reasoning before they become habits.

(Continued)

(Continued)

- Do not crowd problems on a page, as that may be confusing.
- Give extra time to do tests and quizzes.
- Suggest to the family that a homework tutor be employed. The student needs to work through the problems with someone who knows how to do the work. It is better that the tutor not be a family member. The student already feels badly about his inability to do math.
- If time allows, prepare the student for new material by going over it before class or having the homework tutor go over the material in advance.
- Remember that the student misreads problems and forgets how to solve problems. Make sure that the student knows that is part of the condition and not any attempt to get out of work. On the other hand, it simply means that the student needs to work more carefully and check all work.

ATTENTIONAL AND LEARNING PROBLEMS

The classroom teacher, while not the person who makes the diagnosis of learning disability, provides the information and classroom observations necessary for such a diagnosis. You will find that there are also boys in your classes who do not qualify as learning disabled, but who will benefit from assistance similar to that afforded your LD students. You can help these students learn to deal with their problems by structuring their learning experience in such a way that participation is improved. The teacher who utilizes this information will offer a learning environment that

- Provides opportunities for students to explore alternative paths to learning
- Provides instruction in learning strategies that use a student's strengths to compensate for weaknesses
- Provides support for the student who is struggling to learn

6

Social and Emotional Differences

TANK MCNAMARA JEFF MILLAR & BILL HINDS

In each of the schools where I have taught, because I am a counselor, I have been part of the groups that meet to discuss students with problems. For the most part, boys did not come for help even when we offered, but came to the group's attention because their grades had dropped, they were in trouble in the dorms, or we had heard from their families. Occasionally, the senior in charge of a dorm would alert us to some situation. When boys did come to talk something over, there was always some cover story. Many boys who came for extra academic help stayed to talk over personal

troubles. When I began to teach psychology, I got a host of "I have a friend who…"
questions. What interested me was that many of those questions arose out of discus-
sions in the dorm. That told me that the boys were talking with each other about their
problems.

The stereotype is that boys are not open about their feelings and they have a hard time communicating emotional information. One theory is that they may not experience their emotions as deeply as do girls (Geary, 1998). However, there is evidence to the contrary. We have seen in Chapter 1 that as children mature, the amygdala increases more in males whereas the hippocampus increases more in females (Giedd et al., 1997). The amygdala is the part of the brain that responds to emotions, particularly fear and rage. So if the brains of males are capable of intense emotions, why does the contrary stereotype exist? According to one explanation, boys experience strong emotions but are just not able to express them (Cahill, 2003; Sax, 2005).

Are these differences in emotional display learned or biological? Previously, we found that sexual differences become gender differences as variations in biology create distinct responses to environmental stimuli. Communicating emotions is no different. Biology is the driving force, but expectations and beliefs play a part in producing stereotypical behaviors in boys and girls. Because boys find it difficult to articulate their feelings, they are characterized as not having those feelings. If you want evidence to the contrary, look at their physical responses. When boys feel passionately about what they are doing, their voices will get louder, their actions will get more dramatic, and they may literally fling themselves into the activity. Let them use physical means to express their excitement until they get older, and then help them learn to use words to convey their feelings.

Years ago, I believed that most gender-stereotypical behaviors were learned. When my son was born, I was determined that he would be exposed to a wide variety of peaceful playthings and be given toys associated with both boys and girls. When he was four, I found him using a sharp stone to whittle a piece of wood into a pistol. I have no idea where he got that idea, as he was not given any guns as toys, he did not go to day care, and he was not allowed to watch any TV other than what was on PBS. I tried to raise him with both male and female influences. He still crashed his toy cars together and built forts from which to defend our house. He does cook, but that is more because his father cooks than because of my efforts to expose him to traditionally female activities. His boyness came through in spite of my attempts to androgynize him.

In the past decade, focus has been placed on masculinity and the development of boys' emotional lives (Biddulph, 1997; Kindlon & Thompson, 1999; Mac an Ghaill, 1994; Pollack, 1998). The concern is that boys are getting the message that typical boy behavior—loud, competitive, and physical—is bad, and they need to become more like girls—quieter, cooperative, and gentle. There has been an increase in the number of single-sex educational programs for boys, partially in response to a perceived need for havens where boys can be boys, away from environments where their nature is questioned or where the accepted standard of behavior is feminine (Bleach, 1997; Bushweller, 1994; Hawley, 1991). However, with attention to the ways boys cope with the world, help can be provided in the coed setting.

Another consideration is the belief that boys suffer from a lack of appropriate male role models and that school is one place where that lack can be remedied (Biddulph, 1997; Connell, 1996; Mac an Ghaill, 1994; West, 2002). For example, in the library of one boys' school are large poster-sized pictures of a great many of the faculty posing with their favorite book. You would guess that the headmaster and the head of the English department would be there, but it might interest you to see the reading preferences of the head of the science department and the dean of students, a former marine. The message is that everyone reads. The library is a great place for all to find quiet. I have heard boys comment on finding their math teacher deep in a novel or another teacher quietly reading a book from the children's section to his young son.

The boys see their teachers with their families, and they see the respect these men have for their wives. They learn that looking after children is the work of all in a family. I taught a child psychology course where each student was assigned a small faculty child to look after and report on. The boys were fascinated by how the little children thought and behaved, but agreed that they would be less inclined to take the course if there were girls around. They saw how openly distressed a faculty member became when his wife went into very early labor, especially when there was doubt about the baby's survival. They also saw the men in family situations that they might not otherwise have had the opportunity to observe. One afternoon a student entered my class exclaiming, "You are NOT going to believe what Mr. T was doing in the bathroom! He was changing his son's diaper!" I told him that I had been in many women's bathrooms and seen women changing children's diapers, and asked him what the difference was. He stopped for a minute, and replied, "Nothing, I guess, I just never thought of him doing that."

One theory is that in modern society many boys do not have enough time with their fathers. This creates "father hunger" and boys go looking for an older male to serve as a model and a mentor. Unfortunately, many of the older males readily available to most boys are not likely to serve as positive models. Consequently, many boys join gangs, bully others, and fail to develop close ties with others (Biddulph, 1997; Pollack, 1998; West, 2002). One reason for fathers being absent is that they are at work, but in school the men are there—it *is* their work.

Male teachers can provide a variety of role models. My father was a learned professor of foreign languages whose favorite author was Proust. However, many boys helped him haul native fieldstones he used to build a house, and they saw he could wield a pen, a shovel, and a spatula equally well. Yes, the athletic coaches are great role models and many boys' lives are changed by working with these men. Others' lives are shaped by contact with the English teacher who writes thrillers or by the physics teacher whose whacky sense of humor engages the lonely boy.

In addition, the boys see how their male teachers treat their wives, the female teachers, and other females on the staff. That can have a profound effect on a boy who may not be used to seeing women treated with respect and as equals in the working world. Many of the boys who were in my ninth-grade science classes later told me that they were originally disappointed to have a woman science teacher. They believed that somehow a woman could not be as rigorous a scientist as a man. After the class they had changed their minds, and not totally because of what happened in the class. Several boys remarked that they were impressed that the rest of the science department treated me as an equal and came to me for help with problems in areas in which I had more expertise. Boys need role models to learn proper behavior of all sorts, including how to relate to women. If their only teachers are women, they have no models for how to interact with women.

The emotional lives of boys is a topic many schools are beginning to consider. The problem, we are realizing, is not that boys don't have emotions, but that they lack the skills or freedom to express their emotions. Boys believe in the "boy code," the unwritten law that says that boys are not to divulge their feelings, and those who do are weak or not masculine. In addition, boys are not to work hard, because if they do it will look as if they care about what they are doing

(Maccoby, 1998; Pollack, 1998). With positive male role models in school—both teachers and older students—it is likely that boys will see that men can share and let others know what they are feeling. Because boys understand that the male teachers were boys once, they trust the male teachers to understand what they are going through. When boys interact with male teachers on a daily basis, they learn what it means to be a productive member of one's community.

Emotions come into play when children approach puberty. It is not that young children do not have emotions, but that the rise in hormones associated with puberty creates in many children a change in how they experience their emotions. Puberty has a considerable effect on the development of self-esteem in boys. Research has demonstrated that later-developing boys have lower self-esteem than do boys who enter puberty earlier (Duke et al., 1982; Peterson, 1986).

Self-esteem comes from the judgments that we make about ourselves, be they positive or negative. As most children enter adolescence, their perception of their capabilities and their worth takes a downward turn. Generally this has been seen to be true of girls, but boys also suffer (Peterson, 1986) and they are less likely to share these feelings with others. Boys are more confident of their academic skills, so if they fail, they can be devastated. They question their beliefs about themselves, and not infrequently start on the downward academic spiral of "nothing I do is right" (Grossman & Grossman, 1994). Setting a boy up to win or giving him easier work is not the answer, since when he discovers what you did he will think you are convinced he cannot do the work. One of my advisees, who had never had an easy time in science, decided to take physics in summer school so that he could focus on that course. He did very well and I complimented him. I was amazed by his reaction when he replied that the course was really easy and even "science losers" like himself scored high.

The drop in self-esteem is true for girls as well, but the last child in a class to enter puberty will probably be a boy, and he may feel left behind by his peers. In addition, his immature behavior will be all the more noticeable in comparison to his female classmates, who may have begun puberty two or more years previously. In the classroom, this difference in maturity may be reflected in the way students approach learning and how they process information, resulting in students who have widely differing levels of scholarship. Even in a single-sex classroom, this can be a problem. Whenever we brought up the topic of love in my senior psychology class, the more immature boys in the class inevitably snickered as they made a quick link to sex, whereas the more mature students wanted to discuss relationship building.

THE BRAIN AND EMOTIONS

In the past, the general belief was that emotions come from the heart, but in the early nineteenth century an accident to a railroad foreman named Phineas Gage changed the way we think about the source of emotions. Gage suffered a horrendous injury in which a metal spike passed through his head, separating most of his brain from a portion of the frontal lobes responsible for social decisions—how we get along with other people (Pinker, 2002). Amazingly, the accident left most of the rest of his mental functions intact. Before the accident, Gage had been a dependable and steady person, but from that point on he had a hard time governing his temper, he became unreliable, and he was too quarrelsome to work with others. Gage's accident points to the frontal lobes as playing a major role in how reasoned decisions are made. Without that portion of his brain, Gage seemed somewhat like a young child who insists on having his way no matter the cost or how inconvenient it is for others. What this tells us is how important various parts of the brain are to our emotional life.

Unless we are discussing a child's inability to control his emotions, we usually don't connect emotions and the classroom, especially when we discuss boys. The paradox of boys is that, while they won't discuss their emotions, they are extremely influenced by their emotional reactions. We have already covered the importance of the amygdala in boys' emotional responses, especially with respect to aggression. It has been suggested that the differences in brain maturation may be reflected in academic performance (Yurgelun-Todd, Killgore, & Cintron, 2003). More important, the male brain is structured in such a way that the primary source of emotions is not connected to a part of the brain that can talk about them.

What this means in the classroom is that since the brain structures responsible for memory are developing sooner in girls, girls can be better at remembering course content and events. Boys are influenced by their emotions—possibly because they don't express them—and consequently they need to be actively involved and to feel positively about school in order to be engaged in the learning process. In an earlier chapter, we learned that boys are masters of trivia. If they do not remember as well as do girls, how is this possible? Boys are masters of trivia for topics about which they are intensely interested—when they are emotionally engaged in the material, they remember, and remember very well. Without that emotional engagement, boys need help in acquiring memory strategies. In Chapter 4, we discussed some memory strategies that were particularly good for boys. The ones that follow help boys use emotional connections to remember.

Applications for Your Classroom

- Use mnemonic devices with music and rhythm to help boys remember basic facts. Boys enjoy music and are more likely to employ memory tricks that use it. There are a large number of music mnemonics, including the alphabet song, the dinosaur song (a little ditty that describes all the major types of dinosaurs), and the preposition song, which seems to appeal to boys because they find it silly. If there is information that the boys need to know and you cannot find a mnemonic, have the boys put the material to a song or rhythm that they like. The Web site www.songsforteaching.com has a great many similar songs that will be useful for students of all ages.

- Practice memorizing. Have all students memorize poems, particularly if they are funny; Shel Silverstein and Jack Prelutsky are poets whose works appeal to young boys. Older boys may be interested in learning some of the great speeches of war heroes (Washington's farewell to his troops) or famous men (Lincoln's Gettysburg Address). Boys will be eager to memorize material they find interesting.

- Use topics in which the boys are very interested to lead into topics that may be less interesting. If you can't get young boys to read the books on your reading list, see if you can find a comparable book on dinosaurs, or other topics such as sports, war, science fiction, or famous men. Ask your students what their favorite topics are and use those passions to provide a springboard for your lessons.

- The child who calls out answers does so because it matters to him that he knows the answer. Try having teams to answer questions, but limit the answering to one child. This way, even if he is not the "answer man" the child gets the satisfaction of knowing his team knows he knows, but doesn't have the opportunity to dominate the class. Mix the groups up frequently so that children will have the chance to work with all the others. You can use the Academic Tournament or Jeopardy model for this activity. Competition is important to boys, so use it to help them acquire necessary information.

(Continued)

(Continued)

CAUTION

★ Boys have a hard time memorizing lots of material if they do not see any reason for the exercise. Point out that if they are sure of PEMDAS (the order of operations in math problems) they won't make as many mistakes. Reciting the Gettysburg Address in front of the class will help prepare them for speaking in a business meeting. This seems obvious, but boys do not always get the long-term ramifications of learning.

★ Boys will not work for a teacher who they believe does not like them. Usually a boy draws this conclusion based on the teacher's failure to understand how he learns. Boys tell me that teachers they do not like will not listen to their explanations of why they cannot do work the way the teacher wants, or will not respond to their learning needs. The fact that the student may not have discussed these problems with the teacher will not change the boy's attitude toward the teacher. If you find a student shutting down and refusing to work for you, here are some suggestions:
  – Ask the child what the problem is.
  – If you do not get a satisfactory answer or you do not understand the problem as the boy describes it, ask other teachers with whom the boy has a positive relationship.
  – Families can be helpful in understanding the needs of younger children.
  – The school counselor may be effective in helping you and the boy understand each other's position.
  – Including the students in planning classroom activities works well with boys. They like being a part of the planning process, and it will give them insights as to why the lesson is structured as it is.

Impulsivity and Delay of Gratification

Impulsivity in boys is a major complaint of many teachers. Boys will answer without being called on—true, they raise their hands, but they answer the question at the same time. I have frequently remarked to boys who insist on answering without being called on that there is no neural connection between raising the hand and opening the mouth, but usually to no avail. The offender will apologize and two questions later is blurting out answers again. I'd rather have them shouting out answers than daydreaming and not engaging in the lesson, but they can be disruptive.

Blurting out answers is just the tip of the iceberg. Similar behaviors include starting before directions are given, inability to wait one's turn, and saying the first thing that comes into their minds. While boys are very impulsive, most men learn to control themselves. The problem is getting there.

Later prefrontal cortex development is thought to be the reason that boys are less likely to be able to inhibit impulses (Baron-Cohen, 2003; Giedd et al., 1999). This delay in self-control ability is seen in infants as well as in older children (Baron-Cohen, 2003; Maccoby, 1998). Learning to control our impulses and to wait for promised rewards are similar behaviors because, if we are impulsive, we have a hard time waiting to get the promised treat—delaying gratification.

It is thought that the adult brain makes decisions using the frontal lobes and the adolescent brain uses the amygdala (Pinker, 1997). Recent studies have revealed that as adolescents mature, boys and girls differ in the brain structures employed to process emotions, instructions, and procedures. Researchers compared the reactions of boys and girls ages 9 to 17 when presented with pictures of faces that looked fearful. As they matured, the brains of girls shifted from primarily using the amygdala to responding with the prefrontal cortex. Boys, on the other hand, did not show any such shift with age and continued responding in the amygdala (Killgore, Oki, & Yurgelun-Todd, 2001; Killgore & Yurgelun-Todd, 2001). One study found that girls were better at planning and paying attention, and the theory given to explain that difference was the superior executive function of the frontal cortex in girls (Naglieri & Rojahn, 2001). What this reveals is that as girls mature, they begin using the prefrontal region of the cerebral cortex for decision making, while boys continue to use the more emotional amygdala. This is now considered to be a factor contributing to impulsive behavior in boys.

No matter what the reason, boys are less able to delay gratification and to plan actions, and are more likely to be impulsive and less polite (Canada, 1999/2000; Du, Weymouth, & Dragseth, 2003). Girls behave more maturely than their male age-mates, who may be involved in mock fighting, rough-and-tumble play, and name-calling (Maccoby, 1998). The boys have been indulging in this behavior all along, but incidents increase as they approach puberty (Berk, 1997). Even in high school, the younger boys cannot walk down the hall without throwing themselves or shoving others into objects or people. This is usually accompanied by the use of rude names indicating that they like each other. By the time the boys are seniors, this horseplay is much reduced.

The cited research indicates that the root of many poor decisions by adolescents may be that they tend to respond emotionally, without thinking of consequences. We have already discussed that boys' development, both mind and body, is behind that of girls. Adolescent boys are likely to still be using the emotional part of their brain to make decisions after girls have begun to include their reasoning brain. In addition to using their frontal lobes, girls are involving the hippocampus, and that may be why they are more likely to learn from their and others' mistakes.

Reading Emotions

Remember the studies where day-old infants were exposed to two different visual stimuli, one a woman's face and the other a mobile? Judges agreed that the girls looked more at the woman's face and the boys looked more at the object (Connellan et al., 2000). In the second study, twelve-month-old children were presented with videos of cars moving or of faces moving—the boys looked longer at the cars and the girls longer at the faces (Lutchmaya & Baron-Cohen, 2002). This is not news to parents of young boys, and is one reason that *Bob the Builder* is so popular—it's about trucks.

As discussed in Chapter 2, girls are better at reading expressions on people's faces (McClure, 2000). Boys have trouble in this area. My students are convinced that I read minds because I know that they don't understand something when they look confused and start paging through their textbooks. After I tell them that I read their faces and their body language, they still think that what I do is some sort of magic. When we get to the topic of reading emotions in my psychology class, I bring out a set of pictures of people showing different emotions and actually teach the boys how to identify the basic emotions on people's faces.

It is not that boys are unable to read basic information such as a smile or a frown, but they don't do as well with subtle facial expressions such as disgust or disbelief as do girls (Anderson & Morganstern, 1981). Additionally, they don't get the double message from facial expressions and body language that girls can understand. Consequently, if you smile while you are reprimanding a boy, he may only see the smile and not hear the negative message about his behavior.

Applications for Your Classroom

- Use direct statements when giving boys information on their progress. You may know at which behavior you are smiling, but the student may misread your facial expression or miss seeing your smile or frown altogether. The boy who has just spent ten minutes drawing a monster is going to think you don't like his drawing if you frown at him for grabbing a crayon from another child. You need to be specific—"Your drawing is very good, but Peter had that crayon and, if you want it, you should ask him if you may have it for a while."

- Develop signals to indicate approval, disapproval, and other elements of classroom management. For quiet, the teacher can say "one, two, three, eyes on me," and then simply put the index finger on the lips. For older students, the signal is "Give me five." All students raise one hand indicating that they know that (1) eyes are watching, (2) ears are listening, (3) lips are closed, (4) hands are still, (5) feet are still.

- This can be a great opportunity to introduce the basic skills of American Sign Language using signals for stop, go, quiet, and so forth. Learning a language that is not written may be easier for some boys, and that knowledge may provide a foundation for learning reading and writing skills. There is not a lot of evidence for this connection, but some teachers believe it to be true.

- Teach boys to interpret facial cues and body language by having them pantomime parts of a story that the class is reading, directions for some class activity, or appropriate vocabulary. What does someone look like who is horrified? Amazed? Astounded? Have them draw pictures of people who look scared or happy. They can pick out descriptions of emotions from their reading and practice writing about how they feel in journals.

CAUTION

- ★ Boys may be unable to follow verbal directions. If the teacher relies on verbal and facial methods to communicate, such as raising the eyebrows to ask a question or using eye movements to indicate where a child is to go, it may appear as if boys are not paying

(Continued)

(Continued)

> attention when in fact they find the directions ambiguous. Provide directions in at least two ways. When you say the directions, use visual prompts such as one finger for "first, do this," two fingers for "second, do this," and so forth. Then, either write the directions on the board or provide a handout with the directions. In my science classes, I always use a handout listing the steps in a lab exercise. I know they won't read directions at first, but when they get lost, they will refer to the sheet.
>
> ★ Boys may misperceive the message about their behavior if the teacher smiles as she or he reprimands them. The teacher may be trying not to overwhelm the boy with his errors, but this may present inconsistent information. A more neutral facial expression will get a coherent message across.

EMOTIONAL VOCABULARY

Boys don't seem to have many words to describe what they feel. College counselors work hard to help boys find terms to describe themselves other than well liked, good athlete, hard worker, and so forth. We know that boys use less emotional language to describe their feelings, and one explanation is that their environment may be teaching them not to express their emotions (Maccoby, 1998). It is also possible that the environment does not push boys to respond because they have difficulty in vocalizing their emotions. In particular, boys may be taught not to express emotions that may be seen as feminine, but instead to focus on the facts of a situation (Martino, 1995).

Whether or not the source of boys' circumscribed emotional vocabularies is their environment, school is just the place to rectify this problem. Teachers need to start early helping boys widen their vocabularies to describe how people feel about what happens to them.

Applications for Your Classroom

- Using literature studied in class, give the students a passage describing how a character responds to an event in the book. Let them use a thesaurus to search for synonyms for all the adjectives and adverbs in the passage. Older students will then rewrite the sentence using the synonyms, trying to convey the same meaning.

- Teach emotional vocabulary in clusters. Have boys develop lists of words that describe confidence, character, or cheerfulness. That should help them be able to use those words later.
- Since boys tend to describe people in terms of facts, start there when developing a description of a character in a novel or story. Then have them assign emotional words to the fact list. For example, if the character is Johnny Tremain, the fact list can be: hard worker, in charge, secretive about background. The emotional vocabulary that comes from that could be: hard worker—dependable, reliable; in charge—bossy, arrogant; secretive about background—aloof, prickly.
- In classes with very young boys, give them the vocabulary they need to describe how they feel. To a child who has been working to build a tower with blocks: "It must be frustrating when you can't make the blocks stand up." To a class who will not settle down after lunch and has gotten an attack of the sillies: "You all can be so exasperating."
- Give boys the chance to care about something, such as a classroom pet or a school little brother or sister. Encourage them to babysit. Giving boys experience with very young or very small beings will show them that tenderness and nurture are required in some situations and are not limited to girls (Neall, 2002).

CAUTION

★ Some boys will make fun of others who use an emotional vocabulary. It does not matter why these children are uncomfortable with emotionally laden words, but you should help them understand that these words will be important to them later. Have them look for such words in the sports pages of the newspaper or in song lyrics by popular musicians. (Of course, be careful to select songs that don't have words you don't want your students learning!)

AGGRESSION AND BULLYING

Aggression is one of the salient traits of boys, and if you expect boys to be aggressive, they will not disappoint. However, any group of boys will exhibit a wide range of aggression, and while some boys are pushing and shoving to get to the head of the line, there will be others who will stand back and be content to wait. Those who are more obviously aggressive need to learn to temper their aggression so that it is appropriate for the situation and so that they do not force their aggression on others. Part of the difficulty is that boys are well aware that our culture believes aggressive boys are normal and nonaggressive boys are wimps. Actually, the most common pejoratives usually involve referring to the nonfighter as either a girl or a homosexual. This is a problem that needs to be dealt with immediately and early. Some boys will actually have been encouraged by their families to be aggressive and to fight back and will have learned those derogatory terms at home.

In a summer camp, there were several boys who boasted about their prowess on the basketball court, using their basketball skills to put down other students. They played roughly and were proud of it. One female camp counselor played on her college basketball team and the boys taunted her about her skills, saying that even though she was taller, they were better players—actually what they said was that she played like a girl. This situation was made somewhat more difficult because the boys were African American and the counselor was white. She challenged them to a game and it was quickly apparent that her skills were far above theirs. Instead of gloating, she began to show them what she was doing and why her moves were so effective. By the end of the session, the boys had learned to play better. In addition, she had served as a role model, showing the boys how to be aggressive players while at the same time not turning that aggression on peers who were plainly outclassed.

Another problem is that in the present school climate, aggression is often linked to violence. Two boys in the first grade who are roughhousing on the playground may be accused of fighting and sent to the school counselor. It is quite possible that they were just playing, and it is also possible that one was beating on the other. I am always amused when my two male kittens wrestle, as it is so much like those first graders. However, if one kitten gets a bit rough and the other squeaks, they stop immediately. This is the three-part lesson about aggression that boys need to learn.

1. Stop when the other person says to stop.

2. If something hurts, you are to say stop.

3. Stopping or asking to stop does not make you a wimp.

(I'm well aware that this will only work with very young boys, but let's start somewhere. Using animals as models will make this lesson more acceptable.)

For older boys and adolescents who exhibit physically aggressive behavior, do what you can to steer them into organized programs where they are taught how to use that physicality under the close supervision of adults. The Golden Gloves program, Boys and Girls Clubs, school wrestling programs, martial arts, and the like have helped a large number of boys learn to channel their energies at the same time they are learning to be considerate of others.

Point out that acting in this way respects the other person. Boys can understand that being respectful of other people means that they get respect in return—that beating up on someone only means that the other person gets mad and wants to get even. Boys sometimes have a hard time seeing the difference between fear and respect, but it is a valuable lesson worth teaching. Involving older boys in activities with the younger ones has the double effect of teaching both sets of boys how to respect the skills and abilities of the other. Boys tell me that what they really want is to be respected, and sometimes they don't know how to do that. Using role models helps. The models can be either people in the school or people that the students learn about from books.

Most of the children in your classroom will have been exposed to a large number of violent acts through TV, movies, and computer games. Because these sources are extremely popular, students may believe that the behavior is acceptable. A long-term study revealed that the more a boy identifies with a violent character, the more likely it is that the boy will behave violently when he is an adult. This study pointed out that children are more vulnerable to violence the younger they are (Huesmann, Moise-Titus, Podolski, & Eron, 2003). It is important to do what you can to reduce the exposure of all of your students to violent media—but particularly boys.

When a person intentionally uses force, either physical or emotional, against another person who cannot or will not retaliate, that is bullying. In fact, bullies frequently get their way despite who they hurt in the process. Bullying is a major problem, especially in middle school. In 2003, 13.9 percent of sixth graders reported being bullied in school, compared with 6.7 percent of ninth graders (NCES, 2004). Victims of bullying appear to be about equally distributed between boys and girls. This same study noted that 7.8 percent of boys and 6.5 percent of girls reported being bullied. However, in the same year 17.1 percent of boys, but only 8.0 percent of girls reported being in fights on school property

(NCES, 2004). While equal numbers of boys and girls may be victims of bullying, we may believe that more boys are bullied because they are more likely to be involved in fights. Fighting may be a sign of overt bullying, but covert bullying may not be so obvious.

A new form of subversive bullying is growing: cyberbullying. Middle-school students, who are without cars and less mobile than older students, are using instant messaging (IM) and text messaging to communicate with their friends. A growing number of students are using IMs to threaten other students by posting rumors, snide comments, and other demeaning information. This has resulted in serious problems for some children and is thought to be involved in several suicides (Meadows, 2005; Swartz, 2005). Since this activity does not take place at school, why should schools deal with it? The students know each other from school and the information that is disseminated is generally based on school activities. Younger children may learn about the practice at school and believe the behavior is acceptable as a way to control their peers.

Most school systems, if not all, have programs in place to deal with bullying and to impress upon students that the behavior is not acceptable. Children may come to school predisposed to bully because of home factors, including poor parenting and a lack of positive role models. School factors that may make bullying more common include lax adult supervision and implied acceptance of the behavior by adults who fail to do anything to stop the bully. In addition, the presence of gang activities may encourage bullying behavior (Limber, 2003; Olweus, 2001). Make sure your students are aware of the school policy on bullying and do all that you can to enforce it.

You can help your students by creating a respectful atmosphere in your classroom. If a student wants to be a bully, your presence may deter him. But you cannot always be present. Students who are treated with respect will respect each other and the teacher. That is the best way to help bullies learn other ways to deal with their peers.

Applications for Your Classroom

- Providing consistent rules for behavior helps all students learn self-control. Set rules and enforce them. This is more likely to happen if you have no more than five rules. State them in the affirmative, keep them short, and use developmentally appropriate language. Examples might be: Students will be ready for class when the bell rings; students will be respectful of other students' stuff. If the rule is that there will be no bothering other members of the class during seat work, then passing notes and throwing spitballs are both violations and should result in the same discipline, even though the note-passing was less disruptive.

- Do not make exceptions to the rules because you believe a child's motives were not malicious. Boys may believe that you really do not mean to uphold rules or may believe that you do not like them if they are disciplined for an infraction that another child got away with. If a rule becomes too difficult to enforce or it is apparent that the rule needs to be changed, do so, but explain to the students why the change occurred. Do not change rules often. Boys view people who cannot stick to the rules as weak.

- Young boys do not like being thought of as younger than they are and may react with disrespect to a teacher's attempt to speak gently to them, particularly when the child is upset. Boys will respond to being treated matter-of-factly and included in decision making about how to deal with a situation.

- Encourage regular physical activity. Boys benefit from daily exercise and involvement in sports is a good way to accomplish this (Frydenberg & Lewis, 1993). Boys' high schools generally have two or more hours of athletic practice every afternoon, and all students are members of competitive athletic teams. Students who are likely to be victims benefit as well. One rather soft-spoken, willowy young man was having a hard time of it until he joined the cross-country team, where his long legs and lack of bulk were an advantage.

- A physical outlet will help boys control their emotions (Kleine, 1994). Physical education classes can help, but may not be enough for some boys. Martial arts have been successful in helping boys learn to control themselves. Another program involves boys in the percussion section of the school band to help control anger (Currie, 2004). Suggest that a child help a social service agency such as those who build houses for the needy, clean up urban waterfronts, or maintain walking trails.

(Continued)

(Continued)

- If it becomes obvious that a student is bullying, you will need to include the school counselor in your plans to deal with the behavior. Your class is probably not the only place that his behavior has been noticed, and a coordinated effort is likely to be more effective in helping this child learn to respect his peers.
- Humor will help and will defuse the tensest of situations. If this is not natural to you, don't try. Boys have a high standard for humor and will greet poor attempts with derision unless you tell them how awful your jokes are and challenge them to come up with worse ones.
- Name-calling is very common in the heat of an argument and boys will use terms that many groups will find demeaning, particularly females and homosexuals. This is a good place to teach the lesson that name-calling is not an effective way to win an argument and that pejorative terms have value only because the persons involved in the argument agree that the term has a negative connotation. Teach younger boys to argue effectively, stating their points instead of resorting to personal attacks. Older boys may find debate competition a good place to learn the fine points of argument. Search through literature for alternative terms; Shakespeare is full of negative terms whose connotations have changed over time.
- Use peer counselors. This program is used extensively in many schools, where the counselors are known as head boys or head girls, prefects, monitors, and the like. They are usually senior students who have demonstrated that they have the ability to stand firm in the face of peer pressure and are willing to uphold the rules. I have seen prefects break up fights much more effectively than an adult could have done because the combatants may feel threatened by an adult presence when they are misbehaving. Peers serve as effective role models for younger boys as well.
- Do not make accusations by pointing out shortcomings, as boys are likely to become confrontational when accused in front of others. Simply describe the behavior: "Your books have not been put away" or "I don't have your homework for today." You haven't nagged, you have just stated the problem and then it is up to the boy to say how he is going to deal with the problem. When you feel you need to set some limits or

standards, do so in a positive manner: "You are capable of good work" rather than "you never get any work done" (Neall, 2002).

CAUTION

★ Confrontations with students will occur for a variety of reasons. If you challenge the student in front of his peers, he is not likely to back down. The best way is to step outside of the classroom and talk with the student where he does not have the support of the class. If your class is very young, do not step out until someone is there to take your place. Young boys are likely to see this as an invitation to misbehave even if you are right outside the door.

★ Some bullies are experts in fooling adults about their true motives. Be careful in accepting explanations when certain students are involved. However, as a woman in a boys' school, I found that the boys were less threatened by me or by older teachers and therefore were more likely to be straightforward.

★ Homophobia and femiphobia can be made much worse if boys are allowed to use derogatory terms. There are successful football players who have "come out" and women professional boxers. In addition, some male hairdressers are married with children. When it is appropriate, you should not shy away from frank discussions of homosexuality and feminism. Helping boys come to terms with those topics will help them become stronger adults.

COMPETITION AND COOPERATION

If you were to use one word to describe boys in general, competitive would be it. Boys will vie with each other over who is strongest, who is smartest, and who has the most stuff. The usual explanation for this behavior is that it is carried over from the time when the strongest male got all the land, all the resources, and the best females (Geary, 1998). Whatever the reason, if two boys are together, they will compete with each other over some matter. This behavior can create problems in the classroom, or if used properly can help motivate students. Research has shown that for boys, competition helps academic performance (Gneezy & Rustichini, 2004).

You should be aware that there are several types of competition. Direct competition involves a head-to-head struggle with one of the combatants emerging as the victor. Indirect competition involves an individual working to improve his past achievement, what athletes refer to as attaining "a personal best" (Billing, 1980). Cooperative competition exists when groups of people work together for a common goal for the benefit of the group (Bonta, 1997). You don't need to encourage direct competition, but the best ways to engage boys in the learning process use indirect and cooperative competition.

It has been my observation that, in the presence of girls, boys are more likely to engage in direct competition. In single-sex environments, boys are more likely to use cooperative competition, treating the group as an extension of their individual identity. There is a huge social advantage in this—boys in boys' schools learn to be good followers. They understand that only a few are needed as leaders and that the leader depends on those who support him. Boys learn how to identify good leaders and to work with the system to change leadership when it is not effective. For the group to work efficiently, the participants need to acquire effective communication skills so that all have an active part in the endeavor. Boys who only engage in direct competition may not acquire these skills and spend a good deal of their adult life frustrated because they are not included in the few who attain the top positions.

I have little corroborating evidence other than anecdotes for my belief that boys in boys' schools become better communicators. However, whenever I meet the graduates of boys' schools, I ask what they do for a living and whether or not they use communication skills in their job. Do they feel that they are good communicators? What I get is quick acknowledgement that they need good communication skills as part of their work and agreement that they think that they communicate well—usually, they believe, far better than their peers do. Some are surprised when I ask the question because it never occurred to them what the source was for their career success, but they agree that communication skills and their ability in cooperative competition are responsible. These men learned to communicate in the football huddle, in the dorm, and in the classroom because the emphasis everywhere was on the effort of the group.

Sports are the most obvious place where boys compete, and it offers a great venue for boys to learn to win and lose. They learn that the rules are the rules and you can't change them, in the same way that 2 + 2 always equals 4. They learn that unless you really try, you don't accomplish much—that playing for fun may pass the time, but you don't improve your skills that way. They learn to work with others and to be a productive part of a group effort—that divisiveness on a team will guarantee unsatisfactory results. They learn to trust others and to be trustworthy—that if someone makes promises and does not follow through, everyone loses (Swift, 1991).

Applications for Your Classroom

- Use cooperative and collaborative learning exercises in the classroom. You can have boys work together on a project, but you can also have the whole class work on a project. One history class developed a Web site for a Civil War battle that occurred near the school. The boys designed the Web pages by dividing up the chores and worked together to finish the project. When one group returned to school with some spectacular photographs of a reenactment, the boys worked to get permission to use the pictures and included links to the Web site for the reenactment group.

- Working toward a "personal best" is easy in a gym or PE class, but it can also work in an academic area. Boys can keep logs of their accomplishments and chart their progress. Did they bring their reading speed up? Is their comprehension of passages better now? Younger students can chart their progress on graphs, and older students can keep track using a computer spreadsheet such as Excel.

- Competitive competition can be used as well. Spelling or geography bees allow some students to shine. However, remember that some of us can't spell worth beans and others have no interest in the capital of Senegal, so you can also have math bees and vocabulary bees. For the child who isn't very good at any of this, or who has stage fright, it will be better to compete as a member of a small group.

- When you assign group work to small boys, make sure that everyone has a chance to be a leader and a follower. Surprisingly, a quiet child can turn out to be the most effective leader because he can get opposing factions to work together.

- Teachers can call "personal fouls" when a student berates his teammates for not trying hard enough or for not being good enough. Make sure that your students know that personal fouls will result in points deducted from the offending student's score.

(Continued)

(Continued)

- Have the class play academic football. Divide the class into two teams. Each team decides on a quarterback: the student who will answer the questions. If the team answers a question correctly, they get seven points and the other team gets the ball (a try at a question). If the team decides to punt (not answer) or if they are incorrect, the other team gets a try for three points. If the team is not sure of the answer, they may elect to try a field goal: a correct answer earns three points, but the other team does not get a try if they miss. The quarterback is the only person who may give an answer, and part of the exercise is to work together. The quarterback should be replaced at least once during a game and, for younger students, each should have a turn as quarterback. You may want to designate one student as referee to ensure that rules are kept and that no fouls occur.
- It is very important for children to learn to be gracious winners and resilient losers. If one person wins, someone else has to lose, and that is the way it is. Remind your students that losing does not mean they failed. In Olympic speed events, all three top finishers may beat the previous world record, with the gold medalist finishing a bit faster than the rest. You might keep a chart for each child in his folder so that you can show that student privately how well he is doing. This will be particularly helpful for middle-school boys who are beginning to understand the connection between the amount of work they do and the results.

CAUTION

- ★ Some boys are very competitive and will turn any event into a personal competition with the rest of the class. One way around this is to structure the lesson like a "scramble game" in golf. Students work in small groups and each tries all parts. The group score is based on the best score of each individual within the group for each step in the lesson. If the lesson requires several different skills, the competitor will have to depend on his teammates and that will teach him how to work with others.
- ★ Boys may compete in front of peers for attention and control. Putting the chief competitors in different parts of the classroom and assigning them to different groups may help.

> ★ Boys will compete with each other on subjects having nothing to do with what is going on in the classroom, but the competition may affect the way the boys act in class. For example, if two boys are vying for a spot on a team, they may not be good lab partners until that matter is settled.
>
> ★ Most boys will respond to sports metaphors in the classroom, but not all. Make sure that you also use metaphors from other areas popular with boys, such as heroes who can come from space, fantasy, or comics.

PUBERTY

Physical differences are most obvious in middle school, when children are between ages 11 and 14, and it is around then that emotional changes also occur. With the onset of puberty, children begin to seek independence from adults, particularly their parents, and this search is encouraged by peer pressure. School can provide nonparental adults to serve as guides and mentors through this process, helping children make the transition from childhood to young adulthood more smoothly (Eccles, Lord, & Midgley, 1991).

We have mentioned several times that boys and girls have different pubertal timing. The problem is that in middle school most girls are far ahead of most boys, but the range of development can be huge. In a ninth-grade boys' class, one boy had been shaving for a year and was over six feet tall and another had not gone through the voice change and was under five feet tall. Making matters worse, the less developmentally advanced child was several months older than the other student. In a seventh-grade girls' class, there were students with comparable pubertal differences, with one girl looking more like a grown woman and another having not yet begun to fill out.

This difference is hard enough in single-sex classes when girls are comparing their figures or boys are showing their muscles, but a coed class can be devastating for the very early and very late developers. Research has shown rather conclusively that the children at the ends of the spectrum are the ones who are more likely to have trouble in school. Furthermore, it is the early-maturing girls and late-maturing boys who suffer the most (Caspi, 1995; Dubas, Graber, & Petersen, 1991; Goldstein, 2003). The early-maturing girls may be less academically oriented because they are beginning to focus on social matters such as dating, and the late-maturing boys are not at the same level of cognitive development as their classmates and find academics more difficult. In fact, late-maturing boys usually have the lowest academic achievement (Dubas et al., 1991; Duke et al., 1982).

For boys, when their academic problems compound their social inadequacies, the result is the first step on a slippery slope to failure (Peterson, 1986). They are told they can't pay attention, they are messy and disorganized, and they don't read or write well. Now they don't seem to be developing into what society tells them they should aspire to be—the muscular athlete. Many of these boys retreat to their computers where they invent a world they can control.

Another problem for boys during puberty is that they are less likely to find someone in whom they can confide when they have troubles (Berk, 1997). They worry about whether they are developing normally and may want to avoid showering after sports if the school only has communal showers. Lack of adult height is a major concern for boys, and the prospect of becoming a short adult will concern the boy who is slow to develop, even if he knows that his parents are short as well (Goldstein, 2003). Exposure to a wide variety of adults or older students may provide someone whom the child can trust with his problems.

Applications for Your Classroom

- Make sure that the school offers health instruction appropriate to the students' developmental levels. Invite physicians who specialize in men's health to come to talk to your class. When Lance Armstrong, the cyclist, revealed his testicular cancer, my students were very eager to discuss how to perform a self-examination and how to treat the illness.
- Use literature to help boys see that the problems they may be having are not unique and they are not weird for thinking as they do. Books by authors as diverse as Jack London and Gary Paulsen provide boys with realistic characters facing problems similar to ones they are facing. As Harry Potter grows up, J. K. Rowling is having him cope with many issues that boys find familiar.
- Parents of middle-school boys may begin to feel that they are out of the loop, and their sons may act as if their parents embarrass them. You may be the link between parents and child. Have students develop a class Web site and post

examples of good work there. For parents' night, have the students present some of their work or prepare a demonstration of something they have learned in class.

- Encourage boys to seek out someone in whom they can confide. If you see a boy whose behavior takes a turn for the worse—becoming sullen, solitary, or sloppy—alert the counseling department. Ask the child if he wants to talk if you feel comfortable with him and think you have a good relationship.

CAUTION

★ Boys may be thought of as less intelligent if they are the shortest in the class (Duke et al., 1982). However, lack of physical development should not be used as evidence that a boy also lacks cognitive development, as some boys who develop late physically are nonetheless cognitively mature. Teachers need to be aware of this and be on the alert to ensure that smaller boys are treated as equals in the class.

★ Boys may be thought of as more intelligent if they are tall for their age. Early-developing boys should be encouraged to use their energies in positive ways such as community service, athletics, church youth groups, or scouts and 4-H. The problem is that it is tempting for them to be with older students who are much more sophisticated and involved in activities not appropriate for a younger boy. In addition, they are more likely to get into trouble with older students. I have known several boys who were young for their class, but taller than all the rest. Usually, teachers assumed these boys were older and complained about their immature behavior.

★ Boys who are behind the curve in development may spend a lot of time playing computer games or communicating with their friends through IMs. Since they are on the computer so much, they will be interested in learning about program design and other advanced computer skills. Make sure that they have the opportunity to do so.

ALCOHOL AND DRUGS

Combine emotionally based decisions with mind-altering substances and the effect is disastrous. Alcohol reduces inhibitions that—for boys—may not be strong to begin with. That means they may engage in behaviors they know are dangerous. One study compared the incidence of drowning between men and women. Men were far more likely to drink and swim, swim alone, swim at night, and boat without a life jacket (Howland, Hingson, Mangione, Bell, & Bak, 1996).

Research in a variety of populations shows that men, and particularly young men, drink more than women (Lewinsohn, Rohde, & Seeley, 1996; Lorente, Peretti-Watel, Griffet, & Grelot, 2003). Information on students from the Centers for Disease Control Youth Risk Behavior Surveillance System indicates that in 2003 more boys than girls reported using chewing tobacco (11% to 2.2%), being under 18 and purchasing cigarettes at a store (24.2% to 13.8%), using marijuana (25.1% to 19.3%), using methamphetamines (8.3% to 6.8%), using heroin at least once (4.3% to 2.0%), and being offered, sold, or given an illegal drug on school property (31.9% to 25%) (Centers for Disease Control, 2004).

Alcohol and the Adolescent Brain

It has long been known that alcohol affects the brain and nervous system, but only recently have the specific effects on the adolescent brain been discovered. What follows is information from an article (Wuethrich, 2001) on the effect of alcohol on the adolescent brain which contained interviews with leading researchers in the field.

Alcohol seems to affect the memory processes of the younger brain more than those of older brains. Research on young adults, ages 21 to 24, compared to slightly older adults, ages 25 to 29, showed that with a blood alcohol level of .08 percent, the younger adults' learning capacities were 25 percent lower than the older group.

MRIs of young alcohol abusers, ages 14 to 21, showed smaller hippocampi than did those of healthy age-mates. The hippocampus is central to formation of memories.

Slices of rat hippocampal cells exposed to alcohol showed that the higher the concentration of alcohol, the more cell death occurred. Cells from preadolescent rats died at a rate four to five times greater than cells from mature rats. Exposure to alcohol resulted in cell death in the frontal lobes in adolescent rats. Older rats did not show this damage, but the damage in the younger rats was severe. There was also damage in the limbic system. These two parts of the brain play a large part in development of the adult personality. This research has only been conducted in rats, but

---

the effects were serious and the researchers are concerned that similar damage may be occur in adolescent humans.

The major damage seems to be done during withdrawal from the presence of alcohol, so binge drinkers may suffer more damage than social drinkers.

A study compared young alcohol abusers, ages 15 and 16, to non-drinking age-mates on tests of cognition. The drinkers performed about 10 percent lower than did the nondrinkers on tests of memory and problem-solving ability. These subjects are being followed, and recent findings indicate that they are now developing attention problems as well.

Tests of the brain in action (fMRI) of young adults who drink reveal that, when shown words associated with drinking behavior, a portion of the brain called the nucleus accumbens shows activity. If this portion of the brain is stimulated, certain neurotransmitters are released and the individual feels pleasure. Repetition of the behavior that caused this feeling is likely to occur, leading to addiction.

The combination of mind-altering substances and sexual behavior is a growing problem. One study found that students who reported binge drinking were more likely to claim to have engaged in risky sex (sex with multiple partners, sex without a condom, sex leading to pregnancy). Binge drinking was defined as having five or more drinks in a row in the past two weeks for males, or four or more drinks in a row in the past two weeks for females. Students who admitted having a drink were seven times more likely to report having sexual intercourse than nondrinkers (Dunn, Barte, & Perko, 2003). In addition, using alcohol was connected with sexual victimization, with the perpetrator also likely to be a user of alcohol (Felson & Burchfield, 2004; Maxwell, Robinson, & Post, 2003).

Do mind-altering substances affect academic performance? At the very least, substance use results in lower academic motivation (Andrews, Duncan, & Hops, 1994). Scientists are beginning to look carefully at the effect of alcohol on the young brain. It used to be thought that the young brain was better able to repair itself, but it now appears that the younger the brain, the more likely that permanent damage will be done by heavy alcohol use. Moreover, the damage seems to happen most often while detoxification—commonly known as a hangover—is taking place (Wuethrich, 2001). The greater the hangover, the more damage is done, so binge drinkers have more damage than individuals who drink the same amount spread over more days; adolescents are more likely to binge drink (Dunn et al., 2003).

Marijuana users have trouble recalling words in a list, a problem with obvious relevance to schoolwork (Pope, Gruber, Hudson, Huestis, & Yurgelun-Todd, 2001). This particular study did not find that memory problems on these tests persisted, even for long-term users of marijuana, when the individuals had been free of the drug for at least 28 days. However, the researchers agree that memory for words may not be a sufficiently sensitive test to determine neurological damage from marijuana use. Other studies have found that marijuana causes long-term memory disruptions (Hall & Solowij, 1998; Solowij et al., 2002) and psychological dependence on the drug (Stephens, Roffman, & Simpson, 1994). In addition, boys may be interested in knowing that there is evidence linking use of marijuana and reproductive system damage, particularly reduction in testosterone. Additionally, problems have been reported with the production, motility, and survival of sperm in marijuana users (Hall & Solowij, 1998; Peugh & Blenko, 2001; Preboth, 2000).

There is no question that substance abuse is bad for young brains, but it is also likely to do other damage to abusers. Boys are more likely than girls to engage in risky behaviors, including substance abuse, unsafe sex, and reckless driving. Combine competitiveness, aggression, unsophisticated problem-solving abilities, and alcohol with a car and the result is, not infrequently, serious or fatal accidents. Research has shown that boys are much more likely than girls to engage in risky driving practices, yet many who have violated the law do not view their behavior as dangerous. For example, the average speed that boys in one study regarded as excessive was 97.7 mph. In addition, this study did not find that the typical driver's ed course did much to change the students' attitudes toward risky driving. The research suggested that rescinding licenses for violations was a more effective deterrent than fines (Sarkar & Andreas, 2004).

If you don't teach health or drivers' education, why should you be concerned about students' use of drugs or engaging in risky behaviors? If for no other reason, an impaired brain does not learn properly, and such behaviors result in poor outcomes for students. More important, whether you teach kindergarten or twelfth grade, you are in a position to influence how your students view drug and alcohol use and how they conduct their lives. You are not responsible for the way they behave, but you can make a difference.

Applications for Your Classroom

- Provide opportunities for students to evaluate the effects of decisions. This works particularly well in history or social studies, but literature classes can discuss the consequences of a character's actions, and biology classes can analyze the effect of pollution on the environment.

- Help children recognize the consequences of their actions. Failure is not a bad thing, especially if the teacher helps children understand why they failed, what steps they can take to correct the mistakes, and how successful they can be when they do it right. There is a huge difference between failing and being a failure, and school is the time for children to learn that lesson. Our culture leads boys to believe that failing is a blot on their masculinity, and they need to understand that giving up is the real failure.

- Earlier we mentioned how athletic coaches can use sports to help boys practice managing impulsivity as they learn to play a game. In addition, in the process of coaching a game, a coach can help boys see the consequences of actions and model good decision making.

- Be vigilant about drug and alcohol abuse. A national survey of admissions to emergency rooms showed that 49 percent of alcohol-related admissions involved individuals below the age of 21. The number of alcohol-related visits increased from age 13 to age 21, at which time the number began to decrease (Elder, Shults, Swahn, Strife, & Ryan, 2004).

- At the same time, develop good relationships with your students and listen to what they have to say to you. Some of them will be concerned if they know of drug and alcohol abuse and will communicate that in some way to a valued teacher.

- Blow the whistle if you have to. It may damage your relationship with some students, but if you don't say something, they will think you either don't care or don't think their behavior is wrong. On the other hand, you may have been allowed to know about situations because students want you to be aware of the facts. This way it can be an adult who tells, and the students are not labeled as "snitches."

(Continued)

(Continued)

- Educate students about the brain and how drugs and alcohol are more likely to damage the adolescent brain (see box). Invite young (college-age) members of AA, NA, or Alateen to talk to your classes. Folks from Al-Anon are happy to discuss the effects of substance abuse on the family. This will help any students who are in alcoholic families understand that they are not alone in what they are experiencing.
- Above all, do not preach about the evils of drugs. Students are impressed by facts and not by scare tactics. I give my high-school students copies of scholarly reviews of the effects of ingestion of psychotropic substances, and they respond much more positively than if I told them about the effects of drugs. They have seen plenty of peers taking substances with no apparent consequences, and if you try to exaggerate the effects they will not believe anything you tell them.

CAUTION

- ★ Boys are likely to begin abusing alcohol earlier than girls. A study of alcohol abuse found that boys ages 14 to 18 drank more often, started drinking earlier, and drank more overall than girls (Lewinsohn et al., 1996).
- ★ Because some programs do try to frighten adolescents, many students will not believe the truth about drugs. Using stories of adolescents who have had bad experiences with drugs will not work unless the story is delivered by the individual in question.
- ★ The older the student is, the less likely you are to be able to influence his behavior. That does not mean that teachers of twelfth graders should not try; it does mean that teachers in elementary and middle school need to be particularly careful how they introduce material on risky behaviors.

SOCIAL INFLUENCE ON SCHOOL

When former students return to school for alumni events, it can be very enlightening to eavesdrop on them. These men lived together during a formative period of their lives, and it is obvious from their conversations that they have shared their hopes and fears, their feelings, their problems with parents and girlfriends, and their beliefs about what is important. These men are acting in ways not generally thought to be stereotypical male behavior because they are involved in each other's emotional lives. In single-sex schools, there is less social pressure to conform to the accepted standard of gendered behavior. Boys have the freedom to be involved in art, music, and drama at the same time they play soccer, and girls are allowed to be athletes and science geeks at the same time they talk about their favorite novel. Boys and girls are encouraged to express feelings not stereotypically masculine or feminine. In a single-sex environment, boys are still affected by the standards of what society believes is appropriate male behavior, but they are allowed a greater latitude in their behavior (James & Richards, 2003).

However, this is not true for the vast majority of boys in coed schools. Their behavior is judged by societal norms, and if they do not meet the standard they are thought to be not very masculine (Mac an Ghaill, 1994; West, 2002). I teach a college course in child psychology, and in all the sections I have taught, I have had only one male student. The first day of class he said that he was only taking the course because it was the only one he could find that fit in his schedule. During the class, he shared stories about his own small children, but still found it somewhat uncomfortable to take a class that focused on children. At the boys' school, I taught a popular elective in child growth and development. In that class, one of the requirements was to write a case study of one of the faculty children, and in order to do so the boys spent a lot of time with their subjects. When I meet those students later, they always say that that class was one they enjoyed the most in high school.

What kind of behavior is normal for males? What do we mean when we say, "boys will be boys?" Pointing out that a boy is typical for a boy usually means that he is tough, he distrusts adults, he doesn't do anything weak or sissy, he is muscular, he never cries, he plays sports, he doesn't talk very much, and he doesn't act like a girl (Pollack, 1998; West, 2002). Typical boys are described as physical and active; they like excitement and humor, they value courage and justice, and they want to be respected and admired (Neall, 2002). Most important, real boys don't cry.

The pressure for boys to conform to the male stereotype of behavior is much stronger than the pressure for girls to conform to the feminine stereotype (Askew & Ross, 1988; Maccoby, 1998; Pollack, 1998). From the early 1970s, women were exhorted to change their ideas about what they could aspire to accomplish, to take on nontraditional roles, and to widen their horizons. Programs were instituted to encourage women to seek professional degrees and to assist businesses in increasing the number of women hired in management positions. Title IX made sure that girls had the same opportunity to be involved in athletics and other programs in school as did boys.

During the same time, men were told they had to change, but little instruction was provided (Sax, 2005). Boys were pressured to emulate the behavior of girls, or at least that is how it seems to them (Pollack, 1998; West, 2002). The most important point is that men and women are not the same. As Steven Pinker says in *The Blank Slate* (2002), "equality is not the empirical claim that all groups of humans are interchangeable; it is the moral principle that individuals should not be judged or constrained by the average properties of their group (p. 340)." Neither women nor men should feel that their behavior is wrong simply because it does not conform to the stereotype for their gender.

One more comment on equality or the lack of it in our present society. Certainly the glass ceiling exists; women still are not paid at rates commensurate with men, and young mothers are penalized at work for taking time off to be with their babies. However, inside the classroom, because of the way that school is structured and classes are taught, girls generally do better than boys. The problem is that because it is not a place where they succeed, boys may not value what they can accomplish inside the classroom, prizing more highly what they can do outside the classroom. My students will eagerly compare what teachers make to what successful computer entrepreneurs who never graduated from college make. Perhaps engaging boys in the educational process may help them appreciate the fruits of education, and they will value people for what they know and can do, not just for how rich they are or how much stuff they have accumulated.

Pressure to Normalize Behavior

How soon does society put pressure on children to conform to gender-appropriate behavior? Research has shown that, when observing infants, adults will report that they see behaviors stereotypically associated with the gender they believe the child to be, whether or not the baby actually is that gender. If they are told the baby is a boy, they will report that the baby is vigorous and more playful, and if other adults are told that the same baby is a girl, they will report that the baby is cuddly and more sensitive. That information is well known. However, one study reached a different conclusion, finding that observers were more likely to report gender-stereotypical behavior that conformed to the actual sex of some of the babies. It was suggested that there may be observable behavior in some individuals that is typical for their gender

(Burnham & Harris, 1991). This is only one report of the phenomenon, but it opens the door for the idea that stereotypes may be based on real behaviors.

For example, toy selection by children has generally been thought to be learned. Mothers smile when girls pick up a dolly or boys pick up a truck, and frown if the choices are reversed. Children learn which toys are appropriate for them (Roopnarine, 1986). Research on the topic does not speak with one voice, however. It is well known that females who have congenital adrenal hyperplasia (CAH), a disorder that exposes babies to high levels of androgens in utero, prefer boys' toys, prefer rough-and-tumble play, and prefer to play with boys (Hines, 2004). In addition, their drawings look more like those of boys than of girls unaffected by the condition (Iijima, Ariska, Minamoto, & Arai, 2001). These young women are normal girls except for the bath of hormones to which they were exposed prior to birth. This is just one of several genetic abnormalities resulting in individuals who are classified as intersex—neither totally male nor totally female. In most cases, hormonal abnormalities during fetal development are thought to be the cause. However, reports are not consistent on the effect of sexual ambiguity on gender. Some individuals seem content with a gender that conforms to their physical appearance, and others prefer a gender that conforms to their genes (Hines, 2004; Sax, 2005).

In addition, research has shown infant rhesus monkeys conforming to gender-stereotypical play behavior (Overman, Bachevalier, Schuhmann, & Ryan, 1996), indicating that toy selection may be influenced less by society and more by biology. Remember that infant boys preferred to look at trucks, while infant girls preferred faces. Infant female monkeys were much more likely to pick up dolls and infant male monkeys were likely to pick up toys associated with boys. Another study observed chimpanzee daughters who learned termite-fishing behavior from watching their mothers. The chimpanzee sons, who also had mother models for this behavior, did not acquire the same techniques (Lonsdorf, Eberly, & Pusey, 2004).

Our society reinforces gender stereotypes. Each year, I ask my students in child psychology to go to the toy section of a large department store and see if they can find gender-free toys for children between the ages of 3 and 8. They find it is extremely difficult—even the balls are either pink or blue. What amuses me is their descriptions of what they call "the pink aisle," which is full of dolls, craft kits, and other girl-oriented toys, and the corresponding "blue aisle," full of cars, military or police gear, and building blocks.

More enlightened toy stores, where the price tags are considerably higher than those in discount establishments, do have games and other gender-neutral toys, but in large chain stores even some of the board games are designed for one group or the other. I invite you to compare the board games Candyland and Chutes and Ladders. The games are similar, but Candyland has Dora the Explorer on it, leaving no doubt that it is for girls while Chutes and Ladders has a large drawing of a boy on the front. Even puzzles are gendered. For young children, there is a choice between a picture of The Fantastic Four in a blue box and Hello Kitty in a pink one. You will even find a choice of themes for playing cards—Care Bears in a pink box and Teenage Mutant Ninja Turtles in a blue and green box. Remember that the girls' eyes are more responsive to the red end of the spectrum and boys' eyes to the blue end. It appears as if the packaging as well as the theme is designed to appeal to one sex or the other.

As children enter adolescence, there is increased pressure for them to conform to the behavior typical of their gender. This is referred to as *gender intensification*, and it reflects the desire to fit into the standard of behavior set by peers (Halpern, 2000). During this time, children will be most inflexible about what behavior is appropriate, and unwilling to see that there is a wide range of suitable behaviors open to both men and women. Middle-school students, who are on the threshold of adolescence, are therefore most intolerant of anything that implies gender ambiguity. One of my ninth-grade students remarked that he didn't think that pink was an appropriate color for a man's shirt because it was a girl's color. Not long after that, I saw one of the coaches wearing a pink knit shirt and pointed that out to the student. The boy remarked that he bet that the shirt was a gift from the coach's wife. He was not going to change his mind about appropriate attire for men.

This intolerance can affect how a class approaches material. In a coed class, boys may sneer at a discussion of the emotional ties between characters in a book or show no sympathy for people oppressed by tyrants (Pollack, 1998). The boys may become disruptive because they are uncomfortable with the subjects under discussion. I have had this sort of reaction in a boys' class as well, but it is much easier to get the students to examine why they react as they do. With girls in the class, young boys may be more reluctant to talk about subjects that are stereotypically feminine.

What this means is that students will enter your classroom with the understanding that some toys and activities are appropriate for boys and others for girls. And, depending on the messages they are getting at home, they may be very reluctant to engage in any activity that they have been taught belongs to the opposite gender. Boys may not want to help tidying the classroom, and girls may not want to work with blocks. Additionally, boys may have trouble obeying the rules, because society says "boys will be boys" and being good is for girls. This is different from boys who are noisy and exuberant but who know the rules apply to them. Knowing the difference between these two attitudes is very important. When a boy fails to abide by the class rules, talk to him away from his classmates. State what he has done and then remind him of the class rule that he has violated. How to deal with discipline will be covered in Chapter 8, but first you need to know whether a boy violating the rules does or does not believe that the rules are directed at boys.

Applications for Your Classroom

- Make sure that toys and other materials in your classroom are as gender neutral as possible, so that boys will be less likely to reject a toy based on its packaging. Fortunately, those sold for teachers tend to be less gendered, but they may be more expensive. Having a play kitchen that is natural wood or painted white is better than one that is pink and purple.

- If a boy seems reluctant to engage in an activity that has gendered connotations, such as cooking, see if you can put a masculine spin on it. Find male role models to show that real men do cook and tend babies. Male examples in cooking are easy to find—Chef Boyardee, Colonel Sanders, and the Iron Chef are a few. The movie *Mrs. Doubtfire* shows that men can look after children. In a unit on solubility, I was frank about the content of the lesson. We discovered why dirt and grass stained clothes, how soap worked, why dry cleaning was necessary, and why vinegar was so good for cleaning glass. I didn't structure the class to be a lesson on cleaning clothes, but rather a lesson on the practical application of chemistry.

- You can include activities that are not traditionally associated with boys if they are embedded in the lesson. In Chapter 9,

(Continued)

(Continued)

you will read about a cooking project in which the class made and sold dog biscuits; boys were very willing to engage in this activity. One fifth-grade teacher each year had her students do an international project. Each student picked a country and became the expert, making maps, pictures, and a poster showing the major aspects of the country. At the end of the unit, the class sponsored an international fair. They invited their parents and the head of the school to view their posters and sample traditional foods that the children had made. Because the children got to pick their own countries, they were more interested in the project and proud of their contribution to the international meal that capped the demonstrations.

- It is possible that boys may see reading as something that is only for girls. You will find in Chapter 11 a list of authors whose books appeal to boys. Earlier chapters contain several different suggestions about bringing men into the classroom to help boys with reading.

CAUTION

★ Some boys may be scornful of attempts to include them in activities they see as "girlish." They will make derogatory comments and tease the children who do join in. This is hard because the child who does this may have been taught by his parents that boys don't do a certain activity. Don't push him, but remind all students of class rules about respecting classmates, or see if you can redefine the activity so that the boy will see it in a different light. Our chemistry teacher would make homemade ice cream during the summer chemistry class. When a student complained that cooking wasn't chemistry, the teacher renamed the exercise a "freezing point depression" lab, broke the steps up so that students only did a part of the lab, and astounded the students with the product at the end.

★ Older boys in a literature class may have trouble discussing feelings or motives because this is not traditionally masculine. Try stepping the discussion back a bit and shift to a more objective consideration of what the characters do. Start by listing events, then discuss motives. The students will be covering the same material you originally wanted to cover, just starting from a different perspective. For example, talking about the politics of Scotland and the connections between thanes and their king is a good lead-in to a discussion on *Macbeth*. Once the politics are clear, you can then discuss corruption of power and why that happens—which leads to Macbeth's motives.

Pressure to Succeed

The pressure for boys to succeed in life is huge. As one senior boy told me, "Of course I'm stressed. In four more years I have to be ready to start a career so I can support myself and a family, eventually, and I have no clue what I am interested in!" I pointed out that his mother, who was a lawyer, certainly helped support his family, that his father didn't do it all. He replied, "Oh, sure, but the *expectation* for a man to support a family is there." During the past twenty years, the career choices for boys have remained strongly gender stereotyped, whereas the choices for girls have expanded into previously all-male professions (Berk, 1997).

A survey of gifted girls and boys in middle school found that both groups preferred scientific careers, but boys were more likely to have a specific career in mind. Boys felt parental pressure to select a goal, whereas girls stated that their parents would support their decisions (Reis, Callahan, & Goldsmith, 1994). Another study discovered that teachers of early elementary students were more accepting of girls who indicated an interest in cross-gender careers, but did not see that cross-gender careers were appropriate for boys (Cahill & Adams, 1997). Boys feel pressure to select a career early and then feel that they are limited to traditional choices.

In the schools in which I have taught, some families are very obvious in their desires to have their children follow in the parents' professional footsteps. Remember the story at the beginning of Chapter 1 about the boy named Sam who wanted to go to a small college in spite of his parents' desire that he attend a large, prestigious university? It will not surprise you to know that Sam's father was a very successful businessman who credited his accomplishments to the network of associates from his days at a well-known business school. He did not want his son to suffer later for his failure to make the right contacts while he was young. "After all," said the father, "why did I send Sam here? If he goes to the small college he might as well have stayed at home and gone to public school." Even in the community college where I now teach, there are young men who are there because of what their families want and not because of what they want to do.

Applications for Your Classroom

- Starting early, expose all students to a wide variety of career choices. Schools should make the effort help all students widen their horizons, particularly by exposing them to non-stereotypical careers.
- Examine the representations of individuals that your students may see in posters, in their textbooks, and in videos. If the librarian is always a stern-looking lady with a bun and the astronaut is always a man, try to expose your students to a wider variety of role models.
- Suggest that a young man who does not seem ready for college take a "gap" year. It is common in Europe for students to travel or work for a year after finishing high school and before entering college. There are many programs for this, including both academic and practical experiences.
- Invite graduates of the school who are still in college to come to discuss how they are coping with pressure to make career decisions. The graduates may be able to assure your students that changes in major can be made in college and that a lot of students do not graduate with the same major that they declared upon entrance to the school.

CAUTION

★ As a society, we tend to value high-paying occupations over ones that are personally fulfilling. Boys, pushed to make money, may not consider certain choices. Career programs in elementary schools can expose children to choices they might not otherwise entertain later. Having a male teacher in elementary school may introduce a boy to the idea of education as a profession.

★ One concern I hear frequently from families is that they are worried that if their sons take time off from school, they may never return. This is a major concern of some families, and your counseling department may want to address this issue through a workshop or panel presentation.

Anti-Intellectualism

What is so distressing to those of us who work with boys is that they seem so sure of themselves. They brag about their accomplishments and promise to do better. Several studies have concluded that this is simply a way to hide the fact that boys know they are not doing well in school. The braggadocio covers their serious lack of self-confidence as students (Bushweller, 1994; Purkey & Harper, 1995). It appears that the anti-intellectual posturing by boys is simply a way to cover their failures—if they do well, they have no problems, but if they do badly, well . . . they don't care anyway.

Self-handicapping is the practice of protecting yourself from anticipated losses by creating a cause for poor performance. We have all done this—going out the night before a very hard test telling yourself that you can't study anymore. If you do well, you will attribute your success to your relaxed state, but if you fail, well, how could you expect to pass if you party the night before? You have covered all your options. Research shows that men do not rate self-handicapping as negatively as do women and are more willing to accept self-handicapping as an excuse for poor performance (Hirt, McCrea, & Boris, 2003). Additionally, boys believe that teachers value the efforts of girls but not of boys, so why try (Pollack, 1998; West, 2002)?

Another reason many boys underachieve in school is that there is peer pressure to do so. The message is that education is not the proper venue for men, and so boys don't have to work. Boys also stop when they notice that their friends are not working. Studies have found that girls are more likely to talk or study when they get together, but boys are more likely to play sports or just hang around together (Askew & Ross, 1988; Phillips, 1994; Schneider & Coutts, 1985). This can lead to an ever-accelerating spiral of failure; boys who don't work begin to fail, which means they start to avoid school, and you see where this is heading. At the very least, if boys do succeed, they must not appear to be working (Epstein, 1999).

One theory about why this happens is that boys believe some behavior is appropriate for one place and other behavior appropriate for different places. One study reported that boys felt that schoolwork should be done at school and not at home (Holland, 1998). Another study found that boys had a hard time integrating their school life and their out-of-school life and consequently did not often study effectively when they were out of school. The point was that the men in their lives did not work when they came home, so why should the boys (Harris, Nixon, & Ruddock, 1993; Holland, 1998)? The boys did not believe that schoolwork was anything like the work that their fathers did, and so they saw little point in doing it at home.

One study examined how teachers' beliefs about students were related to the students' gender and to their success in school. Both male and female teachers were in agreement about the characteristics of male students who were not academically successful. A leading descriptor was that these students were "easily influenced" (Bennett & Bennett, 1994). If the influence was to study hard, these students would not likely have been identified as academically unsuccessful, so it is presumed that the influence was an academically negative one. Peer pressure was drawing these boys away from academics.

Schoolwide programs to combat anti-intellectualism usually garner sneers from the very groups who are being targeted. You will get better results by discovering who the leaders of these groups are and getting them involved in academic pursuits. That may seem like an unattainable goal, but find an adult who relates to these leaders and work with them to develop programs that will attract the boys.

Applications for Your Classroom

- Anti-intellectualism is easier to manage very early, probably in preschool or early elementary school. Encourage your parents' association or civic organizations such as the Boys and Girls Clubs to offer afterschool programs, especially ones connected to the school curriculum. These would include computer training, explorer clubs, "Odyssey of the Mind" competitions, and the like. Any program that gets students together with adult supervision in an academically positive environment will help.
- Encourage sports programs to build in academic connections. In the days when students had to maintain a certain academic average to compete, boys were more likely to pay attention to their studies. However, if programs are in place to support academic performance by providing tutoring or academic mentoring, academic standards for athletic performance can help. Require the boy who is having academic problems to continue to practice so that he will be ready to compete as soon as his grades improve.
- Develop some way to assess academic improvement or deterioration that is shorter than the typical grading period. Boys will

work for a week, but if they don't have some reward they are likely to slip back again. More immediate reinforcement helps boys connect increases in their effort to positive academic results. This is particularly true for the athletes. You can give older students interim grades or reports. For younger students, develop individual charts that the teacher checks daily. At the end of the week, if the child meets the goal jointly set with his teacher, he gets a reward. The reward can be stickers or pencils—or better yet, time to read a book of his choice. Those who have not met their goal must do extra practice on schoolwork. Older students need to be encouraged to work for the intrinsic value of doing well. The incentive to work is the knowledge that success is its own reward, but some students need that spelled out for them, particularly if they have not experienced much academic success.

- Help boys learn study strategies and work with them to plan study approaches. The student who knows how to study is more likely to do so rather than resorting to self-handicapping.
- Develop a game plan for studying. Get the boys on your study team together after a test to go over the "game film." What did they do right and what did they do wrong? You will be helping these boys develop accurate self-assessment skills.
- Role models can be a powerful influence on boys. If the role models available are athletes or entertainment figures for whom education is not important, the boys will not value education. Men they know well who give them lots of attention and who will work with them can change the way boys view the importance of doing well in school.
- Do all that you can to keep children's grades private. For small children this will be impossible, but point out that grades are a reflection of a lot of factors and are not something to hold over others as a mark of superiority.

CAUTION

★ Even boys with the best of intentions can be recruited into anti-intellectual groups. Adult presence is one of the best preventatives. If you are close to a college or university, inquire if there is a big brother/sister program that will connect boys with males who have succeeded in school.

(Continued)

(Continued)

> ★ Be a safe haven by providing support for boys who want to be in school. Warn boys that the pressure not to work is out there, and help them develop some methods to deal with that pressure when it comes. Use some of the techniques to combat bullying.
>
> ★ Expose your students to individuals who are true experts in their fields, so that they can see their modesty about their abilities. Teach the students to "let their actions speak for themselves."
>
> ★ Some schools have tried to do away with grades, using an elaborate rating system. This simply feeds into boys' beliefs about how well they are doing and does not face them with the consequences of their behavior. My students are usually delighted when I share how hard I struggled with foreign languages and my poor grades as a result. For whatever reason, that is not an area I excel in, but I never gave up and eventually did well enough to get into the college of my choice.

Ability v. Effort

Research has shown that teachers believe the reason girls are academically successful is because of their effort, while boys are successful because of their ability (Fennema, Peterson, Carpenter, & Lubinski, 1990). Students also have the belief that girls succeed because they work hard and boys succeed because they are smart (Epstein, 1999; Tibbetts, 1977). Complicating this is the belief of boys that they are innately more academically capable than girls (Littlewood, 1995). This is the reason that girls think they are going to do badly on a test because they haven't studied enough—even if they know the material—and boys think they will do well on a test because they understand the material, even though they haven't studied enough.

One symptom of this problem is the consistent finding that boys do not have correct perceptions about their academic abilities. For example, it has long been known that boys overestimate their ability in math (Parsons, 1981), and further research has found that boys overestimate their ability in English as well (Bornholt, Goodnow, & Cooney, 1988). Compounding this problem is teachers' support of underachieving students who have long-standing patterns of academic self-deception. The teachers try to put a positive spin on the students' work, and the result is that both the students and the teachers are incorrect with respect to the students' actual ability (Holland, 1998). You will hear teachers say something like, "I know he can do better if he tries," or, "He is a good student, but has hit a bad patch right now." Teachers don't want to run the risk of giving a child the impression that they think he is simply not academically capable enough. So instead, we give them the impression that they are not working hard enough. The problem is that if you are told you are lazy often enough, you might become lazy.

If teachers are responding to students based on beliefs about the interaction of effort and achievement, then sex biases are going to lead teachers to treat students differently (Bennett & Bennett, 1994). In and of itself, that should not be a problem, as everything you find in this book suggests that teachers should respond to individual student needs. If, however, teachers believe that smart boys are capable, then boys are going to continue to believe that effort is not as important as ability, and underachievement will be more and more common. Focusing on helping boys understand that effort is required will do a lot to improve their chances of opening a book when they study.

Before I started examining this area, I tended to look at my students who seemed to be academically capable but who were not succeeding as either lazy or as under the influence of unmotivated peers. In working with these students, I would emphasize that the student could do better, but I was not very specific about what he needed to do to improve. Also, I was willing to let the student convince me that he would work harder in the future. I now know that I need to challenge the belief of capable boys that their ability will get them through, and work with them to find specific steps to increase their academic effort.

Applications for Your Classroom

- Do what you can to help boys have a more realistic view of their abilities as well as of the amount of effort they are putting forth. Focus on what the child does do well, but make it plain that there are other areas with which he is having trouble. It will also help if the families are included in this realistic approach.

(Continued)

(Continued)

- The regular reports sent home to families should be based on observable behavior. I start by mentioning some challenge the student has met or progress he has made before I list his shortcomings. Specifically state what the boy has failed to do, but also include strategies and plans for improvement. List the work that was late or is missing rather than just saying he has not completed all his work.
- Invite families of underachieving students in to talk to all of the faculty involved with their son. Make sure when you do so that this does not become a complaint session, but that the faculty has specific examples of problems and suggestions for helping the child improve.
- If families of underachieving students find it difficult to come to a meeting at the school, go on a home visit. You may be surprised at what you learn about a child from knowing more about his living situation.
- Include the boy in the plans for improvement. Both teachers and families should be involved in monitoring his attempts to work more efficiently, but the primary effort should come from the boy. Younger boys may need reminders, but older boys should be doing this on their own. I find that a regular meeting time with a student, usually just before or just after his class, to review his work for the past week is a great way to keep the boy focused on reality.
- Many boys simply do not know how to study. They need specific instruction in ways that suit their learning style. You will find more information in Chapter 10.

CAUTION

- ★ Families may resist attempts to enlist their help in getting the boy to work at home. For very difficult situations, you may need to include your counseling staff in helping families see how their intervention can help their child.
- ★ Children will live up to or down to your expectations. By high school, students should have realistic views of their abilities. Again, specificity will help. For example, you could say, "Out of four homework assignments that were due this week, you only turned in two. Even though you got good grades on the

ones you turned in, you got no credit for the missing work."
Then have the student figure out his average.

★ Some boys will simply give up. Why should they work when
the teacher thinks they are dumb? Point out that as much as
you would like to become an Olympic-class swimmer, you
simply don't have the ability. That does not mean you cannot
enjoy swimming or that you cannot coach swimming. You still
work to improve your technique because you like the exercise,
but you are aware of your limitations.

SCHOOL AND MASCULINITY

Gender studies have traditionally focused on the issue of feminism,
and there has been little work devoted to studying how school affects
the development of masculinity (Mac an Ghaill, 1994). Máirtín Mac
an Ghaill in England, Steve Biddulph in Australia, and Michael
Thompson in the United States have been some of the leaders in the
area of school and masculinity. In Chapter 11, you will find a bibliog-
raphy of materials by these writers and others. You will notice that
the overwhelming majority of these authors are from England and
Australia, where there is a strong movement to include information
on the development of masculinity in schools.

Far more information and opinions exist on how schools can work
with boys to develop positive senses of masculinity than can be covered here. However, I have included a small sample of what is available. Most of the material used to support the assertions in this area
comes from ethnographic studies: Someone went into a school,
observed how children behaved, and wrote about it using specific evidence to back up assertions. Other works are entirely opinion based.
You will note that the statements in this area are not preceded by
"research has shown . . ." but rather by phrases like "the belief is . . . ."

How can schools help boys develop healthy senses of masculine
self? More important, how can school be involved in this area?
Everything we do, say, or believe is colored by our self-concept, and
part of that concept is gender. As we are shaped into positive and productive members of society, we cannot avoid dealing with how our
gender affects our productivity. As much as we might believe that all
people should be treated the same, we are all different and we need
to understand how our world and our selves are interconnected.

To avoid discussing that topic, or to limit the discussion to one half of this topic—feminism—will not well serve the children we teach.

How did we get into a situation where a discussion of masculinity is necessary? There are two parts to this problem. In the past, most of the focus, both in school and out, was from a masculine perspective. That was wrong. We now need to help children see that there are many different possible ways of looking at the world from a gendered perspective. Schools need to be careful to make sure that all children are included on their own terms. Look to see if in your school there is a high proportion of girls getting the academic awards and of boys getting the athletic awards. If so, the message that is sent to boys and girls is unmistakable.

The other part of the problem is the lack of positive male role models for boys in the world. Some believe that the increasing number of one-parent families (headed almost entirely by mothers) is a major contributing factor (Biddulph, 1997). When boys are in a family composed of their mother and their siblings, they have few male role models. In that environment, boys may define what it means to be a boy as the opposite of what it means to be a girl (Neall, 2002; Pollack, 1998).

Other adults in a boy's life are likely to include female teachers. What may happen is that, in trying to figure out what it means to be a man, the boy may attempt to be as unlike the adult females surrounding him as possible. He may decide that the proper behavior for men is loud, rude, crude, messy, unacademic, unemotional, and uninvolved. The idea that there may be many different types of masculinities is never considered, because there are no role models for other types (Mac an Ghaill, 1994). This is why all the experts state most emphatically that more males are needed to teach in elementary classrooms (Biddulph, 1997; Bleach, 1997; West, 2002).

Having a male teacher makes a huge difference to how boys view art. I have known several varsity football and basketball players who took AP Art (studio) because they were required to take an art elective. The art teacher approached the topic from a mechanical viewpoint. In one exercise, a picture was cut into squares and each student was given one part to reproduce. While the boys were told how to enlarge their square according to the same scale, they were not given any other directions. When each student was finished copying his square, the parts were put together. The resulting picture was a fascinating look at how each student interpreted the piece he was given—a reproduction of the original, but different at the same time. One boy told me that this approach totally surprised him, as he had previously only thought of art as something for girls. It never occurred to him that there might be other ways to approach this subject.

Applications for Your Classroom

- Classroom teachers rarely have much say in the hiring of other faculty, but where appropriate, support the addition of males to the staff, particularly in the classroom. While my son's male third-grade teacher left after one year, the boys in that class still talk about Mr. G. His tolerance of the noisier and wigglier group of boys went a long way toward helping them see school in a positive light.
- If the addition of male faculty is not likely, do what you can to bring males into the classroom.
- Older boys may choose to go to their local elementary school to serve as "book buddies." For the younger boy, the high-school student serves as an academic model, and for the high-school student, being treated like an academic star is great for his self-concept as a student.
- If you are in a large metropolitan area, you may find programs whereby large corporations encourage their employees to volunteer in social service agencies, in local arts programs, and in schools.
- Encourage your parents' organization to provide programs on different types of parenting. Ask local experts such as counselors, pediatricians, or university faculty to debate various approaches to raising children. This will give families and teachers alike new ideas about how to work with the children.

CAUTION

- ★ Boys may become very defensive if they are presented with a model of masculinity that runs counter to what they have been taught at home. It will be wise to introduce a variety of models to your students.
- ★ Families may become very defensive if they believe that their sons are being presented with models of masculinity they believe to be incorrect. Be alert for this possibility. Communication with the parents of your students is the key here.

LEARNING APPLICATIONS

Emotions can interfere with learning, but knowledge about how to use emotions can make the learning experience much more effective.

Group Size

Research shows that in early school through middle school, girls prefer to work in groups of two or three, whereas boys prefer to work together in larger groups. In addition, children through middle school choose to play in same-sex groups (Benenson, 1993). In the larger boy groups, power hierarchies help keep the group work positive. Boys report having more close friends than do girls, and boys are more likely to think of themselves in terms of group membership (Maccoby, 1998).

- Even though boys like to work in larger groups, the goal of the project or the cognitive levels of the students may require smaller groups. In any group work, you should give the students two grades, one for the outcome of the project and the other for individual participation. That way, the hard-working student gets credit for his work, while his partner who did little work will get the same grade for the project, but a poor participation grade.
- In elementary or middle school, you should function as a coach and help prompt the students to solve the problem. In high school, it may be appropriate to let boys work out the leadership roles within the group. Don't step in too soon if it looks like the boys are having trouble figuring out who is in charge. Simply remind them of the deadlines.
- If the exercise works best individually or in groups of two, set the children to work on the task. After several minutes, allow them to get together into larger groups to share and compare what they have done. Assigning group work is most appropriate when
  - Learning a new concept is a desired objective
  - High-level problem solving is required of the group
  - Students are encouraged to explore multiple perspectives of a problem
- Group work is not appropriate when
  - Understanding of basic knowledge is a desired objective
  - Low-level comprehension of facts is required
  - Students are required to memorize, learn by rote, or master a skill (Howard & James, 2003)

Impulsive/Reflective

Students who are more impulsive are likely to respond quickly and make more errors, whereas reflective students take more time and make fewer errors (Jonassen & Grabowski, 1993). In general, boys are more impulsive and girls more reflective, but also younger children are more impulsive and become more reflective as they mature.

Reflective students have more writing fluency and score higher on paper-and-pencil tests. Impulsive students are less likely to plan to use learning strategies, but become less impulsive with haptic training. This involves turning a visual or auditory experience into a tactile experience, such as using sandpaper letters when learning the alphabet or making a map of a major Civil War battle. Interestingly, haptic learners tend to be more abstract in their thinking (Jonassen & Grabowski, 1993).

- Give boys a problem to solve—a puzzle, a lab exercise, a math problem—and have them come up with as many different ways to solve the problem as they can. It helps to start this exercise with a practical example: How many ways can you think of to count a pile of paper clips?
- Have students come up with questions for material that is being covered by the class. The act of coming up with questions will help students think about the material in a deeper way.

Independent Learners

The stereotype is that men won't ask for directions or for help, and while it is not entirely true, I have had boys do something wrong rather than ask me to clarify directions. The belief is that this is a culturally acquired phenomenon, because boys can be taught to ask for assistance. The important thing is for the teacher to give the information in a matter-of-fact manner and not coddle the student: "Do you need help? Here is what you need to know," rather than "Oh, I'm sorry, do you need for me to go over that again, or did you not understand what I meant? Let me sit down with you and go through the material step by step." The latter approach will not appeal to boys.

- Structure the lesson so that at some point the student needs to get information from some source—the teacher, another student, the library. Praise the students for correctly identifying when they lacked sufficient information to complete the task and asking for help.

- Encourage your school to schedule a help period during the school day. This is standard in boys' schools, and some public schools are realizing that it is helpful for all students. You will find that some students need to be required to come for help, but if you make it a positive experience, they will return.

EMOTIONS AND LEARNING

The paradox for boys in school is that even though they are not good at expressing emotions, they learn best when they are emotionally connected to the material. Boys have to like their teacher and the subject in order to put forth the effort to do well in school. School is a safe environment for boys to expand their emotional vocabularies and their emotional repertoire. The problem for boys is that the standards for proper male behavior are less flexible than what is considered proper for girls. Do what you can to help boys learn to find themselves and to learn to withstand the pressure of society to follow one path. The teacher who utilizes this information will offer a learning environment that

- Provides opportunities for students to acquire both the meaning and understanding of a wide range of emotional expressions
- Provides an environment where students can explore different types of masculinities and stand up to peer pressure
- Provides instructional opportunities for boys to experience a wide range of emotions within the classroom, using the written word in language arts, the study of other cultures in social studies, the understanding of physical responses in science, and any similar appropriate use of material

7

Students With Other Risks

George, one of my advisees, came into my office and, with a sigh of resignation, folded himself into the extra chair. I showed him the note that I had gotten a week before from his English teacher, telling me that the student was having trouble in that class. "Can you tell me why I got this note?" George started to say something several times before blurting out "I know everything that happened in the book we are reading, I know who all the characters are, but then he goes and asks me what the theme *of the book is. I told him what happened, but that wasn't good enough for him." The book, I discovered, was Hemingway's* A Farewell to Arms, *which I hadn't read in a long time. "You tell me what the book is about." He was right, he did know everything that happened, but I began to realize that he had not been taught how to find the meaning of the story. I began to ask him some questions.*

"What is the setting of the book?"

"World War I."

"And when was the book written?"

"Just before World War II."

"Do you think that the events leading up to World War II might have something to do with the story?" A long pause. . . . "Oh, you mean that the book is really about the causes of World War II?" I pointed out that Hemingway was very interested in the political situation in the late 1930s. "Oh, that is why Mr. S went on the other day about the Spanish Civil War. Well, why didn't he say so?"

For the rest of the year, George and I met twice a week to work on what he called "Finding the why's in the story." He had come to the boys' school from an inner-city school where he had done very well. Both of his parents had attended college and were very anxious that their son do so as well. I learned a great deal about why many African American males underachieve in school from this young man. In his memory, I pass that understanding along to you.

This book was written as a way to help teachers who are concerned with the difficulties that boys have in school, because many of them, even those with educational advantages, are not succeeding. For boys whose background is not centered on educational success, the problem is doubly difficult. Most of the research in this area has looked at individuals according to their membership in certain cultural, linguistic, and socioeconomic groups that traditionally have not focused on education. The material in this chapter is necessarily broad, and the intent is to assist teachers in finding ways to help students become successful in school despite their additional risks.

One of the things I discovered is that education can be approached in two different ways. George came from an educational setting where students were taught facts and graded on how well they remembered them. The students I was used to working with had been taught concepts and graded on how well they could apply them. Research reveals that families from racial minorities or from lower socioeconomic groups believe that what is important in school is providing students with a safe environment and scoring well on national tests. Parents with college degrees and those in higher socioeconomic groups believe that safety and scores are not as important as the values encouraged by the school (Schneider, Marschall, Teske, & Roch, 1998). Additionally, concerns of teachers in urban classrooms center more on management and on what the children are to do in class, while those of teachers in suburban classrooms center on academics and on the learning process (Townsend, 2000).

My advisee was a very capable student, but he had not been taught how to examine material closely to uncover the underlying meaning. Once we began to investigate the concepts in his lessons, George discovered that he thoroughly enjoyed this sort of academic exercise. No one had explained the process to him, and he did not feel confident enough in his abilities to ask the teacher for clarification. He told the teacher he hadn't read the assignment rather than admit that he didn't know what the teacher was asking. The note the teacher sent to me said that my advisee was not doing his homework, when in fact the problem was that the student did not understand the questions and he was not about to reveal his ignorance to his classmates.

His other problem was that he had not been encouraged to become an independent student. He did what he was told to do, but no more than that. It never occurred to George to review what he had been learning or to come for help unless directed to do so. His study skills were lacking because his education had been focused on having all children do the same lesson. When I showed him how to approach the lesson in a way that used his academic strengths, he caught on very quickly. As we worked together, he learned how to be an autonomous learner. He would e-mail me with questions or stop me in the hall to continue our discussions.

In working with this young man and with other boys whose success in school may be at risk because of cultural, linguistic, or socioeconomic factors, I have come to realize that there are three issues that make a huge difference in whether or not they see school as an appropriate place for them. We have already discussed the important role that teachers play in the success that boys have in school. Boys report that the teacher is a major factor in how they view the class and their participation in it. If you teach elementary school, you can change the course of a boy's life. That is true regardless of the group the child belongs to. It is not that those of us who teach in middle and high schools can't change lives—we can and do—but it is in elementary school that children from backgrounds that do not emphasize the importance of education come to identify themselves as students (Holland, 1996).

The social environment in which the student was raised makes a huge difference. Again, this is true for all students, but for students with economic and social disadvantages, conflicts between their culture and the school culture may mean that their normal behavior is seen as creating problems in the classroom (Ogbu, 2003; Townsend, 2000). When these students are boys, the combination of factors—culture and gender—means that they are the students least likely to succeed.

The third factor that can make a difference in whether a boy succeeds in school is the adults in his life. We have already seen that all boys do better when they have interested men as role models. Even if a boy does not have interested men in his life, having strong women who support the schools and require the boy to do his work will make a difference. Ben Carson, the noted pediatric neurosurgeon, credits his mother for being the prime influence in his educational life. Although she never completed high school, she raised two boys in the projects of Chicago by herself, working two jobs to support them. She made sure that her sons did their work and knew that education was the most important part of their lives (Carson & Murphey, 1990).

This is a complicated issue and one that people have devoted their lives to studying. But no matter what a boy's background, it appears that the major problem any boy has in school is that he is a boy. Deal with that issue first and other efforts to include him in school are likely to be more successful. What follows is a brief discussion of some of the major issues with suggestions gleaned from the literature.

TEACHERS

As a teacher of boys, I have found that the single most important thing that they need is a teacher who can understand them. The important point is not that the teacher is willing to listen—I hope all teachers will listen—but that the teacher can understand the message the boy is trying to convey. Students without strong academic backgrounds may not have the language to express themselves in such a way that the teacher understands what the student is asking

(Townsend, 2000). My advisee did not know the meaning of the term *theme* and was willing to let the teacher think he had not done the work rather than admit that he had no idea what a theme was. George had read the book and was able to give a plot summary, but he had never before been asked to describe the underlying meaning of the story. Once the teacher was aware of the source of the student's problem, he made sure that he explained such concepts so that all students were clear on the meaning. I have found it is typical of boys in general to let the teacher think they have not completed the assignment rather than to acknowledge their lack of comprehension, particularly when they perceive that the rest of the class understands.

Usually one of the identified issues regarding students whose cultural, linguistic, or socioeconomic membership puts them at risk in school is that there is a dearth of teachers with similar backgrounds at all levels. There is little reason to think that this will improve rapidly (Branch, 2001; Townsend, 2000). However, research shows that all sorts of teachers can be very effective with students who are diverse, as long as the teachers are interested in the students and willing to spend the time necessary to understand what the students want and need from them (Davis, 2001; Fenzel, Peyrot, & Premoshis, 1997; Hubbard & Datnow, 2005). The race of the teacher does not necessarily determine how effective the teacher will be with a student of color, particularly if that student is male. One study found that 60 percent of teachers believed that their African American male students would not go on to college. In that study, 65 percent of the teachers were themselves identified as African American, indicating that the race of the teacher did not guarantee a positive attitude toward black males in school (Garibaldi, 1992).

Part of the issue is that teachers need to understand that the behavior of some students may not fit the model of behavior expected in the classroom. Some children may appear to be interrupting or talking back to the teacher, when the behavior is simply part of the traditional culture of many African American families—what is known as "call and response" (Schwartz, 2001; Townsend, 2000). This is actually an indication of a child who is engaged in the lesson. African American children in general may be used to more physical movement (Moore, Ford, & Milner, 2005) and may have louder speaking voices that draw the teacher's attention. When combined with boys' greater activity and aggressive nature, the teacher may perceive behavior as angry and hostile when the child is simply enthusiastic (Grossman & Grossman, 1994).

This particular type of behavior is not necessarily true of Hispanic children and is infrequently true of Asian children, who have been raised to be extremely respectful of the educational process (Goyette & Xie, 1999). One study comparing white, black, and Hispanic males and females in school reported the correlation between grades and self-esteem as a way to measure how strongly students identified themselves as students. By far, those with the poorest identification were the African American males. Except for the area of reading (due to the language barrier), by the twelfth grade, Hispanic males had stronger identification with school than either black males or black females (Osborne, 1997). This study did not uncover the reasons that black males are least likely to think of themselves as students. It did note that by twelfth grade all other groups were reporting roughly the same level of identification, so the problem is most serious for black males. One area that black males did identify with was science, indicating that very practical, hands-on education is appealing to them (Moore et al., 2005; Osborne, 1997).

Teachers need to examine their beliefs about all students. If you have gotten this far in this book, your ideas about why boys behave they way they do in class probably have changed somewhat from when you started. Remember, no matter what their background, culturally diverse boys are boys first. Apply the principles of dealing with boys to *all* boys, regardless of culture, and you will see improvement. If one group of boys in your classes still is not engaged in the learning process, but others are, then look at what that group has in common. If you find a common factor, and are not sure what your best course of action is, talk to other teachers in your school whom your students identify as teachers that understand them. Ask your administration for professional development opportunities to enlarge your and your colleagues' understanding of the diverse cultures in your school. You will find a list of books that may be of help in Chapter 11.

Suggestions From the Experts

- Make sure that students who are at risk hear appropriate praise about their academic ability and promise. When students know that their teachers believe in their ability, they are willing to work harder (Howard, 2003).
- Raise the issues of race and education frankly with your students. They know the problems; they need your insights and advice on how to deal with the problems (Howard, 2003).
- Assist students with language differences in acquiring standard English skills. Help them learn to recognize when it is

appropriate to use standard English and when they may use their own regional speech (Townsend, 2000).

- Examine the way you respond to the students of color in your classroom to ensure that you are treating all students equitably. Research has shown that teachers may give black males less direct instruction, pay them less personal attention, call on them less, give them less time to answer questions, and demand less work from them (Duncan, 1999).

- Find out about your students' lives away from school. Knowledge about your students' outside interests will help you relate to them in school (Townsend, 2000).

- Plan activities in your classroom where students have more physical movement. Interactive lessons are particularly appealing to youth who have an inadequate educational background (Moore et al., 2005; Townsend, 2000).

- For Hispanic boys, pay particular attention to encourage reading skills by giving them books they are likely to be interested in and by working with them in small groups where they do not feel they are noticed by the rest of the class (Osborne, 1997).

- Assist your school in providing appropriate role models for the boys of color (Ford-Harris, Schuerger, & Harris, 1991). These can be teachers, mentors, coaches, older students, community volunteers, employers, or individuals from social service organizations, just to name a few.

- Examine your own stereotypes, preconceptions, and apprehensions about students whose cultural, linguistic, and socioeconomic membership differs from your own, as these might affect your students' achievement or motivation (Ford & Moore, 2004; Howard, 2003). If you see this as a problem, encourage your school to provide professional development programs to help all the faculty in the area of multicultural understanding. This can be a major step forward for your school.

CULTURE

The issue of culture involves several different areas of focus. Your students will probably have in common the culture of the local community. This involves politics, socioeconomic strata, career opportunities, religion, attitudes, and living conditions, to name a few. The culture that some of your students will share is that of their peer group. The focus of the various peer groups may be athletics, arts, academics, technology, or even gang activities. The culture your students will not share, except with those with whom they live, is that of their family. Whether or not they subscribe to the family culture is partially a matter of age—as they grow up, they will move away from the family culture and develop their own—and partially a matter of individual family dynamics. Again, this is true for all students, regardless of race or gender. But a difficulty may arise if you and your students do not share a cultural background, and that may have nothing to do with race. Because I was raised in the rural South, I find that I understand the culture of boys raised in similar areas no matter what their color. Even though a boy raised in the urban North and I share the same color, his culture is very foreign to me.

If you are new to your area, you need to become familiar with the local culture. Read the newspaper, talk to other teachers, get around the neighborhood or area to see where your students will come from. You will also need to make this effort if redistricting brings in students from a new area. Churches, civic groups, and volunteer agencies offer excellent chances to get to know people and to find out what is important to them. You also need to find out the history of education in this area. If redistricting has been contested, students coming to your school may be reluctant to do so and unwilling to become a part of the school community.

This is good advice for all teachers, so why does it appear here? The problem is most obvious if the teacher and the students do not share a cultural or linguistic heritage. In that event, you need to make the effort to become a part of the community because that will open the lines of communication between you, your students, and the families of your students. Although most obvious when you and your students are from different races and cultural backgrounds, this is also true when race is not a factor. I teach a college course in our local high school. I am relatively unknown to most of my students, but each year there are two or three whose parents know me one way or the other. In the first days of school, those students are usually eager to show their classmates that they already know me, thereby rapidly opening the lines of communication. At the community college, where I know few if any of my students, I have noticed that it takes longer for them to begin to open up unless there is a student who has taken a class with me before. That student makes all the difference.

Disidentification

Many boys whose culture does not focus on education do not think of themselves as part of the school. They go to school, but if you ask them about themselves, they do not identify themselves as students. This phenomenon is called disidentification and has its origins in a theory called stereotype threat. The idea is that minorities—and this theory has been applied to women as well as to cultural, linguistic, and socioeconomic minorities—internalize the stereotypes that say that they will not be successful in school. The individuals then do not identify themselves as students as a way to protect their self-identity and self-esteem (Ogbu, 2003; Steele, 1997). To be successful in school, individuals must identify themselves as students and as part of the school community, but in doing so they run the risk of failure. In the case of minorities, that failure would confirm the stereotype—that minorities do not succeed in an academic environment—so the solution to the dilemma is not to try.

An alternative explanation for disidentification, called the oppositional-culture theory, comes from a difference in attitude toward cultural assimilation. Ogbu (1998, 2004) identifies minorities as being either voluntary or involuntary. Those who are voluntary, such as Asians and some Hispanics, want to become a part of the culture and so they internalize the prevailing values of the majority. These cultures encourage their children to become as American as possible and to take advantage of the educational opportunities. Involuntary minorities, such as African Americans and Native Americans, make every effort to maintain their separate identities. These cultures do not encourage their children to be actively engaged in a system that is not responsive to the cultural needs of their children.

There is some evidence that Hispanics who have educationally disadvantaged backgrounds in addition to a language difference may also show signs of disidentification (Osborne, 1997). This may be the reason that Hispanics have the highest school dropout rate (NCES, 2006). When compared to white and Asian students, black and Hispanic students reported less attachment to school, with Hispanics more disidentified than blacks (Griffin, 2002). What effect the possible mobility of the family may have on the Hispanic student was not considered.

While both of these theories make rational sense, there is no agreed-upon method to determine whether or not disidentificaion is the reason that an educationally disadvantaged student is doing poorly. A recent study attempted to determine whether or not either or both of these theories could explain the poor behavior of black students. Students in this study reported that they did identify themselves as students, but at the same time discounted some academic evaluations as not being relevant to or descriptive of them. The stereotype threat theory would explain their beliefs that the academic descriptions did not fit, but would not explain why, at the same time, they identified themselves as students. With regard to the oppositional-culture theory, which is based on whether or not the students come from voluntary or involuntary minorities, findings indicated that while students may oppose school as an institution, they still accept that academic achievement is important (Morgan & Mehta, 2004). The jury is out on this, but the feeling is that the source of minority students' academic difficulties may be more complicated than one theory can explain.

Peer Culture

We have already discussed the major problem in this area, that of anti-intellectualism. Boys in general are inclined to discount the importance of academic success, and boys from certain cultural, linguistic, and socioeconomic groups are even more so. These boys appear "too cool for school" and project a persona detached from emotion and from academics. Their behaviors may be in sharp contrast to the motivated, engaged student, thereby drawing the notice of the administration. When they will not conform to the accepted standard of dress and behavior, they are punished, which then leads them to distance themselves further from school (Yeakey, 2002). They band together to support and encourage each other, which results in a culture defined by their success in areas anywhere but school.

Another group of disadvantaged boys who are marginally attached to school are those in competitive athletics. It is not that black boys are necessarily better at athletics, but sports are a good fit with their culture. Part of African American culture is the feeling of communalism (Sankofa, Hurley, Allen, & Boykin, 2005), and playing sports requires cooperation and team loyalty. Being part of a team can be simply an extension of communalism. Also, we have already mentioned that African American children can be more active and receptive to strong stimulation—what is called verve (Sankofa et al., 2005). Certainly, playing competitive athletics provides a high level of activity and stimulation. If school emphasizes individual competition and quiet demeanor, athletics can be very appealing to the African American boy, as it provides a stimulating group activity. Unfortunately, if athletics is the currency he is using to pay for his identity—and later, in college, literally pay for his education—the time required to focus on athletics may reduce the time available to focus on academics (Messner, 1992). In that case, he will identify himself as an athlete and not a student.

Ethnic Identification

Another part of this complex situation is that boys whose group membership may put them at risk in school who are good students may be accused of voluntarily taking on the racial characteristics of the majority—what has been called "acting white" (Grantham & Ford, 2003; Howard, 2003; Ogbu, 2004). These students feel that they fit in neither world and can be rejected by both black and white students. The most powerful antidote to this problem I have ever run across was exemplified by an African student whose attitude was that his skin color had no affect on his intelligence or his ability to succeed. In fact, when one of our African American students accused him of "acting white" because he worked hard, he replied that he was not "acting white," he was "acting smart."

For other students, ethnic identification may be somewhat different. Children who live in areas close to their country of origin, primarily Hispanic students, are exposed to their traditional cultures and may be a bit more confident about their identity. The problem is that academic success may not be part of that identity. On the other hand, many of the students whose countries of origin are in the Asian-Pacific area may come from families who are likely to be middle-class and for whom academic success is an expectation (Goyette & Xie, 1999; Grossman & Grossman, 1994).

Suggestions From the Experts

- Use musical instruments, rhythm, poetry, role playing, drama, sports, games, learning centers, field trips, and any academic activity that involves movement, music, and stimulation (Moore et al., 2005).
- For students in the primary grades, provide instructional strategies reflecting boys' more active natures. They may view traditional classroom activities, such as imitating the female teacher, or songs and games, as not masculine (Holland, 1996).
- Use cooperative and collaborative learning activities, encourage students to work with other students in tutoring or mentoring, and promote opportunities for students to get involved in community or service activities (Lewis, 1992; Moore et al., 2005).
- Include multicultural themes and activities wherever appropriate in your lesson plans. Integrate this material into your teaching throughout the year as you prepare your students for their life in a diverse society (Ford & Moore, 2004).

- One technique that has been used with great success to foster racial harmony in the classroom is the jigsaw lesson plan. Because students collaborate to solve a problem, this method helps all students be a part of an active educational opportunity that depends on all members of the group for success (Gregory, 2003; Tomlinson, 2001).
- When academics are emphasized and celebrated, it is easier for boys to succeed academically without fear of criticism from other students (Fenzel et al., 1997). It may be easier to focus on academics when students are arranged in smaller groups, as with Freshmen Academies, an academic plan where the ninth grade has a dedicated section of the school in an attempt to allow for smoother transition to high school.
- Include members of the larger community in your classroom. You might invite a local civic leader to speak on the subject of citizenship, a storyteller to share local lore, or an employer to outline the skills necessary to obtain a good job (Townsend, 2000).
- Ask families what they would like to do to help, or who they would suggest as a good resource. The problem is that many families from cultural, linguistic, or socioeconomic groups who have not succeeded in educational settings have limited school involvement because their schedules prevent them from participating in traditional ways—helping in the classroom in lower grades, attending school activities, raising money for school needs, and the like. The more the families feel that they are partners in their children's education, the more positive they will be about school (Townsend, 2000).
- There are many social programs that encourage youth participation. These programs use the connection to the community, together with communalism, to help young people develop their sense of self (Lewis, 1992). Sponsorship can be provided by federal organizations, local religious and civic groups, youth organizations such as Scouts or 4-H, or schools. Encourage your students to take advantage of these opportunities.
- A few programs have been developed to interpret the majority culture for minority students. Some are for recent immigrants, some involve helping students with the college choice process, and some help African American boys to identify themselves as students (Bailey, 2003; Holland, 1996). You may suggest the adoption of such leadership programs by your school to help all minority boys.

ADULTS

For all boys, the presence of powerful role models makes a huge difference in the way that they view any activity, including school. The problem for the boy at risk is that there may not be many men of similar backgrounds in education to serve as role models. The men of color who are in the schools are more likely to be in maintenance, sports, or administration and less likely to be in the classroom (Branch, 2001; Townsend, 2000). In the school year ending in 2000, only 25 percent of classroom teachers were male, but 56 percent of school principals were male. At the same time, 7.6 percent of classroom teachers were black and 5.6 percent were Hispanic. Of the school principals, 11 percent were black and 5 percent were Hispanic (NCES, 2006).

These percentages of male and minority faculty are not reflective of the student body. In 2000, 78.8 percent of school-aged children were white, 15.6 percent were black, and 5.6 percent were of other races. At the same time, 51.6 percent of school-aged children were male (NCES, 2006). Because students spend most of their day in the classroom, the person with whom they have the most contact is likely to be a white female.

School has been the place where children are supposed to learn the skills necessary to succeed in life. The claim is that any child can aspire to any position he wants. All he has to do is try hard enough. The models who have been held up are people who through hard work and persistence, together with a good education, made a better life. Unfortunately for boys of color, school has not provided the academic boost necessary, and the success they hoped and planned for has eluded them (Yeakey, 2002). The role models they find are more likely to be outside of school—usually some highly paid athlete or entertainer from the inner city whose skills were not learned in school.

Unfortunately, strong academic role models for boys at risk may be scarce outside of school. For some, the family culture does not promote success in education, and there may not be a male family member who has succeeded in school (Bailey & Paisley, 2004; Grantham & Ford, 2003). Society at large does not provide many successful role models either. Minority males are usually found in two areas: in the entertainment field, whether sports or music, or in the penal system (Yeakey, 2002).

Some of the successful programs addressing this need are found in schools, but come from areas outside the traditional educational system. Descriptions of three such programs follow.

PROJECT 2000 has been a very successful program in the Washington, DC, area schools, but was begun, funded, and staffed by a chapter of Concerned Black Men, Inc. (Holland, 1996). This program begins in elementary school and provides African American male volunteers working in classrooms to tutor and mentor the students all the way through high school. A house in the neighborhood where the majority of the students lived was purchased and staffed by the volunteers. The house served as a "safe haven," providing afterschool tutoring and other support for older students.

Gentlemen on the Move was instituted in a high school in North Carolina. The students agreed to abide by a set of expectations for behavior, and the program provided extra academic support. In addition, students were required to be involved in community service projects as a way to develop leadership skills. The parents of the students in the program were expected to provide support. They met monthly to discuss how their sons were doing and how they could help the program (Bailey & Paisley, 2004).

Nativity Mission School was instituted by members of the Society of Jesus (the Jesuits) in a Spanish area of New York City and has been so successful it has spread to other cities. This parochial school for the fourth through eighth grades provides as many meals as the student needs, afterschool activities, evening tutoring sessions, and even summer camp. After the boys leave and go to high school, the school serves as a place they can come for help or support (Fenzel et al., 1997). I've taught boys who were a part of the original school, and I have been very impressed with the academic preparation and seriousness of purpose of these young men. They tell me that only because of Nativity have they had the chance to succeed.

These are just three of many such programs around the country. From what I can see, most are successful as long as the adults remain involved and interested. They share some characteristics. All programs

- Emphasize academic progress and provide tutoring to ensure that the students do not fall through the cracks
- Have a set of guidelines and expectations for behavior, with some means to make sure that there are consequences for violations
- Provide mentors and role models in the form of successful men of color who are committed to working with the boys
- Require the students to be involved in afterschool and community activities to foster a sense of belonging to the group and to limit contact with peers who are not involved with the program

The two key points are that there are interested adults and the boys feel like they belong to a special group. This takes effort, involvement, and persistence, but the alternative is that these young men become marginalized and end up in trouble with the law or the victims of crime.

Gangs

Some twenty years ago, a South African national park found itself with too many elephants. The solution was to relocate some younger elephants to another park. A few years later, another problem developed in the second park—the killing of white rhinos. After careful observations, the rangers found out that the transplanted young elephants were the killers. These elephants had been harassing the rhinos by throwing sticks at them, chasing them, and finally stomping them to death. The young elephants banded together in groups led by particularly tough young males, in the manner of street gangs. Finally, a suggestion was made to bring in a number of mature male elephants to see what effect they would have on the young elephant thugs. In short order, the older males asserted their authority and the young elephants, after a few futile attempts to stand their ground, yielded. According to the source, the young elephants "started following the older bulls around—obviously enjoying the association with the adult males, yielding to their discipline, and learning from them proper elephant behavior." The absence of older males left a void that the juveniles tried unsuccessfully to fill, and when the older males were reintroduced the young elephants were more than willing to follow their lead (Raspberry, 1999).

Just like the young male elephants, boys also need authority figures to help them learn proper behavior. You will notice that in the story, the older elephants did not try to persuade the younger elephants to behave better. The senior elephants were sure of their authority, physically able to take over, and tolerated no mess from the younger elephants. The article describing the situation with the elephants pointed out that this method might be effective in dealing with human street gangs as well.

Gangs do exist and will create problems in your school. However, remember some points made earlier: Boys like to work and play in groups, they are competitive, they are aggressive, and according to some theorists they are in need of male role models. Those factors go a long way toward explaining why boys like to congregate in groups, develop hierarchies within those groups, and use membership in the groups to define themselves. Just because boys are members of disadvantaged populations does not mean that they are predisposed to join a gang. However, if they do not identify themselves as students, joining a gang is a way to acquire an identity.

If there are active gangs in the area where your students live, you have gang members in your school. This is a problem that the school must deal with through unified approaches. Remember the elephants; one of the best ways to deal with gang behavior is through programs whereby men are actively engaged with young boys doing real work in the community. Some programs have focused on upgrading the school playground, building access ramps for local elderly or handicapped residents, cleaning up abandoned lots, refurbishing bicycles for local children, and using common land in developments to grow vegetables for residents. Each of these programs is a joint effort resulting in a tangible and useful product. This is something to which the boys involved can point with pride, and it is the development of pride in one's own efforts that will help the most. If you have the chance, suggest such programs to help the boys in your school.

Suggestions From the Experts

- Encourage the participation of families and members from the community in school programs. The more that children see successful adults, the more likely they are to believe that they can also succeed (Townsend, 2000).
- Help develop a comprehensive school behavior policy, support the maintenance of school rules, and support programs designed to assist chronic offenders (Schwartz, 2001; Townsend, 2000).
- Encourage programs that help students at risk identify with those in higher education by inviting college students from similar groups into your classroom or supporting tours of historically black colleges and universities (Grantham & Ford, 2003).
- Require academic extracurricular programs that will expose students to mentors in the community. Give credit in your class for students who are involved in shadowing or internship programs (Grantham & Ford, 2003).
- All adults in the school should play an active part in helping marginalized boys feel like they are a part of the school. The students should be expected to be respectful of the adults, but the adults should also be expected to be respectful of the students (Bailey & Paisley, 2004; Holland, 1996).

BOYS WITH CULTURAL, LINGUISTIC, OR SOCIOECONOMIC DIFFERENCES AND SCHOOL

Part of the lack of success of boys from diverse groups in education begins with their gender. Regardless of race, many boys are having trouble in school. Add to that the problem of race, and the situation of these boys is a national shame. The solution begins with teachers who are committed to teaching all the children in their classrooms, regardless of gender or race. The teacher who utilizes this information will offer a learning environment that

- Provides educational opportunities for all students, not just those who are successful
- Provides support and assistance to students who may, because of race or language barriers, think that they are incapable of learning, or that education is not important for them
- Provides the opportunity for all students to develop personal aims and goals by encouraging interaction with a wide variety of successful adults who can serve as role models and resources

PART III

Strategies and Resources for Teaching the Male Brain

8

Classroom Management Strategies

Baby Blues

SOURCE: ©Baby Blues Partnership. King Features.

When I teach the study skills class in summer school, I start the first day by greeting the students, telling them my name, and announcing the title of the course. Then I ask the boys, "What do you think you are going to learn in this class?" Inevitably, they look at each other to see if anyone else has an answer. Usually, a boy will reply, "well, we are supposed to learn how to be better students." So I ask them what they think good students look like. This initiates a discussion about what it means to be a student that gets them involved in the class from the beginning. At the end, I give them my class rules. I have only two. It drives me nuts when students are late to class, especially since this class meets first period in the morning. So the first rule is don't be late to class. I point out that if they are late, they will give me back that time by being early to the next class. And, if they continue to be late, they will come in earlier and earlier until they can meet the deadline. If that means that I have to get to school early, even at 6:30 A.M., I will do that, and I have. The other thing that drives me nuts is students who don't care about their work. So the second rule is don't look like you are not working. I realize that students may not work, but just don't let me see it. If I become aware that a student is not working, he will come in early to do all the required work and extra work as well.

Most of my students have told me that I was a bit scary on the first day, but that as they got to know me, they found out that I was pretty cool. But, as one boy put it, "I also knew that you meant business." The old adage, "start as you mean to go on" applies to classroom management. If you are too easy at first, under the impression that students will like you better, boys especially will take advantage of that, and you will find that you are not the person in charge of your class.

I am very careful not to step across the boundary between teacher and student. Consequently, it is much easier for me to keep class order. When teachers ask me why I don't want to be friends with my students, I reply that the students have plenty of friends. What they need is a teacher, and I can't be both. Friends are there to help you through life and to share your experiences. Teachers are there to create a learning environment responsive to each student's needs. Yes, you will share some experiences in the classroom and students may confide in you. That is not because you are friends, but because they need you to be a trustworthy adult. What you want is to foster a mutually respectful, honest, and friendly atmosphere. When you do that and provide educational experiences that engage the students, you will be managing your classroom.

Classroom management is not about control. Visitors to my classes are sometimes dubious about what is going on. One day, the head of school walked in to find me in one of the student seats and one of the students at my desk. We had been discussing how an engine worked and I discovered that the student in question knew a great deal about how lawnmower engines worked because he had a summer job mowing lawns. So, I told him, "you know a lot more than I do on this subject, you tell us how they work." He did a very good job, and even the head of school was impressed. The class was under control because the students were engaged in what was going on in class, not because I was in the front of the classroom.

I have always said that what goes on in the classroom is a collaborative venture. Both the teacher and the students have to be a part of the lesson. Learning takes place when everyone in the classroom is an active part of the process, not when the students are merely doing what they are told. Earlier, we discovered that boys learn best when they are emotionally connected to the material—when they like the subject and/or the teacher. That is the key to getting boys to behave (remembering that their good behavior may not look like ideal behavior). Boys engaged in the learning process are going to blurt out answers, initiate discussions that seem totally off the subject, and argue with the student in the next seat about the right answer.

One lesson that the American school system seems to teach well to boys is how to hate school. Ask boys in kindergarten how much they like school and most will tell you how much fun their classes have and what they learned yesterday. Ask a sixth-grade boy the same question and you are likely to find that he does not like school and cannot wait to get out. The problem is that in kindergarten, the boy was encouraged to move around his classroom and get physically involved in learning opportunities. In sixth grade, lessons primarily take the form of seat work, and the boy who responds best to active learning environments is bored and restless.

HOME INFLUENCE

Let's start at home. After all, children's outlook on school is partly a product of their environment and the attitudes toward school they learn from their families. Most important, research shows that parental involvement is directly related to children's academic success (Hill et al., 2004; Hortacsu, 1995). These studies measured parental involvement by how often parents attended parents' meetings, came to parent information sessions, or assisted with functions at school. The researchers commented that it is difficult to measure at-home parental involvement because of the dependence on self-report, whereas at-school involvement could be tracked.

The mere presence of a parent may make a difference. One study examined the effect of fathers on children's college entrance exam scores and found that noncustodial fathers had little effect, even if the children reported that their fathers were supportive and involved. Fathers in intact families had direct effects on exam scores, although the effects were influenced by ethnicity and income (Furr, 1998). For African American boys, the lack of effective male role models in the home was seen to directly depress academic achievement (Rodney, Rodney, Crafter, & Mupier, 1999). Much of the literature on helping boys develop into good citizens as well as competent students focuses on the necessity for good male role models (Biddulph, 1997; Kindlon & Thompson, 1999; West, 2002). Research would seem to confirm the notion that many boys need frequent contact with a supportive male to succeed in school.

The mother is also very important. Research has shown that the educational level of the mothers affected the school behavior and achievement of students more than did the educational level of the father (Hortacsu, 1995). Remember, also, the role that Ben Carson's mother played in his success. Certainly, in most families children spend more time with their mother, and it is usually the mother who is the educational contact for the school. However, please make sure that if the family wishes for the father to be the primary school contact that you make every effort to facilitate that.

When our son was small, I was teaching and my husband was self-employed. It was much easier for him to leave work if our son was sick and needed to leave school than it was for me. Even though the school was not large, we had to make a point every year to make sure that he was the first person listed to be called. In addition, my husband was the homework parent. Since I am a teacher, we thought it would be better for the parent who was not an education professional to manage homework, because I might be tempted to teach him instead of just supervising. The problem was that when we went to parents' night, the teacher usually directed her remarks to me. If both parents come to a meeting with the teacher, assume both are equally involved in their son's progress.

I have discovered that some fathers are reluctant to talk to teachers or to be an active part of their son's education. Some of that reluctance is due to their own problems in school. I have been told by fathers that because they did not do well in school they let their wives be in charge of the children's education. It is also possible that on parents' night fathers do not come because there are mostly women involved—teachers and mothers. Fathers tell me that they enjoy coming to parents' night at the boys' school because there are more men to talk to. Encourage fathers' groups or have specific fathers' nights. Have class fathers as well as class mothers. The class fathers could be in charge of developing a reading group, teaching the students to play chess, or preparing a meal for the students. For children without fathers, being around other men is very positive. You can encourage male staff, grandfathers, or older brothers to come to the reading group or fathers' nights as well.

Above I mentioned that the father's effect on the child's educational progress is affected by ethnicity and income level. More important, parents in different social and economic groups express different expectations for what they view as appropriate outcomes of schooling. Parents from lower socioeconomic groups value schools that are safe and provide the basics of learning. They look at school as a place that assists children in passing the minimum standard hurdles so that the children will be able to earn a living. Increasingly, that means preparing children for college. Middle-class parents expect more from schools, hoping that their children will be exposed to a wider variety of opportunities. They see the purpose of school as enlarging their child's knowledge base (Schneider, Marschall, Teske, & Roch, 1998).

In addition, parental discipline is a factor. A study of adolescent academic performance found that parents with a low level of education were less effective disciplinarians, resulting in behavior problems for boys in the sixth grade. The problem behaviors continued into the seventh grade and were seen there to have a negative effect on the boys' academic progress (DeBaryshe, Patterson, & Capaldi, 1993). Another study found a direct connection between poor home discipline and grade retention, in part because undisciplined children were not likely to do their homework (Rodney et al., 1999). It is not uncommon for parents of children who are not doing well to believe that the problem is caused by the system, by other children, or by a teacher who does not understand the child.

Your best way of dealing with parents who see others as the problem is to communicate with the family early and often. Send home weekly progress notes for all the students. Be very specific about what children have done and failed to do, and use the "sandwich" approach. Put the meat of your message, the negative concern, between two slices of bread, positive statements about what the child has done. You are not sugarcoating, but you are likely to get the parents to listen better if they know when they talk to you that the first thing you say about their child will be positive.

At least one study found that teachers did not welcome family involvement in school and preferred for families to help with homework or school fundraisers (Ramirez, 2001). The administration in the school studied wanted to include families, but the teachers had sent a clear, if unwritten, message to the families that they were not welcome. If you think this is a problem, directly invite the families of your students to help in your class. You may be warned by some teachers to beware family overinvolvement, but you may be able to show your colleagues that families can help.

A noted Australian educator identifies five important factors in getting boys to behave: (1) Having a dad who cares, (2) providing firm rules, (3) caring, (4) getting boys out of doors, and (5) praise (West, 2002). Share that with the families of your students, as they can do a lot to help.

Applications for Your Classroom

- Do what you can to provide male role models for the boys. Older boys may find a mentor outside of school, through a formal program, involvement with sports, or a job.
- Encourage families to come to school for teacher conferences and other programs.
- Suggest that high school students babysit younger siblings during teacher conferences so that adults in the family can come for meetings.
- Your counseling department may be able to start a family group to help parents get involved in their children's education.
- Basic rules applied consistently will go a long way toward helping all children. Most important, your classroom should be a place where the students can trust you and each other.
- If getting homework completed is a problem, refer students to an afterschool program that helps students do their homework before going home. If such a program does not exist in your area, make a suggestion to your administration to start one. If that is not possible, work with the student and family to develop a schedule for the student to make sure that homework is properly completed.

CAUTION

★ Lack of involvement by families is difficult to address because you end up preaching to the converted. The families who come to school programs for families are frequently the ones who are least in need of assistance. Home visits can help. Remember that family members may not come because of language barriers, because of conflicts with work schedules, or because they did not have successful experiences in school themselves.

DISCIPLINE

The best classroom management plan is based on learner engagement. The more involved your students are in what is going on in the classroom, the less time they will have to misbehave. I realized that my ninth-grade students usually misbehaved when I was lecturing. They rarely gave me any trouble during lab because they were involved with the activity. My seniors, on the other hand, were better able to sit and take notes for a whole class period, although they did need some time to discuss the material at hand. It was a matter of my providing a learning environment that responded to the developmental level of my students. Even then, I had some students who had trouble abiding by the rules, but not many.

Absolutely the only way to handle discipline is to state the rules very clearly and then consistently apply them (if it seems like you have heard this before, I think the point bears repeating). Earlier, I recommended that there be no more than five positively stated rules for the classroom and that the teacher be very consistent in applying them. If your list of rules is long and complicated, it will be difficult to enforce them—think Ten Commandments and not the Internal Revenue Code.

Your five positively stated rules will not cover every incident in the classroom, so you will need to help children learn to interpret how those rules are applied. For example, if the rule is to treat each other with respect and one child shoves another's books off a table, you will need to help the children see how respecting others means respecting their stuff as well. Boys have more trouble with what they perceive as ambiguities in rules, so the teacher must be consistent in applying them.

The five positive rules can also be applied to the whole school, as with the rule "all in the school will treat each other with respect." This can start with the magic words "please" and "thank you," from teachers as well as from students. You may be surprised at the response. I teach a college-level class at the local high school, and during one semester, each time I went to school I would pass a group of boys getting their last cigarette before school. Each day I said "Good morning, gentlemen." For about a month they ignored me, but I persisted. Finally, one day, one replied, "Good morning. Ma'am." Toward the end of the semester, I was walking through the hall and came across an exuberant group of students. As I passed, the group parted to let me through. When I said "thank you," I realized that the leaders were the boys I passed each time I went to school. I treated them with respect, and they treated me with respect.

At the elementary school my son and I attended, each teacher shakes hands with each student as they exit the classroom for the day—prekindergarten students through the eighth grade. Some teachers accompany that with "thank you for your hard work today," or "have a good afternoon," but do not say the same thing to every student. That practice was started by the founder, who was my kindergarten teacher. I remember feeling so important because an adult shook my hand. Because I give my students the same respect, I find that they reciprocate—and not just to me, but to each other.

One of the most frequent complaints from students about discipline is the wail that "it's not fair!" Part of the problem is that girls and boys understand fairness differently. After years of teaching boys and girls, I think I recognize the difference. For girls, fairness is achieved when equality is attained. They want to make sure that each child is treated the same. For boys, fairness is less about equality and more about clarity. They need for the rules to be specifically stated ahead of time.

Maintenance of Discipline

Before you begin this section, you may want to review material on behavior control. This includes behavior management using rewards as well as punishment. Here, we use the term punishment to mean a response to a child's behavior that is designed to reduce the chance of that behavior being repeated. That can mean giving a child something he doesn't like, such as detention, or taking away something he does like, such as attention.

There are differences in the ways that boys and girls view behavior control (see box for an explanation of terms). In one study, second graders, sixth graders, high-school students, and college undergraduates observed videos of a variety of parental discipline scenarios. As a group, these students agreed that induction—asking a child to imagine how his behavior affects someone else—was an effective method of controlling a girl's misbehavior, but that power assertion would be more effective with boys. In addition, girls viewed induction more positively and boys viewed power assertion and attention withdrawal more positively. What is even more interesting is that the males in this study (remember they were in second grade through college) viewed the parent who used power assertion or attention withdrawal as more fair and more sensitive to the child than the parent who used induction (Barnett, Quackenbush, & Sinisi, 1996).

Behavior Control

There are three major forms of behavior control.

Induction occurs when an adult points out to a child the effect his unruly behavior has on others. "Don't hit Tommy. It hurts him. How would you feel if he hit you?"

Power assertion occurs when the adult makes the child behave. In class, power assertion is likely to be used when the rules are invoked. "It is against the rules for you to hit anyone."

Attention withdrawal occurs when the adult removes attention from the child because of the child's misbehavior. This can include the "time out." "You are to sit in the chair in the hall and do this review sheet. You may return in five minutes."

I have found that boys, particularly middle-school boys, see induction as weak. One boy who behaved well in my class got into trouble with another teacher. The boy complained to me that he didn't know what the rules were in that teacher's class, unlike my class where he felt that my expectations were clear. I asked him what that teacher said to him that he found difficult to understand and he replied, "Mr. S is always asking me if I understand how my behavior bothers other students. I don't know, I'm not them. If he wants me to stop, he should say so instead of making me guess."

I think I know where the problem occurs. Remember fight-or-flight and tend-and-befriend? The first is the way males react to stress, and the second is the way that females react to stress. Female teachers, who are in the overwhelming majority in elementary school, use induction because it works with them: It asks the student to relate to the others in the group—a tend-and-befriend method. They also use attention withdrawal because they see that method works. They don't want to use power assertion because they are concerned that invoking the rules will be too confrontational and cause a student to react badly. The problem is that boys don't relate well to others in the group in moments of stress, such as being reprimanded for bad behavior. They react well to power assertion because it gives clear signals—just what the child who reacts with a fight-or-flight response needs. Boys and girls are very different in this area, so teachers need to develop gender-responsive methods to discipline their students.

If a boy is frequently accused of a transgression unfairly, he may well become defensive and even angry (Heyman & Legare, 2004). He will treat adults with suspicion, and this may escalate. If you ask direct questions and treat the boy with respect, you are more likely to get an honest answer. What I do is state the obvious and wait for an explanation. I once walked into my classroom to find a desk overturned and several red-faced young men sweeping up a broken light fixture. I said, "OK, gentlemen, the three of you are here, the desk is overturned, and the light fixture is broken. Who would like to tell me how this happened?" I accused no one of anything. It turned out that there was a bee in the room; one boy had been standing on the desk trying to hit it with a shoe and got the light instead. I thanked them for their consideration in trying to rid my classroom of the bee. After cleaning up, we spent a little time brainstorming alternative ways to get the bee.

Forms of Discipline

"Time out" as a way to get students to behave is an honored method and can work well. The idea is that separating the student from the classroom removes the reinforcement he gets from his classmates for his unruly behavior. Sending the child to sit in a chair outside the door sounds like it will work, but it may not. For some students, being out of class and not having to work is a reward. In addition, if there are other children in the hall, they are likely to start conversations, and may actually misbehave in order to get put out of class. Most important, make sure that any handheld games are confiscated before the child is sent to time out.

Most other forms of discipline are going to involve the school administrator who is in charge of discipline. Each school has its own methods of disciplining students; these may include detention, Saturday school, in-school suspension, and out-of-school suspension. You need to be very familiar with the consequences of misbehavior and how those consequences escalate for subsequent violations.

Suspension is an expanded version of time out. It may not be very effective, especially for boys who do not see school as a positive place. If they feel negatively about school, suspension may seem like a reward. One study suggested that in-school suspension, together with Saturday school, may be a viable alternative, providing continuous attendance and increasing the chance of the boy improving his attitude toward school—particularly if time is used for remedial work (Rodney et al., 1999). However, suspension is a complicated issue with legal ramifications, and each school system will have its own way of dealing with this disciplinary method.

Applications for Your Classroom

- Follow the guidelines for classroom rules that were described in Chapter 6: five rules, clearly stated in the affirmative and consistently applied.
- Boys will respond positively when you comment on their good behavior, as long as you are specific. Do not, however, make a big deal about this. "Thanks for being so cooperative today" will get better results than pointing out each instance of their cooperation.
- The more input boys have into the school rules, the more likely they will be to abide by them. More important, if they are part of drafting the rules, they will begin to develop an appreciation for ambiguities.
- You can't rewrite the rules every year, but you can support a student government system. Do what you can to assist students in working on substantive issues, and try to help make sure that the students have a say in more than just what type of ice cream is served at lunch.
- Treat boys—actually, all students—with politeness, even when reprimanding them.
- Prepare a child to go to time out.
  - Review the rules, such as "no talking" or "no playing with hand-held electronic games."
  - If there are other children in time out in the same hall, remind the child to turn the chair so that it faces the wall. This will make it more difficult for them to talk to each other.
  - Have a time out bucket. Put review sheets, worksheets, and/or a book in the bucket. As the child exits the classroom, he picks up the bucket and now has a task to do while he is absent from the classroom. That means his time is not wasted, and if he knows that being in time out will not excuse him from work, he may be more motivated to stay in class.
- Do not be tempted to isolate a child who is a constant problem in class by putting his desk so that he is separate from the rest of the class. He is likely to become the center of class attention because he is more visible.

(Continued)

(Continued)

> ## CAUTION
>
> ★ When families and school provide a united front, the boys will follow the rules. Make sure that families are kept apprised of any situations, so that they can support the school's disciplinary decisions.
> ★ Develop a family mentor group. Parents of children who have been in trouble and who have turned around can help other parents much better than can the teacher.

TECHNOLOGY

Boys are very facile on the computer, frequently knowing much more than any adult in the school about how to use various programs and access the Internet. The way your school deals with this issue will vary tremendously depending on the age of your students. However, even some elementary-level students may have the skills to sneak past any system you have in place to keep them from accessing questionable sites. In fact, some will try to figure out how to get around a system just to show they can.

You should have a committee in place to delineate the rules and ethics for computer use in your school. That committee should be composed of at least one librarian, one IT person, several teachers, and several students. That group should be responsible for developing an acceptable use policy—a set of guidelines for proper computer use. Additionally, the group will need to develop methods to make sure that all students and faculty are aware of the rules governing ethical use of the Internet and penalties for misuse. There are legal ramifications for some behavior, such as the limitations on downloading music, and your students should be very aware of what can happen to them even though they are minors.

Part of the problem is that students will be aware of some legendary behavior that they may be tempted to recreate or even improve on. For example, a story circulated around our school about a boy at another school who was hired right after graduation by a computer security firm because he had hacked into their computers just for the fun of it. It only took him several hours to find a weak point. His school had strict rules against hacking, but the school never caught him at it until he already had his diploma in hand and a contract for a job based on those skills. I have no idea if that story is true or not, but my students were convinced that it was and saw it as a challenge.

Applications for Your Classroom

- Be familiar with your school's rules and regulations for the use of the computer and make sure that your students understand how that applies to your class. This includes plagiarism and the purchase of previously written papers.
- In high schools, you probably should include several students on the IT committee. Their needs may surprise you.
- Give lessons in netiquette: the proper and polite way to use the Internet so that others are not offended by what you say or what you send to others.
- When you assign work that involves using the computer as a resource, build into the assignment some assessment for proper use. Part of the rubric for grading the research paper for my psychology classes includes proper citation of Internet sources. I am happy for the students to use the Internet, but they must give credit for the work of others, whether it is published in a book, in a journal, or on the Internet.
- If you teach in high school, make sure that your school subscribes to one of the services that allows you to search for similar strings of words in documents on the Web. If boys know that you will search for previously published work, they will be less likely to use it.

CAUTION

★ Be alert to the possibility that students may attempt to bypass the school regulations on Internet use. Be ready to confront the student about his infraction when you find it, especially if he is accessing sites forbidden by your school computer use regulations.

★ As aware of the Internet as most students are, you will find some who are not. Do what you can to ensure that all students have the same facility with the computer and that all students have easy access to a computer when it is necessary for schoolwork.

★ Check with the experts in your school if you are not very familiar with all of the possibilities on the Internet. Your students may try to skirt the school use code by convincing you and others that what they are doing is acceptable.

CLASSROOM MANAGEMENT
AND LEARNING

Learning can take place only when students are engaged in the learning process. Boys who are misbehaving are not learning the lesson at hand, and it is important that classroom management facilitate the learning environment. The teacher who utilizes this information will offer a learning environment that

- Provides enough structure to allow students to work, but not so much that students spend a great deal of their time focusing on abiding by the rules
- Provides support for parents in their efforts to discipline their sons
- Provides models of ideal behavior and actively discusses the outcome of certain behaviors

9

Content-Specific Suggestions

SOURCE: Photographer: Daniel Grogan, Grogan Photography. Used with permission.

In our summer school, I teach a study skills course and run the tutoring program. Helping students master factoring equations or diagramming sentences makes me examine how I teach, and I end up doing a better job during the winter, when I teach science. One evening in the summer, we had an influx of students who came for tutoring for a grammar quiz, and both of the summer interns were working with those students. Two students needed help in working with word problems, so I gave them some easy ones to see where they were having trouble. Another student appeared needing help in balancing chemical equations, and neither of the interns could be spared to help with this issue. So I moved the mathematicians and the chemist to the opposite ends of the largest tutoring room and worked with both. At one point, the chemist had a breakthrough and I knew he needed me to help him solidify his new-found knowledge, even though the math students were stuck on their problems. The teacher on duty came through, and seeing my difficulty stopped to see if he could help the math students. Now, you have to know that this man was an English teacher, and I knew that he had had trouble with math in high school. I focused on the chemistry problem, and when the student was sure he understood I turned back to the math students. The English teacher had gone, but the students were hard at work on the word problems. One looked up to tell me, "Mr. B was a lot of help. He just pointed out that a word problem translates into an algebraic sentence. The verb is the operator, the subject goes on the left, and the object goes on the right!"

◆◆◆

Just because I was trained as a science teacher doesn't mean I don't have something to offer to a student working with language arts, just as the English teacher had a suggestion for the students working with math problems. However, you ought to know, if you hadn't already guessed, that most of the students needing help with grammar were boys and the two students working on word problems were girls. It is not that boys are all that great with word problems or that girls totally understand grammar, but review courses in summer school are generally filled with students who have the most trouble with a subject. Pointing out that algebra equations are similar to sentences helps students whose verbal skills are strong. The boys having trouble with grammar were not absolutely sure about the parts of speech, so we used a more objective way to introduce these concepts to them. The interns had them working on a game we devised, called Grammar Poker. Words were printed on colored cards and dealt out to the students around a table. The intern then asked them to build a sentence by selecting cards and putting face down a yellow card (article), a red card (noun), a green card (verb), a blue card (preposition), a yellow card, and a red card. They would then turn the cards over and read their sentences, which inevitably turned out to be hilarious.

By manipulating the words, the boys got a clearer picture of how a sentence was structured and where each part of speech went. We used each student's academic strengths to help them understand material that may have been initially presented in a way that was difficult for them.

What follows are some suggestions on how to approach each discipline, using the theory and research that was presented earlier. In Chapter 11, you will find a list of some materials I have found useful as well.

ENGLISH/LANGUAGE ARTS

Reading is a major issue for many boys. Most do not get in the habit of reading early, and when their skills finally catch up to the girls they have begun to focus on other ways to pass their time. They read only when required to. However, the more children read, the more fluent they become with language.

✓ If you can, encourage all families to read to every child every night. Even if you cannot get the parents to start doing this until their children enter kindergarten, it is well worth the effort. Children see that their parents value reading and that is a huge influence on the children. Teach the parents to sit the child in their lap, put the book in the child's lap, and then run their finger under the words as they read. Through simple exposure, children read to in this way learn that reading is left to right, top to bottom, and they learn the difference between a period, a question mark, and an exclamation point, among other lessons. If you are good at mouth sounds, you can take a page from Victor Borge, the Danish comedian, who had a routine of different sounds for periods, commas, colons, and so forth. Let the child say those sounds when you get to them as you read. It will help him pay attention, and he will begin to notice the difference.

✓ Choose books that appeal to all children. Just as boys do not like reading *Romeo and Juliet*, girls do not like *Julius Caesar*. Both, however, usually like *The Tempest*, but for different reasons. Boys will certainly read a book with a girl as the main character, but she has to be involved in action. *Mrs. Frisby and the Rats From NIMH* is a favorite, as is the *Redwall* series, which has several heroines. Boys are usually attracted to nonfiction, biography, science, space topics, and action stories.

✓ Develop a culture of readers. Start a reading club based on common interests or as a father/son activity. If a child does not have a resident father, perhaps he could pick another male friend or invite an older boy to be his partner. The point of this being an all-male group is to impress upon the boys that men read, they read on a variety of topics, and they can talk about what they read.

✓ Boys approach the writing process in a different way than girls. One suggestion is to think about writing as *driving the narrative* (Thomas, 1997). Car themes appeal to many boys, and they understand that you need a vehicle (the plot), a road map (the outline), and a place to go (the conclusion). Along the way, you need to look at the scenery (tell about the location and what is going on) and perhaps take a detour or two to make the story more interesting. Boys are interested less in character development and more in what happens.

✓ Ask boys to react to something that happens in a story. Don't ask them how they feel about it. You get a similar response to your question, but boys are interested more in action than emotions so asking for a reaction is clearer to them.

✓ Dictation is an exercise used in most foreign language classes, and it is just as good for building skills in one's native language. Start by reading a sentence and have the students copy what you read. This is not as easy for some as it sounds. As the boys get better at the task, you can increase the length of the passage (reading portions at a time). This trains the boys to listen to the sounds of language and will help them in learning to take notes from lectures.

✓ *First lines/last lines.* Select first and last sentences from books, plays, short stories, anything that suits your class—but things they have not read yet. Ask the students to match up the first and last lines. Can they detect the author's style, language, or some other factor that helps them figure out how the lines go together? The students might also try to figure out what happened in between. With some help, boys may want to read the parts in between.

✓ Give students short quotes from a work of literature. Have them put the quotes in chronological order and explain why the quotes go in that order; this works very well with Shakespeare. The exercise helps boys see the structure of the story—what my mother, a great English teacher, referred to as the underlying mechanics.

✓ Use a version of mind maps to help students grasp the relationships among characters in a story. Write the main character's name in the middle of the page and the other characters around. Then draw lines indicating the relationships among characters using specific references to the story.

Vocabulary/Spelling Games

✓ *Word finds*. Hide vocabulary words in lots of other letters. As the complexity of the game increases, the words go from being horizontal to vertical, to diagonal, to backwards. While this may seem rather simple, it helps boys learn to recognize letter patterns. This will help with their slower processing speed, as will the following suggestion.

✓ *Scavenger hunts*. Bring in newspapers or magazines and have students see if they can find vocabulary words in preset categories: quantities, animals, occupations, action verbs, and so forth.

✓ *Word squares*. For upper primary grades and up, use grids with four or five squares on a side, with a letter in each square. The student is to make as many words as he can using letters that are contiguous. At the beginning, the words will be fairly obvious. As the complexity of the game increases, students can use words in a variety of directions, finally reversing across a letter to use it twice. This and the suggestion following are aimed at increasing spelling skills.

✓ *Alphagrams*. Make cards from three-by-five-inch file cards cut in half. Put one letter on each card, shuffle, and deal to the students. At the beginning, each student should get five cards, then six, then up to eight. You may want to deal vowels separately so everyone gets at least one, and this will initiate a discussion of the importance of vowels in spelling. You can also make cards with double letters, such as *oo, ll,* and *ee,* or diphthongs such as *ou, ea,* and *ow* when those show up in your lessons. It is tempting to use tiles from a Scrabble game, but I have found that the tiles are small, slippery, and easily thrown.

✓ *Roots and stems*. For each new vocabulary word, have the boys find out from the dictionary what the etymology of the word is. Have them keep lists of root words, prefixes, and suffixes according to word origin. A roots and stems bee has teams competing to figure out the meaning of words that can be made from their lists.

✓ *Phonic fun*. Select a group of words from your vocabulary lists. Have the students write the word you say. Tell younger children to change some letter of the word and write the new word. For example, if the word is *boy*, have them change the *b* to *t*. They should say the new word. For older children, direct them to change sounds in a word. For example if the original word is *shoe*, tell them to change the *oo* sound to the *oh* sound and write the new word—they should write *show*. This helps link sounds to spelling.

✓ *Replacements*. Have students list their vocabulary words according to parts of speech. Find a short story or passage from a book and copy it for the students, marking out the words you want replaced. The students will select appropriate replacements. Younger students will need you to tell them which part of speech is appropriate, but older students should be able to tell from the context which part of speech is needed. Class discussion might center on how the meaning of the passage is changed by the choice of replacement.

Grammar Games

✓ *Diagramming sentences*. For boys, this is the best way to learn the parts of speech. Use magnetic words from a kit or make your own from magnetic sheets. Draw the appropriate lines on a magnetic board (some wipe boards are also magnetic) or use metal (but not aluminum) cookie sheets and have the students put the words from a sentence in the appropriate places. Give students a handful of words and see what sentences they can make from the words and then diagram the sentence. This takes a visual task boys already like and makes it a hands-on experience.

✓ *Scavenger hunts*. Give the students a list of specific parts of speech, such as the possessive form of a proper noun or a participial phrase at the end of a sentence. Using stories the students are reading or passages provided for the game, have students try to find the specified parts of speech. There may be several correct answers for each target, which should initiate good class discussion. This helps with processing speed and reading comprehension of written passages.

✓ *Abundant Adjectives*. Give the students a list of nouns, such as dog, book, tree, and the like. Give them a time limit to see how many adjectives they can write down that could apply to each noun. With a list of verbs, this can be played as Abundant Adverbs. The exercise helps boys expand their active vocabularies.

Writing Exercises

✓ Copy passages from any text the students are currently reading and remove all the punctuation marks. Have the students put in the correct marks. Discussion might focus on how a difference in punctuation changes the meaning of the passage. Focusing on the mechanics is easier for the boys and will lead to a discussion of how the grouping of words changes meaning.

✓ Enlarge sentences copied from the newspaper or your textbook and allow each child to pick one. The students then cut the sentence apart, separating all words and punctuation marks. They then swap sentence bits and see if they can figure out how the original sentence read and where the punctuation went. You can also provide plastic bags with two sentences in each bag and see what sentences the students can come up with. Competing in small groups to see who finishes first will increase boys' interest in this exercise.

✓ *Following directions.* Each student selects some small—but multistep—activity in the classroom, such as taking some books from a desk and moving them to another location. The student writes out a complete set of directions for the activity. Then the students pair up to try to follow each other's directions. At no time can the writer help the student trying to follow the directions. If the directions do not produce the desired activity, the directions should be rewritten until the activity is correct. This helps boys learn to read directions as well as to pay attention to body language, since they have to be able to detect when the directions are resulting in the wrong decision.

✓ *Write my epitaph.* Have the students work in groups. Each group is assigned one of the characters in a book or story being read in class. The students are to come up with an appropriate epitaph for the gravestone of that character. The epitaphs will be posted around the classroom and the students will try to figure out who each character is from the epitaph. Because epitaphs are very short, this gives writing practice to the student who is reluctant to write very much.

✓ *Dulos Poetry.* (Dulos was a French poet of the seventeenth century.) Write two pairs of words that rhyme, such as *cat/hat* and *bent/rent*. The students are to write a four-line poem using those words as the last words in each line, in either an *aabb* or an *abab* rhyme scheme. Boys are much more willing to deal with poetry when it is framed in this way, as it seems more mechanical. Older boys may prefer to write sonnets for the same reason.

The next three suggestions were presented at a boys' school conference by a teacher from Trinity Grammar School in Kew, Australia (Everett, 2003).

✓ *Student research competition.* This is for Grade 7 or 8. Use crossword puzzles or some other puzzle that requires general academic knowledge. Divide the students into groups (the teacher who developed this exercise uses groups of four) and set them to work solving the puzzles. The puzzles should be a challenge for the students but possible to solve with some research. Enlist the help of your librarian to help the students learn how to use the various sources in your library. This will work better if you have some incentive, such as gift certificates to your local bookstore, and if you post the winners from year to year.

✓ *Write for action.* This is for Grade 9 or 10. Boys have trouble framing a persuasive argument for a point of view. In this activity, each student picks some cause about which he feels strongly. He is to research the history of the matter and to frame a persuasive argument in favor of his side. He then writes letters to some real person who can make a change. These may be letters to the head of the school concerning the dress code or to the head of a company that was reported polluting a local stream. The letters are to request a response, and the exercise is not completed until the letter is answered. That means that the boys need to think carefully about who would actually provide a meaningful reply. If replies are not forthcoming in a reasonable amount of time, the boys are to send another letter, enclosing a copy of the original letter and requesting feedback. The boys learn how to write a business letter, a persuasive argument, and a request for response.

✓ *Love and Lust Poetry.* This is for upper-level students in Grades 11 or 12. Engaging boys in the subject of poetry can be difficult. The version of this exercise described here uses three poems: "she being brand" by e.e. cummings, "Paradise by the Dashboard Light" by Jim Steinman, and "A Valediction: Forbidding Mourning" by John Donne. Quite a wide range of selections, but they all deal with lust and love, and two have cars thrown in as a bonus. The students enter the class quietly, they are given copies of the cummings poem, and the poem is read out loud by a classmate. They then turn the copies of the poem over and discuss what they think the poem might be about. How the poem is structured and how that may drive the meaning of the poem is also considered. The teacher then tells the boys that there is something to be discussed that is not usually a topic of consideration in class. At some point, someone will offer "sex." Have them reread the poem in light of the discussion. Do the same with the second and third poems. If you have the boys respond to the exercise in some formal way, you might have them assess the poems according to SPECS (subject matter, purpose, emotion, craftsmanship, and summary) and SLIMS (structure, language, imagery, movement, and sounds).

✓ Humor is a great way to engage boys in literature. Good literature does not have to be serious. Jack Prelutsky and Edward Lear write very amusing poetry that boys like. Boys do not find Mark Twain as funny as they used to, but there are some great Twain short stories they will like. Middle-school boys can analyze jokes, particularly ones with puns such as knock-knock jokes, to see how they are structured. Studying limericks can be risky, but there are some classics you can use to introduce them to the genre.

✓ Since boys prefer to read about real events and real people, select a well-written biography or autobiography instead of a novel for one required book. One boys' school requires students to read a national news magazine as part of an ongoing unit on current events in their history class. The English department picked up on this and assigned one column from the magazine each week as part of the boys' regular reading assignment.

MATHEMATICS

Usually, math is not a problem for boys, so when there is a problem, it is made worse by the boy's expectation that he should be able to do well in the subject. As we have already seen, dyscalculia is no respecter of gender, and the sooner the boy who has trouble in math knows that the better.

✓ Cuisinaire Rods are probably the best aid to teaching math skills that exists. They work best with students in early elementary school although I used them one time to help a student who was having trouble with the concept of volume. The student could not grasp that $3 \times 3 \times 3 = 27$. So we took 27 little cubes from the set, stacked them up in a cube three blocks on a side and counted how many little cubes were in the larger cube.

✓ If the student having trouble in math has good verbal skills, have him read the description of how to do the problem in the textbook. Usually math is taught from the examples in the book, but an explanation of the steps is written in the book as well.

✓ Understanding the meaning of math terms can be very important, so you might have the students develop a math dictionary, where they write each new term down, describe what it means, and provide an example. Some students do not realize that "multiplied by" and "times" refer to the same operation.

✓ Where logic is the problem, I recommend giving children logic problems. There are several different types and all are useful. Doing logic problems helps students learn to solve problems in a way that is not connected with math, but they will find it easier to follow the steps in math problems as a result. Actually, this exercise is good for all students. So many children have little experience in solving problems, and working with logic gives them practice. Most children have a great deal of fun with these.

✓ If the student is having trouble with multistep problems, have the student write out each step. Example: (1) write the equation in standard form; (2) move all variables to the left side of the equation; and so forth.

✓ In geometry, use different colored pencils to trace each figure. This helps pull the various figures apart.

✓ In both algebra and geometry, use different colored pencils to do different steps and the same colors to do the same steps in each problem. Alternatively, students can use different colored highlighters to identify the steps of problems.

✓ In word problems, box or highlight the words indicating the operation, underline the words indicating what the problem is looking for, and circle all numbers, whether in digits or in words. This will help the child translate the words into math. It makes the sentence look more mechanical, which the boys have less trouble with.

✓ Some students may have trouble with basic calculations. There is no way around this except for practice, but if you approach it in a positive way, so will they. It is essential that all students become comfortable with doing mental math—basic calculations in their heads. You will find various programs that will teach this skill. Each child can have a skill mastery sheet and get a sticker when he masters each step.

✓ *24.* This game is available from most teachers' supply stores, or you can make your own from square cards (three-by-five-inch index cards cut in half) on which you put four numbers. The students are to make 24 by adding and subtracting all the numbers, and there may be more than one way to achieve the goal. More advanced students may have double-digit numbers and may use multiplication and division. Students in algebra can use the numbers as exponents.

✓ *PEMDAS.* This exercise teaches students the importance of order of operations and is for older elementary and middle-school students. It is similar to 24 except that the numbers are placed horizontally and the student is to use order of operations without changing the position of the numbers to make a true statement. For example: 3 8 10 6 5; answers: $(3 + 8) = (10 + 6 - 5)$, or $(3 + 8 - 10) = (6 - 5)$. You can use problems from the text by removing the operational signs. For younger students or novices, you may want to point out the answer and have them figure out how they can get there. Older students will try to come up with as many different solutions for the same group of numbers as they can. This can be a competition.

✓ *Math projects.* Develop some practical problems involving several different calculations and assign groups of children to work on solving the problems. At the end, the students are to present their solutions to the class. At the boys' school, we made this a formal affair, inviting the head of the math department, a science teacher, and the assistant head of school to question the students on their findings. The problems can involve the physical environment of your school. We gave students a meter stick and told them to figure out how much money it would take to resod the infield of our baseball diamond. They had to go to the Internet to find out how much sod cost and how much installation cost. The major problem is that sod is generally sold in square feet (not meters). Another problem involved an irregular parking lot at the school. The boys were to figure out what the best arrangement would be for parking using standard parking lot dimensions, and how much it would cost to repave the lot. Again, we gave them a meter stick, but the standards for lot size and the cost for resurfacing are measured in feet. Boys love the competition and using math on real problems.

✓ *Practical math.* Students who have trouble with fractions and percents are better able to do the same operations if the problem uses information based on real situations.

✓ *School statistics.* Have the students collect all the numbers you and they can think of about their class (younger students) and/or the school (older students). These numbers could include how many students are in each class or in the school, the range of ages or heights in the class or school, and so forth. The students will then display the numbers in various ways. A younger class might make each person a colored square of paper and paste those squares in appropriate columns. An older class might use a spreadsheet to display the data and develop a picture of what the truly "average" student looks like.

✓ *Money.* Young children need practice in counting money and making change. Having a pretend store in the classroom works well and shows children how money is managed. One class got in the business of baking dog biscuits to make money for a class trip. The teacher helped the children figure out how to expand the recipe and how to determine what they needed to buy. Once the children knew what their costs would be, there was a lively discussion of what they should charge for the biscuits, which taught them a great deal about overhead and hidden costs. One father who ran a successful business came in and worked with the students on marketing and advertising. Two parents helped with the actual manufacture of the biscuits, which were made in the teachers' lounge (how to write letters to get permission for all of this was a language arts lesson). Some students made the biscuits, some students designed the labels (an art lesson), and some students packaged the finished product (math). Admittedly, the project took on a life of its own, but the students still talk about how much fun it was and the teacher talks about how much the students learned.

✓ *Measurements.* This exercise is primarily for younger students. Students should be careful to record units of measurement as well as the value of the measurement.

> *Length.* Provide large pieces of paper and have the students lie down on the paper so that you can outline them. Then they will measure each part of their drawings and write the

measurement on each part. If you use both English and metric measurement, the students will get used to both. Measure the dimensions of the room, the contents of the room, and so forth.

Volume. Provide several different methods to measure volume, such as measuring spoons, cups, graduated cylinders, beakers, and so forth. Again, using both English and metric systems will let students get used to both systems easily. Provide lots of things to measure, such as sand, dried beans, rice, Legos, paper clips, and so forth. Peas or marbles will roll, and water may cause a mess. You could have this lead into a cooking lesson.

Weight. Provide simple ways to measure weight from a bathroom scale to an electronic balance. Lots of items lend themselves to being weighed from pieces of paper to books to the students themselves.

HISTORY/SOCIAL STUDIES

The advantage for boys is that they like history because the material involves real events or real places. They like social studies less, usually because the emphasis is on the people. If you focus on the place or the events, the boys will be more interested.

✓ Because texts in these areas can be wordy, they present an excellent chance to teach the skills of skimming and scanning. Yes, I know you want them to read the entire lesson, but your choice may be between having them skim the entire lesson or only reading one page out of four assigned.

✓ If boys have a hard time with traditional note taking, teach them webbing as a technique for taking class notes. Then, have them place the information in a web using different concepts as the center of the web. History and social studies are the best place for boys to learn this strategy, as the material is frequently presented in a way that makes it easier to arrange in a web. If you are not familiar with webbing, ask the learning specialist at your school to come to your class and teach you all the technique.

✓ Use the concept of Venn diagrams to have students sort information into different, but somewhat overlapping, groups. This approach works very well to answer those questions that begin, "Compare and contrast. . . ."

✓ In social studies, before beginning a unit on a landmark event like the Battle of Gettysburg, give each boy, or pair of boys, one of the famous generals to become expert on. Give them some basic directions as to the information they need to collect, and let them loose to do the research. When you present the material, let each expert tell his general's part of the story. Boys are attracted to the fact that the events really happened.

✓ Have students create a time line or family trees for famous people or events. Iconic representation is easier for boys to grasp. To help boys learn events in order, place each event on a separate card and shuffle them, then have the students sort the cards into the correct order.

✓ *Write the headline.* Have the students work in pairs. Each pair will be assigned one event from the material being studied in class, and their task is to write an appropriate newspaper headline for that event. The headlines will be posted, and the students will try to figure out what event is depicted by each headline.

✓ *History debate.* Pick several debatable topics from the material being studied, such as declaring independence from England (should we have done that?) or the outsourcing of work by American businesses (should there be sanctions on that practice)? Select a group of students to be debaters—usually three or four on a team—and arbitrarily assign sides with a flip of a coin. Each side gets ten minutes to figure out how they are going to defend their position. Then the debate begins, and each side gets five minutes to argue that position. Once each side has spoken, they each get two minutes of rebuttal time. The rest of the class discusses the positions taken and decides who has won the debate. It is important to get across the point that the side that wins may not have a popular opinion, but did a better job of presenting and defending their position. You can assign the preparation of these debates as homework and have several debates in one class period. One of the important lessons from this exercise is that there are no "right" answers to problems and that every viewpoint has many different aspects. The other valuable lesson is that the boys will learn to argue without fighting. We all need to know how to disagree constructively, listening to all sides, and the competitive nature of boys means that they may have some trouble with this concept.

SCIENCE

Again, this is a topic that boys usually like because it concerns real events and because much of the material can be manipulated or at least seen. When boys enter my ninth-grade physical science class telling me that they don't like science, I generally find that their earlier instruction involved memorizing lists of facts and not conducting experiments. The whole point of science is to expose children to the world and have them see what happens. If you stand up in front of the class and tell them what has happened, you are teaching history, not science. What I find bothers many teachers about approaching science from an experiential viewpoint is that, when you have children learn from experiencing science, you can't control what they are learning and they don't always get the information they are supposed to learn. Actually, that is true for any method of instruction, but science experiments sometimes seem so out of control.

Years ago, Sherwood Githens, my professor at Duke University, taught me how to teach science, and his method has worked for me for many years. There are three main principles:

1. The best way to teach science is to show it. It only takes two minutes for the class to find their own blind spots in their eyes. Someone will ask why the blind spots exist, you tell them, and the students will remember that concept far better than if you had spent ten minutes lecturing and showing diagrams.

2. Don't waste your breath telling boys everything that should happen in an experiment. They won't listen for long anyway. Githens's rule is that the teacher gets five minutes or less to show how to set up an experiment and warn about dangers. After that, set them to work and then you just answer questions. I have had many teachers tell me that students need to have an experiment explained before they do it so that they understand what is going on. That is true for most girls, because they see the whole problem and need to know where the steps fit in before they begin. Boys only see the steps and cannot grasp the whole problem until they have all the facts they will get from the experiment. Once the experiment is completed, boys need to discuss what happened so they can figure out the concept for themselves.

3. After the lab exercise, help students discuss their findings and come to conclusions. You are not to give them the correct answers, but guide them to the right place. When I asked Dr. Githens what I was to do when the students were wrong in their analysis, he said, "Don't tell them they are wrong. You won't change many minds that way. Show them where they made incorrect assumptions or conclusions and set them on the path again." Once we have finished with the unit on density of liquids, I bring out a toy that is like a liquid hourglass. You turn the toy over and colored drops slide through a clear liquid down a ramp to the bottom of the container. When the colored liquid has run out, you turn the container over and it does the same motion in the opposite direction. The question for the students is, "Which liquid is water and which is oil?" The little drops appear made of a viscous liquid so the boys usually decide that they are oil. I don't correct them; I simply remind them to think about what they know about the relative densities of oil and water. A few seconds later, one student will exclaim, "Oh, right, the colored drops have to be the water because water is denser than oil." Boys love this approach. Challenging them to use what they know is so satisfying for them that they are willing to learn the facts so that they can solve problems.

✓ Take a hint from the Odyssey of the Mind competition (which boys love) or the *Junkyard Wars* TV show. Give kids a variety of objects and challenge them to use the objects to build something with a connection to the topic you are studying. Remember the trebuchet my son built for his history class—that could also have been part of a physical science class.

✓ Leaf collections are a great exercise; it is the putting them neatly in a book that boys have trouble with. Let them use a scanner to post pictures of their leaves on a class Web site, complete with a description of where the leaf was found, what sort of plant it is from, and any other interesting facts about the leaf or the habitat of the plant.

✓ Bug collections are also great, but you can't scan a bug and retain its three-dimensional properties. See if you can get someone to donate cheap digital cameras to the class and have the boys take pictures of their bugs. This also works with birding (although they may need a zoom feature to get clear pictures of the birds).

✓ Young boys like to be the "weather guy" for the school, reporting on the prediction for the day as well as what the weather was like yesterday. If your school will not let students speak on the intercom system, or you don't have such a system, post the weather each day outside the door of your class—with "Weather Guy today is . . ." on the bottom.

✓ If you don't know the musical group *They Might be Giants*, your students will. This is a group of musical nerds, many of whose songs can be used in a science class, especially their first hit, "Particle Man."

✓ Growing plants is a bit boring, but it is great fun to see what happens when you expose the plants to different conditions. Try watering the plants with Kool-Aid or blowing air constantly on them from a fan. Compare these experimental plants with some grown in standard conditions. The boys will learn a great deal about how plants function by figuring out how the different conditions changed the plant.

✓ Having living animals in the classroom is, as we mentioned in the unit on bullying, a great way for the boys to learn to take care of smaller, more fragile creatures. Assign boys to teams to be responsible for different parts of the classroom—which will include taking care of the resident hamster or goldfish. This will be more successful if each team does a bit of reading about proper care and develops its own care plan for the animal.

FOREIGN LANGUAGES

✓ The inherent problem here is the auditory issue. Remember that boys don't hear as quickly as girls or hear softer sounds as well. If you are teaching a conversational course, you may find that for the boys who have trouble learning a language this way, they may do better in a traditional book-based course, at least while they are learning the basics.

✓ The earlier that your school can start introducing a foreign language, the better it will be for the boys. This is somewhat true for all students, but for boys with language fluency problems, starting earlier gives them more time to learn.

✓ If you are comfortable with another language and want to introduce it to your early elementary students, select one nonacademic activity that will always be done in the other language. For example, they could always speak Spanish while they are eating lunch or French while on the playground. Starting early and making it a game will help introduce your students to another language.

✓ Many students use flash cards to learn vocabulary, but for some students, reviewing vocabulary totally orally does not work. Have them write the words they are to know on the left side of the red line on a piece of notebook paper and the meaning on the right side of that line. Close the paper by folding lengthwise just past the writing. Fold the paper back so that there is a seam right at the red line. You will now be able to see only the list of vocabulary words because the folded paper will cover the meanings. The student will then write the meanings next to each word. When he is finished, he can pull the paper straight and compare what he wrote with the correct meaning. The advantage here is that this is an active learning exercise and the student is learning the material the way he is likely to be tested—in writing. This method can also be used to learn verb conjugations. The student should do this in reverse, with the English meaning on the left side of the line and the foreign word hidden.

✓ The German teacher at the boys' school each year had groups of four of her third-year students write a screenplay in German and film it. With a digital camera, the boys got to do multiple takes so they could get the pronunciation right, and they could (and did) add interesting effects. Because it was an all boys' school, they had no trouble dressing up as any character needed for the story line, and the stories, while using simple vocabulary, were universally funny.

FINE ARTS, MUSIC, AND DRAMA

Boys may believe that the arts are for girls and not for them. I am always surprised at that belief as, historically, artists have been overwhelmingly male. Of course, a major reason is that women were not given the chance to be artistic, but that is the subject for another book altogether. Research has shown that boys in a single-sex environment are more likely to be engaged in the arts and in other areas stereotypically thought to be more suitable for girls (James & Richards, 2003; Ólafsdóttir, 1996).

I found Carl, one of our football players, hard at work in the art studio one Sunday afternoon in early April. I asked him what he was doing, and he replied that he was trying to finish his painting, which was the last part of his portfolio for Advanced Placement studio art. I asked him what he thought he would be doing if he were at home and he said, "Probably driving around with my buddies or going to the movies." I admired his art and then asked him if his friends at home knew that he painted. Carl said, "No, it's not something they would understand. They think that painting is for girls or sissies. If I painted pictures of football players, they might accept it, but not this." "This" was an almost abstract landscape showing the mountains after a storm seen in the distance from the campus. The colors were strong and the effect was striking.

✓ For boys, make art as active an activity as possible. Working in clay helps strengthen hands as well as providing a tactile experience that appeals to boys. One boys' school offers sculpture in soapstone and another offers ornamental welding.

✓ Photography appeals to boys partially because of the use of a camera means they don't have to be neat to get a good picture. With the advent of digital cameras, there is immediate feedback, which appeals to the impulsive student.

✓ The use of Auto-CAD (automated computer-aided design) is growing in the architectural and engineering fields, and boys who are well versed in it will have an employable skill as well as a way to express artistic ideas.

✓ Music appeals to boys even though they like it louder than the adults do. Start boys with the new musical tubes that produce a sound when struck on any surface. Number the tubes and put a number pattern on the board for them to follow. They will be delighted to have produced "Twinkle, Twinkle, Little Star." An older and very successful version of this is provided by the Orff music system; the students use wooden xylophones and follow numeric patterns to produce music.

✓ Drumming is increasingly popular, and boys are particularly drawn to this form of music. There are many different approaches to drumming and as many different programs. An American musical group that uses drumming in a different and musically important way is Rusted Root. Research found that drumming can be successfully used in group treatment for very angry boys to help them control their anger (Currie, 2004).

✓ Combine photography or videography and music. My son's music teacher had all students in his introduction to music course shoot a video and provide the accompanying appropriate music.

My son's group did a video of a day in the life of the head of school—somewhat tongue in cheek. They were thrilled when the head agreed to let them shoot in his actual office and finally allowed them to video him walking away down the hall—and then he turned around and gave the Richard Nixon two-handed victory wave. The students were so tickled that they chose the music from Gilbert and Sullivan's *Pirates of Penzance*, which begins "I am the monarch of the sea . . ." to accompany this move.

✓ One way to persuade boys to pick up classical instruments is to give them examples of the use of the instruments in nonclassical contexts. Some popular rock groups have violinists—the Dave Matthews Band for example—and the soundtracks to most movies use a wide range of musical instruments. If they like a really neat sound, they might just be willing to pick up the English horn so they can make that sound.

✓ Boys like musical instruments that appear to need a great deal of strength to play—it must seem more masculine. Some of those are the tuba, percussion, and the bagpipes.

✓ The boy soprano has a beautiful voice and usually loves to sing—until girls join the group. As long as it is just the boys, they are perfectly happy singing. See if your school will allow a separate boys' chorus and girls' chorus. They can perform together sometimes, but the boys like to perform by themselves, especially if the music appeals to them. What music will appeal to them depends on what is popular at the moment and what all of the other children in the area like. Most boys' choruses combine modified dance moves with their singing—think Motown.

✓ Boys either like to dance or they don't, but few boys like classical dance. Tap and hip-hop, on the other hand, can be very popular with boys. Use videos of Savion Glover or Gene Kelly to show them what an extremely masculine man looks like tapping.

✓ Young boys like acting. They usually are not shy about being on stage and their louder voices can more easily be heard. In addition, they love to dress the part, especially if the costume involves a sword, helmet, dramatic cape, or big boots. Boys begin to drop out of drama in middle school as their voices become unreliable and the girls get taller. You can lure boys back in high school if they think the part is cool. We had a huge turnout for a production of *West Side Story* when the boys found out that the cast would learn stage fighting from a professional stage combat instructor. *Cyrano de Bergerac* brought out another large group, attracted by the promise of being taught the basics of fencing.

COMPUTER SKILLS

You will find many boys sitting in front of a computer playing computer games and sending instant messages to their friends. Before the invention of the personal computer, the middle-school boy used his superior skills with moving objects (Halpern, 2000; Kimura, 2000) to throw, catch, and bat a baseball, or play chess, or build and fly model airplanes. Now, however, that same boy is glued to the computer or Game Boy and fighting off hordes of attacking ninjas, driving very fast in a Grand Prix race, or building empires by invading other countries. This facility with computers is based partially in the boys' preference for looking at mechanical objects, partially in their ease with mechanical reasoning, partially in their ability to solve problems quickly, and partially in their skill with moving objects. The boys become so at home on the computer that they quickly learn how to use it in a wide variety of modes of communication—and the quicker the better. Boys who won't read have found graphic novels that seem much like their computer games. Boys who won't write a paragraph will spend an hour writing back and forth with a friend via instant messaging. They don't have to worry about spelling or grammar, just getting their point across.

✓ Allow boys the chance to do more schoolwork on a computer. Students with dysgraphia may already be using a laptop in class to take notes. Boys in general may enjoy using the computer for this purpose.

✓ Many boys are self-taught in graphics, and they are much more likely to work on school projects if they can use these skills.

✓ Teach the class how to use the computer to research and organize facts. Do an Internet scavenger hunt for the topic of the day. History is easy, as you can ask them to find the date and location of an event, the names of people involved, and the outcome. The assignment should require the students to find the same information in two different sources so that they can verify their data. In English, if they are studying *The Old Man and the Sea* they can look for information on the Gulf Stream and Cuba.

✓ Some boys only use computers for games and surfing the Web. Unless they are encouraged to use the computer for class, they may not do so because they do not see it as something academic. The first student I taught who was identified with dysgraphia would not take notes in class on his laptop because no one else was doing it. When he got to college, he began to use his computer more often because he saw lots of students with their laptops in class.

✓ Care must be taken to make sure that boys do not spend too much time on the computer. That is a problem that the school may help families address through the parents' group.

INDIVIDUAL DISCIPLINES AND LEARNING

The problems that many boys have with individual courses can be overcome if they use their active learning styles to approach topics that are more traditionally taught in a passive manner. The trick is to find out what the students like to do and can do well and apply those techniques to other courses. It is very important for teachers to understand that the best way for a student to learn material may not be the way that the teacher finds easy. The teacher who utilizes this information will offer a learning environment that

- Provides instruction in a variety of approaches and helps each student find his best way of learning
- Provides a model for other teachers to expand the ways that they present their material
- Provides learning opportunities that depend upon active participation

10

Effective Teaching

SOURCE: Photographer Daniel Grogan, Grogan Photography. Used with permission.

In some schools, there is one full class period every day when teachers are in their classrooms and students can come for help. The theory is that if a student is having trouble in a subject, he can come to that teacher for extra instruction. The problem is that I teach ninth graders, and they rarely come for help unless required to do so. One day, I waited until ten minutes before the end of consultation for Harry, a student I had told earlier in the day to come to see me. When he came in, he never even sat down, but just announced his presence. I invited him to sit down so we could work on the material he was having trouble with in the health class. "I promise I'll work harder," he told me. When I asked him what he was doing to study, he looked a little puzzled and replied, "I'm studying the book." So I asked Harry to tell me specifically what he did when he studied the book. He looked a little uneasy and then told me that he read it. "And what else do you do?" I asked him. I'll never forget his response. "What else is there to do but read the book?"

━━━━━━━━━━━━━━━━━━━━━━━◆◆◆

During my years of teaching boys, I became aware that boys don't do a very good job of discovering the best ways to learn. We saw earlier that once they find a method, they tend to stick with it even if the method does not work, and they are less likely to try other methods (Connell, 1996; Stumpf, 1998). Harry was typical of many boys I have worked with in that it never occurred to him that studying meant anything else but reading the material.

My ninth-grade general science course had no book. The course was composed of daily lab exercises followed by class discussion. When I discovered that most of my students were not taking notes during the discussion, I began to include a lesson on note taking early in the course. The students were so used to having a book with all the answers in it that they were not ready to acquire information for themselves. Once I gave them specific instruction, my students were better able to extract information from class discussion in other classes.

What I discovered from years of teaching boys is that I needed to provide a variety of classroom experiences to ensure that they acquired the information, concepts, and skills that were the subject of the course. In tutoring students, I find that one of the best approaches is simply to help a boy view the material from another standpoint. If the textbook is the problem, I will ask questions that can be answered through a search of the Internet, or have the student interview me on the topic.

When I talk to teachers about including all sorts of learners in the curriculum, I usually get asked for specific examples. I am a science teacher so it is easy for me to come up with examples in science, but in other classes it is more difficult. What follows are suggestions using several well-known theories. I will briefly explain the theory and then give examples using what we know about how to teach the male brain. Remember that these theories can be considered lenses through which to view the instructional process. Some teachers have found these approaches helpful and others have not, but they may suggest different ways to approach your students and are designed to help you implement the principles of teaching boys in coed classes. In each of the examples, activities specifically targeted for the boys are in bold, but the lessons are designed for all students.

Research has shown that when the activities in class are interesting and enjoyable, and give students some choice in what they do or how they do it, students are more engaged in school. Additionally, boys report lower levels of enjoyment and interest in school than do girls (Gentry, Gable, & Rizza, 2002). The suggestion was made that teachers through grade 8 might bear these findings in mind when planning classroom activities to ensure that all students—but boys particularly—are engaged in the tasks at hand.

DIFFERENTIATED INSTRUCTION

According to Tomlinson (2001), "a differentiated classroom provides different avenues to acquiring content, to processing or making sense of ideas, and to developing products so that each student can learn effectively" (p. 1). When you change how you present information and what you ask students to do in response to their individual needs, you are differentiating instruction. The theory is that one instructional strategy will not reach all learners because they all have different skills, strengths, and educational backgrounds. In my ninth-grade science class, I have students who want to know whether I prefer the data from the lab displayed in a graph or a chart working with students who have never written a lab report before in their lives. The problem is how to teach those who have limited science lab experience without boring the students who have been doing this for years. By providing instructional opportunities for each type of learner, all students can learn and make progress in the same classroom.

At first, differentiated instruction can seem overwhelming to the teacher. After all, who has time to provide a variety of approaches for every lesson? The usual suggestion is to do one unit. See how that goes—what the successes are and what needs work. Then the following semester or even the following year, plan another lesson using this technique. Integrate the instructional plan into your teaching slowly, as you have time. Proponents of differentiated instruction will tell you that as you become more adept at thinking this way, you will find it easier and easier to produce instructional opportunities for your students based on this design. While the initial planning for instruction can seem time-consuming, the actual teaching becomes more straightforward because instruction becomes more efficient.

For teachers in high school, some of what follows may seem as if it does not apply to what you do in the classroom. Look at the examples to see how reading and writing exercises can be adapted for a more active learning style. You may not want to do as much as is suggested in these plans, but think about how you can incorporate activities that are visual and hands-on in your lessons.

Components of Differentiated Instruction

According to Tomlinson (1999, 2001) and Heacox (2002), the following are key components of differentiated instruction.

Qualitative approach. Differentiated instruction is more qualitative than quantitative. I am thrilled when the novice science student turns in a two-page lab report with one hand-drawn graph, and am just as thrilled when the more experienced student turns in a four-page report with computer-generated graphs. By the end of the course, I expect both students to have improved their reports.

Presentation. Differentiated instruction offers each student several different ways to approach the learning process. Some students learn best from written material, others do better with hands-on activities. I differ the presentation of material—at the very least, every class involves some lecture, visual representations of the material together with notes written on the overhead projector, and reading something about the topic. My students may get information from a lab exercise, from research on the Internet or in the library, from working with a group of classmates on a project, and from ancillary materials I share with them, as well as from their textbook.

Product. The product that the students present varies as well. Students may be asked to write a paper, give an oral report, put the material in a chart or graph, prepare a debate, design a game, draw pictures, solve puzzles, or write questions, just to name a few. There are many ways for students to demonstrate their mastery of the material, and tests are but one.

Assessment. Assessment is an ongoing process in my classroom. My ninth graders have a daily opportunity to show their progress, while I may assess my twelfth graders only twice a week. I am not a proponent of pop tests because, for the most part, they seem to be used to uncover students who have not done their homework. There are better ways, such as having students turn in their homework—of course, that means the teacher *must* look at it and return it the *next day*. Why? Remember the material on behavioral management. In order to help children learn good behavior, reinforcement must be quick and positive. The same is true for learning lessons. If a child turns in work, he needs to have your assessment of that work while he still can remember why he did what he did. If you return papers several days later, some children will look at their papers and wonder why they responded as they did. That requires a little planning on your part to make sure that you don't end up with a paper from every one of your students at the same time.

The assessments I use may be as simple as asking questions during class or asking the students to respond to the chapter questions in their textbook. I frequently ask students to write a paragraph explaining one of the points that we went over in class. That helps the student who says, "I understand when you discuss it in class, but then can't remember it on the test." In a ninth-grade math class, students may be asked, "What are the steps to solving a rate and distance word problem?" In a twelfth-grade English class, students may be asked, "Where does the title of the story we are reading come from?"

Multiple approaches. Another key component of differentiated instruction is the use of varied instructional approaches, including reading, writing, building models, conducting debates, delivering reports, and the like. Material can be presented to the whole class, to a small group, or to an individual. The combination of approaches is what makes differentiated instruction effective (Heacox, 2002; Tomlinson, 1999, 2001).

For public school teachers who need to see how these components can fit within national standards testing requirements, I have included a section of the Virginia Standards of Learning for seventh-grade English. These standards conform to the national norms and are used here just as examples. You will find references to these particular standards in the sample lesson plans.

Selected Standards of Learning, Commonwealth of Virginia

English, Grade 7

Oral Language

7.1   The student will give and seek information in conversations, in group discussions, and in oral presentations.

7.1.b Communicate ideas and information orally in an organized and succinct manner.

7.1.c Ask probing questions to seek elaboration and clarification of ideas.

7.1.e Use grammatically correct language and vocabulary appropriate to audience, topic, and purpose.

7.2   The student will identify the relationship between a speaker's verbal and nonverbal messages.

7.2.a Use verbal communication skills, such as word choice, pitch, feeling, tone, and voice.

7.2.c Compare/contrast a speaker's verbal and nonverbal messages.

Reading

7.4   The student will read to determine the meanings and pronunciations of unfamiliar words and phrases.

7.4.a Use roots and affixes to expand vocabulary.

7.4.b Recognize analogies and figurative language.

7.4.c Identify connotations.

7.5   The student will read and demonstrate comprehension of a variety of fiction, narrative nonfiction, and poetry.

7.5.a Describe setting, character development, plot structure, theme, and conflict.

7.5.b Compare and contrast forms, including short stories, novels, plays, folk literature, poetry, essays, and biographies.

7.5.e Draw conclusions based on explicit and implied information.

7.5.g Summarize text.

7.7   The student will apply knowledge of appropriate reference materials.

7.7.a Use print and electronic sources to locate information in books and articles.

7.7.b Use graphic organizers to organize information.

Writing

7.8 The student will develop narrative, expository, and persuasive writing.

7.8.a Apply knowledge of prewriting strategies.

7.8.b Elaborate the central idea in an organized manner.

7.8.c Choose vocabulary in information that will create voice and tone.

7.8.d Use clauses and phrases to vary sentences.

7.8.e Revise writing for clarity and effect.

7.8.f Use a computer to plan, draft, revise, edit, and publish selected writings.

7.9 The student will edit writing for correct grammar, capitalization, punctuation, spelling, sentence structure, and paragraphing.

7.9.a Use a variety of graphic organizers, including sentence diagrams, to analyze and improve sentence formation and paragraph structure.

7.9.c Choose pronouns that agree with antecedents.

7.9.d Use subject-verb agreement with intervening phrases and clauses.

7.9.e Edit for verb tense consistency.

SOURCE: Virginia English Standards of Learning, Grade 7, www.doe.virginia.gov/VDOE/superintendent/Sols/English7

In Figure 10.1, you will find a sample differentiated instruction lesson plan for a unit on *Johnny Tremain*. Typical of such plans, you will see that there is a chance for students of differing abilities to engage in a higher or lower level of work. Remember that the prize for being a very capable student should not be more work than the rest of the class. Instead, very capable students should have work that is more interesting. On the other end of the spectrum, the student who has trouble with the material should not be given less work, but work that is designed for his educational ability. Again, material that will work well with most boys will be in bold type.

The theme in language arts for this made-up unit is "everyday heroes"—the class is using a wide variety of sources to find ordinary people who do heroic acts as part of their daily lives. In the column marked Additional Material, Challenge 1 refers to material that is somewhat challenging; it is appropriate for students who find the assigned work moderately easy and have finished the assigned material. Challenge 2 refers to material that is very challenging; it is appropriate for students who need further ideas to tackle.

You will notice that the products vary from reading, writing, and making maps to working on the computer and working in groups. One way to implement this curriculum is to set up stations around the classroom geared around these different activities. Students would work at a particular station until they had met their product requirements. You can also have students work in groups at each station, with the students not moving to the next station until all in the group have completed the basic requirements.

Each student would have an individual plan of completion for the unit, and students involved in the additional challenges could be allowed to skip some of the basic product requirements if what they are doing covered the same material in a different way. A student who reads slowly may be very good at mapmaking. That student may only meet the basic requirements for the reading section, but work on the highest challenge for the visual section.

The advantage of differentiating instruction is that each child can meet basic standards while the more capable children can be involved in activities that will stretch their abilities. In addition, children whose abilities vary across the curriculum will have the chance to excel in their strengths while they work on their academic weak points. If this approach appeals to you, I suggest that you consult some of the sources listed in Chapter 11 for a more extensive explanation.

MULTIPLE INTELLIGENCES

In his theory of Multiple Intelligences, Howard Gardner proposed that, instead of being one concept, intelligence is composed of several different approaches to the world (Gardner, 1983). He described different intelligences or ways that we can learn. For the purposes here, we will use eight of the intelligences. Gardner's point is that intelligence involves far more than what has traditionally been the focus of education—reading, writing, and calculating. Teachers have found it very useful to think in terms of multiple intelligences when developing curricula or planning specific programs, and have discovered

Figure 10.1 Sample Differentiated Instruction Lesson Plan

Purpose: To improve reading and writing skills and to understand how people's behavior is influenced by the events around them.

Standards: English, Grade 7 Standards of Learning addressed in this unit are

Oral Language = (7.1) give and seek information in conversations, in group discussions, and in oral presentations.

Reading = (7.5) read and demonstrate comprehension of fiction and nonfiction and (7.7) apply knowledge of appropriate reference materials.

Writing = (7.8) develop narrative, expository, and persuasive writing.

Learning Objectives: 1) Students will be able to summarize the story, identify major characters, and discuss the events in chronological order. 2) Students will be able to use research to separate fact from fiction and to write a report on the differences. 3) Students will be able to describe how the main character is an everyday hero using specific references from the story.

Curriculum Goals	Proficiency Objectives	Product	Additional Material
Make progress in reading ability	Improving reading fluency	1. Score at least 80% on test of **vocabulary** from story. 7.4.a-c 2. Demonstrate increased reading fluency on three out of five paired peer trials. 7.2a, 7.5	Challenge 1: Read *Mr. Revere and I* by R. Lawson. 7.5 Challenge 2: Read *Paul Revere and the World He Lived In* by E. Forbes. 7.5
Understand interactions of people and events	Recognizing causes and effects	1. **List the major events** in Johnny's life in the book. 7.8.a-f and 7.9 a, c-e 2. Give an **oral report** on one event and describe what effect that had on his life. 7.1.b, 7.1.e, 7.2.a	Challenge 1: Write a report on how the events changed Johnny. 7.8 Challenge 2: Why is Paul Revere so important if he didn't finish his ride? 7.8
Develop visual thinking	Visualizing setting	1. Using a **map of Boston** in 1776, place on it location of major sites. 7.5.e 2. On the same map, identify where **the battles** occurred. 7.5.e, 7.5.g 3. Confirm the battle locations with information from your history book. 7.7.a, 7.7.b	Challenge 1: Construct a **floor plan** of Mr. Lapham's house and shop from the description in the book. Challenge 2: Make a **map of the movements** of Johnny, Revere, and the British soldiers on 4/18/1776
Develop critical thinking skills	Distinguishing fact from fiction	1. Use the **Internet** to discover which characters and events are real and which are made up. 7.7.a, 7.7.b 2. Read "The Midnight Ride of Paul Revere" by W. W. Longfellow and memorize the first two stanzas. 7.5.b. **Recite** in front of the class.	Challenge 1: Make a **chart** comparing the events in the poem to the events in the book. Challenge 2: Compare the account of Revere's ride in the poem with that in the book and in the book on Revere. 7.5, 7.7
Apply curricular theme	Identifying heroes	1. In groups, find evidence in the book that Johnny is an everyday hero. 7.1.a, 7.1.b 2. Each group will be assigned a character and will **debate** who best typifies the everyday hero. 7.1.c, 7.1.e	Challenge 1: Show **graphically** that Cilla is an everyday hero. 7.8 Challenge 2: Write a comparison of Johnny and the main character in *A Wrinkle in Time*. 7.8

that, using this theory, they can better meet the educational needs of all of their students.

The concept of Multiple Intelligences works well with boys because of the emphasis on intelligences other than verbal and quantitative. Earlier, in Chapters 3 and 4, we discussed how boys do better when learning opportunities are less focused on large amounts of written material and more focused on visual information and opportunities for manipulations. Many of the activities in the sample unit require a student to look for something specific in the story to answer a question. That approach reduces the amount of verbal information they must process and gives them a visual task requiring a physical response. You will remember from Chapter 6 that boys do not use a lot of emotional words. Asking them to find details that will support a statement or belief is much easier. Once they have the evidence, you can lead the whole class into a discussion of the motives or events that produced those details.

Another reason that using Multiple Intelligences works well for boys in the classroom is that they respond well to activities involving physical activity, such as drawing, singing, making charts, or demonstrating what a character did. Using Multiple Intelligences as a framework will help the teacher develop classroom exercises that reach a wide variety of student interests and abilities.

Tasks for Each of the Intelligences

The first three of Gardner's intelligences are related to conventional educational tasks and goals. What follows are lists of educational tasks directly related to each of the intelligences. You will find that some tasks appear on more than one list. For example, debating appears as an application for verbal intelligence because the debater must be able to put words together easily to make his point; debating also appears as an application for logical intelligence because the debater must be able to arrange his facts in such a way that he makes his point. When you find a task that appears on more than one list, you will generally discover that a larger proportion of your class will be engaged in that task.

Following are the eight intelligences, with examples of academic applications.

Verbal.   Reads, writes prose and poetry, discusses, listens, memorizes words, spells, builds vocabulary, speaks, debates, tells stories, communicates, plays word games

Logical.	Calculates, solves problems, reasons, analyzes, experiments, organizes, determines relations, finds patterns and sequences, debates, uses symbols, plays chess and strategy games
Visual.	Navigates; sees patterns; understands spatial relations; arranges; makes maps, charts, and graphs; builds models; draws; visualizes; solves puzzles; has good mechanical skills
Musical.	Uses rhythms, recognizes and composes music, appreciates poetry, sings, whistles, keeps time, uses rhyme to learn, plays instruments, makes sound effects
Kinesthetic.	Moves well, acts, plays sports, uses and understands body language with hand gestures, excels at hands-on learning, dances, does charades and sign language, experiments in lab, demonstrates coordination
Naturalistic.	Grows plants, takes care of animals, observes nature, discovers patterns, classifies, sorts, determines similarities and differences, show appreciation of environment, understands systems
Interpersonal.	Works with others, has leadership skills, organizes and works in groups, makes friends, respects others, resolves conflicts, interviews, communicates
Intrapersonal.	Understands self, is introspective and intuitive, sets realistic goals, understands own motivation, demonstrates planning and self-discipline, has clear values and strong will, is metacognitive

Most boys do well with applications drawn from logical, visual, musical, kinesthetic, and naturalistic intelligences.

In Figure 10.2, you will find a unit using Multiple Intelligences in relation to *Johnny Tremain.* Although each assignment specifies an activity for every intelligence, in practice you would pick several intelligences for each assignment, making sure that by the end of the unit all of the intelligences will have been addressed.

LEARNING MODALITIES

You will remember that in Chapter 2 we examined how boys' sensory systems—hearing, vision, touch, smell, taste—differed from those of girls and mentioned some modifications that can be made in class to respond to those differences. One paradigm used to frame instructional

(Text continued on page 233)

Figure 10.2 Sample Multiple Intelligences Lesson Plan

Purpose: To improve reading and writing skills, and to understand how people's behavior is influenced by the events around them.

Standards: English, Grade 7 Standards of Learning addressed in this unit are

Oral Language = (7.1) give and seek information in conversations, in group discussions, and in oral presentations.

Reading = (7.5) read and demonstrate comprehension of fiction and nonfiction and (7.7) apply knowledge of appropriate reference materials.

Writing = (7.8) develop narrative, expository, and persuasive writing.

Learning Objectives: 1) Students will be able to summarize the story, identify major characters, and discuss the events in chronological order. 2) Students will be able to use research to separate fact from fiction and to write a report on the differences. 3) Students will be able to describe how the main character is an everyday hero using specific references from the story.

	Verbal	Logical	Visual	Musical	Kinesthetic	Naturalistic	Interpersonal	Intrapersonal
Skills	Reading, writing, listening	Calculating, problem solving, reasoning	Sense of direction, patterning	Recognition of music, use of rhythms	Physical activities, movement	Care of animals, categorizing, analyzing	Working with others, leadership	Self-understanding, knowledge of direction of life
Assignment 1: Read the first two chapters Week 1: Mon.–Wed.	Write a paragraph on what it means to be an apprentice. 7.8, 7.9	Find out the **rules** of being an apprentice.	**Draw** the silver sugar bowl using the description.	What would it sound like in the silversmith's workshop? 7.7	**Tape your fingers** together and try to write your name or pick up a cup.	Find out why the mark of John Coney, silversmith, was a rabbit. 7.7a	In groups, **debate** whether or not Johnny's leadership conflicts with his apprentiship.	List some of the ways that the author lets you know that Johnny does not understand himself very well.

Figure 10.2 (Continued)

	Verbal	Logical	Visual	Musical	Kinesthetic	Naturalistic	Interpersonal	Intrapersonal
Assignment 2: Read Chapters 3 and 4 Week 1: Thurs. and Fri.	How is the cup a symbol of Johnny's identity? 7.5, 7.8	**List the facts** used to argue for and against Johnny having stolen the cup. 7.8, 7.9	What is a coat of arms? The Lyte arms has a rising eye. **Design your own coat of arms.**	What sort of music would Miss Lyte and her friends listen to?	Cut letters into a potato and use them to **print your name.** How do we print papers today?	Limes were very precious and very useful for sailors. Use the **Internet** to find out what disease limes cured and what a "limey" is.	Johnny calls people bad names. How does that get him into trouble? Do you think that is bullying? **Suggest ways** to help Johnny get his point across without bullying.	Why does Johnny feel two ways about Mr. Lyte? 7.2, 7.5
Assignment 3: Read Chapters 5 and 6 Week 2: Mon. and Tues.	How is the "Tea Party" a metaphor for the war?	**List the events** that led up to the Boston Tea Party. 7.7, 7.8	Newspapers of the period had political cartoons. **Draw a cartoon** about the Boston Tea Party.	**Memorize** the first two verses of "The Midnight Ride of Paul Revere" by Longfellow.	Find out on the **Internet** how big a tea chest was. If it were full of tea, could you lift one? 7.7	How do you look after a horse and put a saddle and bridle on one? 7.7	**Debate** the effectiveness of the Sons of Liberty. 7.1, 7.2, 7.7	How do Johnny's ideas about himself change as he works with the Sons of Liberty?
Assignment 4: Read Chapters 7 and 8 Week 2: Wed.–Fri.	How does Cilla help Johnny grow up? 7.5, 7.8	**List examples** of Johnny's behavior that show he is growing up.	**Draw a family tree** of the Lytes and put Johnny in the right place.	Who is the fiddler in Chapter 7?	Write and **give a persuasive speech** arguing that taxation without representation is unfair.	How did Goblin's nature save him from the British? 7.5	How does Goblin help Johnny get along with other people?	Why does Johnny say "this is the end" when he is at the Lytes' house? 7.5

(Continued)

Figure 10.2 (Continued)

	Verbal	Logical	Visual	Musical	Kinesthetic	Naturalistic	Interpersonal	Intrapersonal
Assignment 5: Read Chapters 9 and 10 Week 3: Mon. – Wed.	What might it have been like to live in Boston during this time?	What was the **military strategy** used by the British to overcome the Colonials? 7.7	**Mark all the battles** with their dates on a map of the Boston area.	Find out what kind of **drums** the British used for their soldiers. What would they sound like?	**Go to the library** and find out which of the characters in the story were real people and which were made up.	How did the **uniforms** of the British make them targets for the Militia and what did the Militia wear that concealed them? 7.7	What is the proof that Johnny becomes a part of the Sons of Liberty?	Why do Johnny's feelings toward Dove change? 7.1, 7.2
Assignment 6: Read Chapters 11 and 12 Week 3: Thurs. and Fri.	Describe how in helping the cause of liberty, Johnny gets his own liberty. 7.5	**List the evidence** that shows Johnny is now acting like a man and not a boy.	**Find pictures of the battles** at Lexington and Concord. How does the description in the book fit with the pictures?	Learn to whistle "Yankee Doodle Dandy."	Find in your hand where the scar tissue was on Johnny's hand. 7.7	**What is camouflage,** and how does Johnny use Pumpkin's red uniform to hide? 7.7, 7.5	Compare and contrast Johnny's leadership at the beginning of the story with his leadership at the end.	**Give a talk** outlining the evidence that Johnny is now a man. 7.1, 7.2, 7.5

SOURCE: Virginia Department of Education. (2005). English standards of learning. Retrieved July 26, 2005, from www.doe.virginia.gov

activities is that of learning modalities. In this instance, modality refers to the various sensory sources of information presented in class. While smell and taste are certainly ways that we get information, the usual methods of receiving information in class are through our visual, auditory, and kinesthetic senses.

There are two types of visual information. One involves words, which requires decoding—recognizing letters and being able to connect those letters into words that have meaning. The other involves icons—pictures, symbols, and representations that we recognize and can obtain meaning from. Therefore, the four learning modalities are visual/verbal, visual/iconic, auditory, and kinesthetic (Thies, 1999). Here are some activities associated with each modality.

- Visual/verbal—reading, writing, journaling, developing vocabulary, spelling
- Visual/iconic—using graphs and charts, highlighting, using symbols, pictures, and patterns
- Auditory—listening, singing, working in groups, giving a speech, using rhyme
- Kinesthetic—hands-on activities, lab exercises, making models, demonstrating

If you are not sure what learning modalities your students use, two versions of a short assessment are found in Chapter 11. One is for elementary school teachers to fill out about their students, and the other is for middle- and high-school students to fill out on their own. A student has to have a certain amount of self-awareness before he can answer the questions accurately, and you will be the best judge of which instrument is best for your students. You may find that some older elementary or younger middle-school students need your help in filling out the form, but it can offer insights into how they learn best.

When using learning modalities to frame instructional activities, try to use at least three of the modalities for each lesson. It is easy to develop kinesthetic activities for subjects that involve hands-on learning, such as math and art, but much harder to develop verbal activities for these subjects. Conversely, language arts and history lend themselves to verbal activities, but developing hands-on activities may present a challenge.

Remember that boys do not develop verbal skills early and their hearing is not as acute as that of girls, so their primary learning styles are usually visual/iconic and kinesthetic (Honigsfeld & Dunn, 2003). Planning activities for either modality will help young boys access the material. Additionally, most tests and assessments are primarily verbal.

(Text continued on page 236)

Figure 10.3 Learning Modalities Unit for *Johnny Tremain*

Purpose: To improve reading and writing skills, and to understand how people's behavior is influenced by the events around them.

Standards: English, Grade 7 Standards of Learning addressed in this unit are

Oral Language = (7.1) give and seek information in conversations, in group discussions, and in oral presentations.

Reading = (7.5) read and demonstrate comprehension of fiction and nonfiction and (7.7) apply knowledge of appropriate reference materials.

Writing = (7.8) develop narrative, expository, and persuasive writing.

Learning Objectives: 1) Students will be able to summarize the story, identify major characters, and discuss the events in chronological order. 2) Students will be able to use research to separate fact from fiction and to write a report on the differences. 3) Students will be able to describe how the main character is an everyday hero using specific references from the story.

Assignment	Visual/Verbal	Visual/Iconic	Auditory	Kinesthetic
1) Read the first two chapters Week 1: Mon.–Wed.	Read assigned pages. Start vocabulary lists. Write a short paragraph about what it means to be an apprentice.	Prepare a **chart** showing the relationship of all of the characters met so far. **Draw** a picture of the silver bowl.	The first page is all about sounds. What do you think that would sound like? How does it sound to shape silver?	Find out the process to make silver objects. **Use clay to make** a bowl like the silver one Johnny is making.
2) Read Chapters 3 and 4 Week 1: Thur & Fri	Read assigned pages. Write a short paragraph about how the cup is a symbol of Johnny's identity.	What is a coat of arms? The Lyte arms have a rising eye. **What would your coat of arms look like?**	Assign parts and **act out** the courtroom scene at the end of Chapter 4.	**Tape your fingers together** and try to write your name. How well do you write with your other hand?

Assignment	Visual/Verbal	Visual/Iconic	Auditory	Kinesthetic
3) Read Chapters 5 and 6, Week 2: Mon. and Tues.	Read assigned pages. How does the horse, Goblin, change Johnny? Is the change for the better or worse?	Research political cartoons from the period. **Draw your own cartoon** about the Boston Tea Party.	Divide the class into Whigs and Tories. Each side should research their viewpoint on the Stamp Act. Then **debate** the act.	A widow's peak is inherited. **See if there are any students** with widow's peaks and have all students check their families for the characteristic.
4) Read Chapters 7 and 8, Week 2: Wed.–Fri.	Read assigned pages. Read Patrick Henry's "Give me liberty or give me death" speech. How does this relate to Chapter 8, section 5?	**Make a web** of all the people in the story, with Johnny in the center. Draw lines to show how characters are connected to each other.	What is alliteration? Why does Cilla say there are some men she could not marry because of alliteration?	**Write a speech persuading** the audience that taxation without representation is unfair.
5) Read Chapters 9 and 10, Week 3: Mon.–Wed.	Read assigned pages. How does Johnny's attitude toward Dove change, and why?	**Draw a picture** of the British soldier's uniform. Why was the uniform a problem fighting in America?	Read Longfellow's "The Midnight Ride of Paul Revere" **out loud** and memorize the first two stanzas.	**Go to the library** and find out which characters in this story are real and which are made up.
6) Read Chapters 11 and 12, Week 3: Thurs. and Fri.	Read assigned pages. Telling lies is a theme in the book. Which ones get Johnny in trouble and which don't? What is the difference?	**Make a map** showing all the battles in the Boston area. Mark their dates and mark how the soldiers moved about.	Learn to whistle "Yankee Doodle Dandy." Use your fingers to **drum on desks** and try to sound like a fife and drum corps.	Assign sides and **debate** whether or not Johnny should have told the lies he did all through the book.

Planning other forms of judging how well a student has learned the material will help all students. Oral reports will benefit the auditory learner, charts and tables will benefit the iconic learner, and acting out the story or demonstrating some event will benefit the kinesthetic learner. You will find a sample lesson plan for *Johnny Tremain* using learning modalities in Figure 10.3.

UNIT DESIGN

In their book *Understanding by Design,* Wiggins and McTighe (1998) describe an approach to curriculum and assessment design that starts at the end and moves backwards. The idea is that the best way to teach is to first decide what it is you want your students to know—what should they recognize, comprehend, and be familiar with? Once you have the end in mind, then you decide how you are going to determine or assess that your students have demonstrated that knowledge. It is important to consider a wide variety of assessment methods, including long- and short-term assessments, structured and fluid assessments, and evidence collected over time as well as that from a specific time such as the end of a unit. Finally, instruction can be framed so that the students gain the knowledge and information the teacher believes is important to know.

An obvious complaint about this method of design is that it emphasizes tests and pays less attention to the process of learning. In fact, the focus is on what students are to come away from the learning experience with, not on their grade in the class. This design actually encourages teachers to develop a wide variety of approaches and to utilize different techniques to ensure that all students have the chance to learn.

In addition to turning the process of curriculum design on its head, the principles of backward design also involve several steps that help the teacher rethink the planning process and result in a more comprehensive curriculum. Following an identification of the state standards that will be addressed by the unit, Wiggins and McTighe present six ways of identifying when students have developed true knowledge. These "six facets of understanding" (1998, p. 44) are

- Explanation—can the student give details and describe events, facts, and data?
- Interpretation—can the student relate the information to other situations, give metaphors, or provide examples?

- Application—can the student translate the information to novel situations, adapting the principles to the new context?
- Perspective—can the student see the information from the point of view of another?
- Empathize—can the student come to understand how that other feels or perceives the information?
- Self-knowledge—can the student understand what he does not do well and what is easy for him to understand based on his own perspective and learning style?

The third step, in which the teacher plans activities and learning opportunities to ensure that the students can understand the information, is based on what Wiggins and McTighe call the WHERE design principles:

Where are we headed?—this is a preassessment to find out what information students have and what they want to learn about the subject.

Hooks—this is the presentation of information designed to increase the interest of the students in the information.

Explore and equip—this is work designed to assist the student in building understanding in the subject.

Refine and think—this asks the student to review the information and reassess what he knows.

Exhibit and evaluate—this is the presentation of final projects, tests, or other means that the teacher has identified at the beginning of the process to indicate that the student has reached full understanding.

You will find a lesson plan for our hypothetical language arts class using backward design in Figure 10.4.

EMPOWERING BOYS AS LEARNERS

The purpose of this book is to provide teachers with ideas, options, and techniques that will make their classrooms more welcoming to all kinds of learners. We all know that by enlarging our repertoire of

(Text continued on page 242)

Figure 10.4 Sample Unit Design Lesson Plan

Virginia Standards

7.1 The student will give and seek information in conversations, in group discussions, and in oral presentations.
  b) Communicate ideas and information orally in an organized and succinct manner.
  e) Use grammatically correct language and vocabulary appropriate to audience, topic, and purpose.

7.5 The student will read and demonstrate comprehension of a variety of fiction, narrative nonfiction, and poetry.
  a) Describe setting, character development, plot structure, theme, and conflict.
  e) Draw conclusions based on explicit and implied information.

7.8 The student will develop narrative, expository, and persuasive writing.
  b) Elaborate the central idea in an organized manner.
  c) Choose vocabulary in information that will create voice and tone.

Enduring Understandings or Unit Learning Objectives

1. SWBAT communicate ideas and information orally in an organized and succinct manner.

2. SWBAT use grammatically correct language and vocabulary appropriate to audience, topic, and purpose.

3. SWBAT describe setting, character development, plot structure, theme, and conflict.

4. SWBAT draw conclusions based on explicit and implied information.

5. SWBAT elaborate the central idea in an organized manner.

6. SWBAT choose vocabulary in information that will create voice and tone.

Facets of Understanding

Explanation: SWBAT identify accurately the format, text structure, and main idea. Interpretation: SWBAT examine the key characters through a time line to identify characters' influence on plot. Application: SWBAT effectively design a map of Boston describing movements of the troops. Perspective: SWBAT identify the point of view of both the American and the English side about the causes of the Revolutionary War. Empathy: SWBAT openly discuss classroom leadership issues relevant to plot and character development. Self-Knowledge: SWBAT demonstrate self-awareness with respect to classroom issues such as false pride and bullying.

WHERE for Boys

(Teacher Considerations and Questions to Address)

W. Where are you headed?	H. Hook your students	E. Experiences	R. Reflect and Rethink	E. Evaluation
Introductory Discussion: Have students write a paragraph on how they think they would act if they were in charge of other students to do a task.	Hooks: Provide boys with foam balls and divide them into two teams. One team has to stand in the middle of the room and the other team can hide behind their desks. Have them throw the balls at each other.	Reading assignments in text followed by classroom discussion. Students will view a video on the Boston Tea Party.	Prompts: Thought questions relating to how the change in Johnny's behavior during the story was related to his experiences.	Unit test with various types of questions. Product: Map of Boston with description of troop movements.
Ask students to describe bullying giving specific, but not personal, examples: for instance, is it bullying when someone takes another kid's lunch without permission?	Have boys tape the fingers of their dominant hand together and try to write. Discuss the difficulties.	Students will produce a time line for each major character. The students will comment on who is present at each of the crucial points in the story.	Discussion about what "freedom" means to Johnny personally and to America as a country.	Product: Time line, accuracy and completeness. Product: Student group work will be based on completeness of the map,
Performance Criteria: Content—Describe accurately the major events in the story.	Differentiation Strategies: When boys are working on their projects, allow them to find their own space to work together; that may mean	Students will produce a map of Boston showing both Johnny's and troop movements. An accompanying document will reference the points in the story.	Relate the experiences of the British soldiers in America to those of American soldiers in Iraq in Iraq. List similarities and differences.	on specific references in the document, on interpretation of information from the book, and on presentation of data.
Process—Collaborate on development of map of Boston.	sitting or lying on the floor. Divide students into two groups for a "book bee."			Product: Book bee score.
Quality—Spelling, grammar, and neatness are part of the polish of the writing assignments and report. Detailed information on the time lines and map is required. Presentations must be completed.	The teams will have three members and will compete on knowledge of the subject for prizes (stickers, a free homework pass, etc.).	Students will be assigned to either the British Army or to a group of Minutemen. The groups will recreate some of the battles using signs for battle sounds (BANG for a rifle, BOOM for a cannon).	Revisions/Rehearsals: Peer review of time lines to check for accuracy. Check calendar every other day to keep students on track to meet deadlines. Students will submit rough drafts of the document accompanying the map.	

(Continued)

Figure 10.4 (Continued)

WHERE for Girls

Introductory Discussion:	Hooks:	Reading assignments in text followed by classroom discussion.	Prompts:	Unit test with various types of questions.
Have students write a paragraph on how they think they would act if they were in charge of other students to do a task.	Give girls pictures of Boston before the Revolution and have them describe what they would wear if they had lived then.	Students will view a video on the Boston Tea Party and discuss solutions options for the problem.	Thought questions describing the change in Johnny's attitude and how that was reflected in a change in his behavior.	Product: Solutions to the problem of taxation other than a "tea party."
Ask students to describe bullying giving specific, but not personal, examples: for instance, is it bullying when someone makes unkind comments about another when that person is not there?	Have girls tape the fingers of their dominant hand together and try to write. Discuss the difficulties.	Students will identify the crucial events in the story and then describe who is present at each event and what their part was.	Discussion about what "freedom" means to Johnny personally and to America as a country.	Product: Identification of crucial events and the influence of individuals present.
Performance Criteria:	Differentiation Strategies:	Students will be divided into groups and each group will be assigned a different character. The group will develop a biography for that character based on specific references to the text.	Relate the experiences of the American people in Boston in 1776. What was their life like? Find out what the conditions are for people in Iraq at the moment and compare the experiences.	Product: Student group work.
Content—Describe accurately the major events in the story.	Make sure that groups of girls are in twos or fours, not threes. Divide students into two groups for a "book bee." The teams will compete on knowledge of the subject and each team will confer before answering, so that all students in the team agree with the answer.		Revisions/Rehearsals:	Product: Book bee score.
Process—Collaborate on development of a map of Boston.			Peer review of time lines to check for accuracy.	
Quality—Spelling, grammar, and neatness are part of the polish of the writing assignments and report. Detailed information on the time lines and map is required. Presentations must be completed.			Check calendar every other day to keep students on track to meet deadlines.	
			Students will submit rough drafts of the document accompanying the map.	

Assessment Plan

National or State Standard	Learning Objective or Essential Understanding for the Unit	Learning Experiences (Assignments, Instruction)	Assessment Methods (Evidence should include self-assessment)	Performance Criteria or Grading Standards	Accommodations or Modifications for Gender Differences
The student will read and demonstrate comprehension of a variety of fiction, narrative nonfiction, and poetry. a) Describe setting, character development, plot structure, theme, and conflict. b) Draw conclusions based on explicit and implied information. The student will develop narrative, expository, and persuasive writing. c) Elaborate the central idea in an organized manner. d) Choose vocabulary in information that will create voice and tone.	1. SWBAT describe setting, character development, plot structure, theme, and conflict. 2. SWBAT draw conclusions based on explicit and implied information. 3. SWBAT elaborate the central idea in an organized manner. 4. SWBAT choose vocabulary in information that will create voice and tone.	Reading assignments in text followed by classroom discussion. View a video on the Boston Tea Party and discuss alternative actions. Students will produce a time line for each major character and note who is present at each of the crucial points in the story. Students will produce a map of Boston and accompanying document showing Johnny's and troop movements with specific references to the story. Students will be divided into groups and assigned a different character. The group will develop a biography for that character based on specific references to the text.	Unit test with various types of questions. Product: Map of Boston with description of troop movements. Product: Time line, accuracy and completeness Product: Solutions to the problem of taxation other than a "tea party." Product: Identification of crucial events and the influence of individuals present. Product: Student group work. Product: Book bee score.	**Test will be 10% of the unit grade.** Homework completion will be 10% of the grade. **Map will be 10% and accompanying paper referencing specific references to text to support map will be 5%.** Or Discussion of problem of taxation without representation will be 5% and suggestions for other solutions will be 10%. **Time line will be 5%.** **Analysis of characters on time line will be 10%.** Or Identification of crucial events will be 5%. Analysis of characters present during those events will be 10%. Score on book bee will be 5%.	**Movement of students in class will be encouraged and the teacher will create different locations in the room where students can work in groups.** **Competition among the students will be used to check knowledge of facts.** **The teacher will use parallels between our War of Independence and the war in Iraq.** Begin each unit with a discussion of the general concepts that will be covered and what the outcomes will be. Focus on how the students can relate to the characters in the story. Encourage collaborative work with small groups of students working together.

SOURCE: Wiggins & McTighe. (1998). *Understanding by design*. Alexandria, VA: Association for Supervision and Curriculum Development.

methods and approaches, we can do a better job in our classrooms. The best part is that we will help all of our students, not just the boys who are having trouble.

The real challenge is to encourage students to become autonomous learners. As we have noted before, boys do not develop study strategies independently and rely on the teacher to tell them what they need to do. As school becomes more complicated, one lesson to be learned by all students is how best to approach the learning process and adapt their study strategies accordingly. This is not something that boys do well. Here are two suggestions that may help your students.

The first is to teach them to think in terms of their learning modalities. Boys grasp the concept of learning modalities well, and if you help them see how to adapt their lessons in a way that makes sense to them, you will have taught them the most valuable lesson of all— how to teach themselves. The figure on learning modalities earlier in this chapter will give you some suggestions for ways to help your students. In fact, many of the suggestions all through this book are based on turning auditory and visual/verbal tasks into kinesthetic and visual/iconic ones. Additionally, you will find a brief assessment to identify learning modalities in the next chapter.

Not only do boys not develop a variety of study strategies on their own, they generally do not develop a variety of test-taking strategies (Stumpf, 1998; Tallent-Runnels, 1994). I have found that when I go over the following hints with my students they are delighted to have a variety of methods to attack a question. In my classes, we refer to the rules of taking multiple-choice tests in a similar fashion to the way the boys refer to the rules of playing soccer. When boys have direction and structure, they do so much better.

TEST-TAKING STRATEGIES

While we make every effort to give our students a variety of ways to demonstrate what they have learned, national standardized tests and other landmark tests continue to benefit primarily the verbal learner. Consequently, many students have trouble taking tests and, as they progress through school, may develop anxieties about taking tests. Helping children develop test-taking strategies will give them a variety of approaches to use when they take tests.

Test anxiety is frequently a problem for the student with poor test-taking skills and learning some strategies will help the student gain control in the testing situation. All forms of anxiety are helped when the sufferer is prepared and believes that he has some skills he can use in the relevant situation. However, if the anxiety is severe—the child gets noticeably pale, sweats, trembles, cries, becomes belligerent—before or during a test, refer the child to your school counselor for assistance. Learning relaxation techniques and test-taking strategies has helped many students overcome serious testing problems.

Beginning Strategies

Step 1. Determine which types of questions are easier and which harder for the student. The easiest way to do this is to sit down with the student and several of his tests. Look at the items he has the most trouble and the least trouble answering.

Ask him:

- How did he study for the test?
- What kinds of questions did he study for?
- How does he go about answering the questions?
- What did he think the question was asking?

If the problem is one of lack of study strategies or test preparation, help students acquire better study strategies. The learning style assessment in the following chapter will help you and the student discover how the student prefers to learn. For example, a student who prefers to learn through a visual modality can study by preparing charts and tables of the information.

Step 2. If the student's problem is that he does not understand what response the question is asking for—a common difficulty—there are several steps that will help.

a. Have the student read the question out loud to you and ask him what the answer should look like. Some students are not aware that essay questions require complete sentences or that questions asking for an outline do not.

b. Make sure that the student understands what is meant by terms such as discuss, describe, compare and contrast, diagram, outline, define, list, summarize, and so forth.

c. Have the student prepare questions for the material. Strangely enough, when students do this, they frequently find that they understand what other questions are asking for.

d. During a test, when the student gets to the type of item with which he has difficulty, have him come up to your desk or step outside with you and talk over strategies for answering the item. You don't want to know what he is going to put in his answer, but how he is going to organize his answer.

Step 3. Adapt study techniques to the type of test anticipated. Studying material in the same way that you will be asked to recall it uses what psychologists call context-dependent memory. For example, parents frequently help children prepare for a spelling test by calling out words and having the child spell the word out loud. However, if the test is written, the poor speller may have trouble writing down the correct spelling if he has practiced his spelling out loud. If the test will be written, the better technique is for the parent to call out the words and have the child write down the answers. If the child is preparing for a spelling bee, then the child should spell the word out loud. Copying notes is an old technique that works well for some students, as does taking notes from the notes—called squeeze-notes. The advantage is that when the student gets to the test, he has a memory of having written the material several times before.

Step 4. Encourage study groups. When boys get together, they rarely do so to study. Good students will acquire this skill later in their academic careers, but usually because a group of girls invited them to join. Teach this strategy to your high-school students by inviting them to participate in a "study huddle," "academic network," "geekfest," or whatever metaphor fits the group you are working with.

I have found that boys are particularly reluctant to admit when they have test anxiety and will make excuses such as "I didn't study." That may well be true, but find out how the boy approaches studying to determine if his study habits are effective for him.

Strategies for Specific Item Types

The first step is to read the directions—this is the most underutilized hint. Directions may help provide clues for how to answer the questions. Frequently, tests ask the student to answer three of five questions, or the like, and answering all of them will take up time, at the very least. Boys frequently do not read directions, and one thing I have done with my younger students is to make them read the directions out loud, in unison, before they are allowed to start the test. If one person reads the directions out loud, the others will simply start to look at the questions.

Objective Questions

- Answer objective questions first. Information that will help answer other questions may be found in objective questions.
- For true/false questions, look for criterion words such as never, always, most, least, some, frequently, rarely, and the like. The more extreme the criterion, the less likely the statement is to be true, and the more ambiguous the criterion, the more likely the statement is to be true.
- For matching questions, read the right-hand list first, then the left-hand list all the way through. The student should match the choices he is sure of first, and cross out the items in the right-hand list that have been used. Then compare the remaining terms and definers to solve the rest of the problem by eliminating choices known to be incorrect. Do not draw lines from terms to definers, as the resulting web will be hard to interpret.
- For multiple-choice questions, direct students to cover the choices, read the question, and try to provide an answer for the question. Then have them look at the choices. If their answer is there, they know they are correct. If their answer is not there, have them look at the choices and see if they can immediately see the answer. If they cannot, direct them to move on and leave the question for the moment. When they have finished the section, they should go back and go through the same process again. Their brains will have been thinking about the question even if they are not aware of it, and the answer will frequently jump out at them.
- For completion questions, direct students to read the sentence carefully to see if they know the answer or if they can determine the answer from cues in the sentence. Pay particular attention to grammar, as this will give hints. Check to see if the word or phrase to be supplied starts with a consonant or a vowel (the blank is preceded by *a* or *an*) or if the word is to be plural. If the student is still not sure of the answer, they are to leave the question and come back to it later—they may be surprised to find that they can then think of the answer.

Essay or Free-Response Questions

- Read all parts of the question first. Because they are field independent, boys have particular trouble in reading questions and may not see how different parts of a question can work together.
- Decide what kind of answer is required. This will be determined by what the question asks for, such as to discuss, describe, analyze, justify, and the like. If the question asks for the student to compare and contrast, using a Venn diagram will help. Put information that is shared in the intersection of the circles and information that is unique to each topic inside the circles, but outside the intersection. The student then has all the information already organized to write the essay. At the very least, have the student outline the answer, as that will keep him on task and let the teacher know that the student really did understand the question if he runs out of time.
- Restate the question in the first sentence. This helps provide structure to the answer and gives the student a place to start.
- Be careful not to use circular reasoning. This happens, for instance, when a term is used to identify itself and does not indicate that the student knows what the term means. I frequently ask my psychology students to define random selection, and many will answer something like, "random selection occurs when subjects are randomly selected to participate in a study." The student does not actually have to know what either random or selection means to provide that answer.
- Help students learn to "read" the teacher. Point out parts of the material that you have stressed and help them understand that the test will focus on that material. Boys frequently have more trouble with this concept, but if you can show them how to hunt for the clues and how to build the case—use a detective metaphor—they can acquire the skill.

FINAL WORDS

What I hope to accomplish with this book is to alert teachers to the fact that boys and girls do not think and reason in the same ways, and that affects what happens in the classroom. Just because a boy is not doing well in your class, do not assume he is not working or that he is misbehaving on purpose. Look carefully at what he is doing. See if there is some other explanation for his behavior; he may have a different approach to the world. On the other hand, he may be doing what he is doing because it bothers you. You have to learn to figure out the difference. If you are not sure, find someone in your school who has experience working with boys and have that person observe the child.

For a boy, it is the teacher who makes the difference. They see the teacher as the primary motivator, the one who makes the lesson interesting or not (Younger & Warrington, 1999). Boys respond to energy and caring. They want to do well, and it is up to us to give them an environment in which they can learn.

The most exciting times I have ever had in a class are when a student develops an inner fire to learn. When that happens, you know that you were a part of providing either the fuel or the spark, and that is why you teach. Boys, and girls, need their teachers to guide them, to encourage them, and to help them find their way. Your students are lucky to have you as their teacher.

11

Resources and Other Helps

All through the previous chapters, I have frequently told you that you would find help at the end of the book. Well, here it is. You will find in this chapter lists of reference books, lists of curriculum helps, lists of study aids, several learning assessments, and a rubric for grading a written paper allowing for poor handwriting.

◆◆◆

BOOKS OF INTEREST

Obviously, none of these lists is exhaustive, but they contain books I have found to be useful. For any who think a book should have been included and wasn't, please send me your suggestions in care of the publisher.

Books for Teachers

Some of these books are either English or Australian and you may be able to locate them by going to the Web sites for Amazon in England (www.amazon.co.uk) or Amazon in Canada (www.amazon.ca).

Askew, S., & Ross, C. (1988). *Boys don't cry: Boys and sexism in education.* Buckingham, England: Open University Press.

Bleach, K. (1998). *Raising boys' achievement in schools.* Stoke on Trent, England: Trentham Books.

Grossman, H., & Grossman, S. H. (1994). *Gender issues in education.* Boston: Allyn & Bacon.

Hawkes, T. (2001). *Boy oh boy: How to raise and educate boys.* Sydney, Australia: Pearson.

Neall, L. (2002). *Bringing the best out in boys: Communication strategies for teachers.* Stroud, England: Hawthorne Press.

Sax, L. (2005). *Why gender matters.* New York: Doubleday.

Skelton, C. (2001). *Schooling the boys: Masculinities and primary education.* Buckingham, England: Open University Press.

West, P. (2002). *What IS the matter with boys?* Marricksville, Australia: CHOICE Books.

Books on Masculinity

Biddulph, S. (1997). *Raising boys.* Berkeley, CA: Celestial Arts.

Hoff-Sommers, C. (2000). *The war against boys: How misguided feminism is harming our young men.* New York: Simon & Schuster.

Kindlon, D., & Thompson, M. (2000). *Raising Cain: Protecting the emotional life of boys.* New York: Ballantine Books.

Mac an Ghaill, M. (1994). *The making of men: Masculinities, sexualities, and schooling.* Buckingham, England: Open University Press.

Pollack, W. (1998). *Real boys: Rescuing our sons from the myths of boyhood.* New York: Random House.

Books of Cognitive Gender Theory That Are Readable and Interesting

Baron-Cohen, S. (2003). *The essential difference: The truth about the male and female brain.* New York: Basic Books.

Halpern, D. F. (2000). *Sex differences in cognitive abilities* (3rd ed.). Mahwah, NJ: Erlbaum.

Hines, M. (2004). *Brain gender.* New York: Oxford University Press.

Kimura, D. (2000). *Sex and cognition.* Cambridge: MIT Press.

Maccoby, E. E. (1998). *The two sexes: Growing up apart, coming together.* Cambridge, MA: Harvard University Press.

Books for Specific Teaching Ideas

Brunson, T. K. (2002). *Differentiated instructional strategies: One size doesn't fit all.* Thousand Oaks, CA: Corwin Press.

Erlauer, L. (2003). *The brain-compatible classroom: Using what we know about learning to improve teaching.* Alexandria, VA: Association for Supervision and Curriculum Development.

Fashola, O. (2002). *Building effective afterschool programs.* Thousand Oaks, CA: Corwin Press.

Gregory, G. H. (2003). *Differentiated instructional strategies in practice: Training, implementation, and supervision.* Thousand Oaks, CA: Corwin Press.

Smilkstein, R. (2003). *We're born to learn: Using the brain's natural learning process to create today's curriculum.* Thousand Oaks, CA: Corwin Press.

Smith, M. W., & Wilhelm, J. D. (2002). *"Reading don't fix no Chevys": Literacy in the lives of young men.* Portsmouth, NH: Heinemann.

Sousa, D. (2003). *How the gifted brain learns.* Thousand Oaks, CA: Corwin Press.

Tomlinson, C. A. (1999). *The differentiated classroom: Responding to the needs of all learners.* Alexandria, VA: Association for Supervision and Curriculum Development.

Tomlinson, C. A. (2001). *How to differentiate instruction in mixed-ability classrooms* (2nd ed.). Alexandria, VA: Association for Supervision and Curriculum Development.

Winebrenner, S. (1996). *Teaching kids with learning difficulties in the regular classroom.* Minneapolis, MN: Free Spirit Publishing.

Wolfe, Patricia (2001). *Brain matters: Translating research into classroom practice.* Alexandria, VA: Association for Supervision and Curriculum Development.

Books Providing Multicultural Resources

Banks, J. A. (1999). *Introduction to multicultural education* (2nd ed.). Boston: Allyn & Bacon. [This is a basic textbook on the subject.]

Caplan, N. S., Choy, M. H., & Whitman, J. K. (1991). *Children of the boat people: A study of educational success.* Ann Arbor: University of Michigan Press.

Davis, L. E. (Ed.). (1999). *Working with African American males: A guide to practice.* Thousand Oaks, CA: Sage.

Denbo, S. J., & Moore B. L. (Eds.). (2002). *Improving schools for African American students: A reader for educational leaders.* Springfield, IL: Charles C Thomas.

Fordam, S. (1996). *Blacked out: Dilemmas of race, identity, and success at Capital High.* Chicago: University of Chicago Press.

Hopkins, R. (1997). *Educating black males: Critical lessons in schooling, community, and power.* Albany: State University of New York Press.

Ladson-Billings, G. (1994). *The dreamkeepers: Successful teachers of African American children.* San Francisco: Jossey-Bass.

Ogbu, J. U. (2003). *Black American students in an affluent suburb: A study of academic disengagement.* Mahwah, NJ: Erlbaum.

Valenzuela, Angela. (1999). *Subtractive schooling: U.S. Mexican youth and the politics of caring.* Albany: State University of New York Press.

Books That Supply Curriculum Ideas

I'm not a believer in worksheets, but the following books contain a great many ways to approach learning in a hands-on way. You might take a look at those that pertain to your courses and see if you could use some of the ideas. There are many similar books. Once you start looking for these, you will find lots of others.

Verbal Skills

Blanchard, C. (2002). *Word roots: Learning the building blocks of better spelling and vocabulary.* Levels A and B. Seaside, CA: Critical Thinking Co.

Sack, A. (2003). *Shortcut to word power: Essential Latin and Greek roots and prefixes.* Berkeley, CA: Optima Books.

Umstatter, J. (1994). *201 Ready-to-use word games for the English classroom.* San Francisco: Jossey-Bass.

Umstatter, J. (1997). *Hooked on English!* San Francisco: Jossey-Bass.

Umstatter, J. (1999). *Ready-to-use paragraph writing activities.* San Francisco: Jossey-Bass.

Umstatter, J. (1999). *Ready-to-use prewriting and organization activities.* San Francisco: Jossey-Bass.

Umstatter, J. (1999). *Ready-to-use revision and proofreading activities.* San Francisco: Jossey-Bass.

Umstatter, J. (1999). *Ready-to-use sentence activities.* San Francisco: Jossey-Bass.

Umstatter, J. (1999). *Ready-to-use word activities.* San Francisco: Jossey-Bass.

Umstatter, J. (2000). *Ready-to-use portfolio development activities.* San Francisco: Jossey-Bass.

Umstatter, J. (2001). *Grammar grabbers!* San Francisco: Jossey-Bass.

Umstatter, J. (2002). *English brainstormers!* San Francisco: Jossey-Bass.

Umstatter, J. (2004). *Words, words, words!* San Francisco: Jossey-Bass.

Math Skills

Harnadek, A. (1991). *Cranium crackers: Critical thinking activities for mathematics.* Pacific Grove, CA: Critical Thinking Books & Software.

Muschla, J., & Muschla, G. R. (1999). *Math starters!* San Francisco: Jossey-Bass.

Serra, M. (1992). *Mathercise Classroom warm-up exercises: Books A and B.* Berkeley, CA: Key Curriculum Press.

Critical Thinking

Parks, S., & Black, H. (1988). *Building thinking skills.* Pacific Grove, CA: Critical Thinking Books & Software. [This series has several levels: Primary, Book 1, Book 2, Book 3 Figural, and Book 3 Verbal; each level has a student book and a teacher book.]

Seymour, D., & Beardslee, E. (1990). *Critical thinking activities in patterns, imagery, and logic.* Palo Alto, CA: Dale Seymour Publications.

Steig, William (1968). *C D B!* New York: Trumpet Club.

Steig, William (1984). *C D C?* New York: Trumpet Club.

Logic

Petreshene, Susan S. (1985). *Mind Joggers! 5 to 15 minute activities that make kids think.* San Francisco, CA: Jossey-Bass.

Williams, W. (n.d.). *Quizzles* and *More Quizzles.* Palo Alto, CA: Dale Seymour Publications.

Workbooks for logic exercises, available from criticalthinking.com:

Mind Benders A1, 2, 3, 4, B1, 2, 3, 4, C1, 2, 3

Think A Minutes, books 1 and 2, levels A, B, and C

Workbooks for logic exercises, available from MINDWAREonline.com:

Venn Perplexors, Perplexors, Noodlers, Logic Links

Books for Boys

There are a lot of books that appeal to boys, if you go looking for them. A list of authors follows, but there are many others as well. I have not divided this by age as, for example, a young boy who is an active reader will find books by Roald Dahl to be fun, and an older boy who is not a facile reader will like the same story just as well and not be insulted by a book that he sees as babyish. I know *Goosebumps* by R. L. Stine is not considered great literature, but boys will read it and sometimes the issue is to get their noses in a book. When they have a choice, boys prefer books that are scary, gross, adventuresome, fantastic, real, or violent. They like to read about true crime, sports, animals, space, vehicles, computers, true facts, or other boys. For a great source, consult Kathleen Odean (1998), *Great Books for Boys: More Than 600 Books for Boys 2 to 14* (New York: Ballantine).

Boys will like books by Douglas Adams, Orson Scott Card, Tom Clancy, Stephen Crane, Roald Dahl, Jack Gantos, The Brothers Grimm, Ernest Hemmingway, Tony Hillerman, Brian Jacques, Rudyard Kipling, Jon Krakauer, Jack London, Gary Paulsen, Dav Pilkey, Daniel Pinkwater, Terry Pratchett, J. K. Rowling, Louis Sachar, Richard Scarry, Maurice Sendak, Jon Scieszka, Lemony Snicket, John Steinbeck, R. L. Stine, Mark Twain, Jules Verne, and Paul Zindel.

RUBRICS

The advantage of using grading rubrics with boys is that they clearly define what the standards are for success. Giving the students the rubrics ahead of time will forestall complaints that "You didn't tell us what to do," or "You graded my paper differently from his." I use rubrics to grade college research papers. They are less specific than this, but no one complains about losing 10 points out of 150 for major spelling errors when they were given the rubric at the beginning of the class.

LEARNING STYLE ASSESSMENTS

One of the problems in teaching boys is finding out what their learning strengths are. What precedes are two versions of an assessment you can use to design study strategies for your students.

Learning Styles Preference Inventory, Elementary School

This version is for teachers to take for young students. How do your students process information? Does their learning style match your teaching style? By completing the inventory below for each of your students, you will gain greater insight into their preferred learning modalities. This knowledge can help you differentiate instruction and meet your students' needs.

Learning Styles Preference Inventory, Secondary School

How do you process information? Does your learning style match the way your teacher is presenting the material? This inventory will

Table 11.1   Rubric for Book Report, Middle School

	4 points *Excellent*	3 points *Good*	2 points *Satisfactory*	1 point *Needs Work*
Identifies book and author	Very clear; spelled correctly	One is correct, other missing or misspelled	Neither is totally correct	Only one is mentioned
Synopsis of the plot	Has all major events described in own words, in order	Most of the major events are included or not totally in own words	Some of the events are included or wording copied from book	Not clear what happens or missed the main idea of the story
Favorite character: names the character and describes at least one major event in the book where the character appears	Complete description	Name correct, description is incomplete	Either name or description is totally missing	The only part included is incorrect
Connects favorite character to theme (ongoing class discussion)	Gives specific examples	Examples are general	Examples are not clearly linked to character	Examples do not apply to the character
Organization: follows outline	Sections clearly defined	Correct order but sections not clear	Some attempt at following outline	No attempt at following outline
Grammar and Spelling	Totally correct	Fewer than 5 errors	Between 5 and 15 errors	More than 15 errors
Neatness (includes handwriting)	Better than any previous efforts	Obvious attempt at neatness	Some progress with neatness	No attempt at neatness

help you gain insight into your preferred learning modality, which will help you select learning strategies for individual courses.

Another way to discover means of assisting students whose learning approaches may not fit with the rest of your class is to use the multiple intelligences paradigm, discussed in Chapter 10.

Table 11.2   Learning Style Preference Inventory, Elementary School

Read each statement, and enter the appropriate number for the response that applies to the student.

      Often (3)   Sometimes (2)   Seldom/Never (1)

Visual Modality

_____ The child remembers information better if he can look at it (handouts, flashcards).

_____ The child stares intently at the teacher when the teacher is talking.

_____ The child seeks out a quiet place to work or turns his back to the class to work.

_____ The child can remember where information is on a page, but can't remember what the page says.

_____ The child does not remember directions given verbally; directions need to be written down or seen.

_____ The child remembers signs and landmarks when telling how to go somewhere.

_____ The child does not always understand jokes or mixes up words that look the same (*like* and *bike*).

_____ The child doodles and draws pictures on his work.

_____ Even though the child pays close attention when the teacher is talking, he has a hard time remembering what the teacher says—but remembers what the teacher did.

_____ The child color codes his work, frequently uses colored markers, or shows use of color in his work.

_____ *Total*

Auditory Modality

_____ The child has messy papers and his backpack is cluttered and unorganized.

_____ When the child reads, he uses his index finger to track his place on the line.

_____ If directions are written on a page, the child does not follow them well.

_____ The child can remember directions if the teacher says them.

_____ Writing is difficult and the child would rather tell a story than write it.

_____ The child often mixes up homonyms because they sound the same (*hear* and *here*).

_____ The child likes to be read to rather than read for himself.

_____ The child quickly understands verbal emotional cues; for example, he knows that someone is angry by the individual's tone of voice.

_____ The child has a hard time reading smaller print and prefers to read larger print, even though his vision is fine.

_____ The child rubs his eyes often or squints when he reads, even though his vision is fine.

_____ *Total*

Kinesthetic Modality

_____ The child starts to work before he has read or heard the directions.

_____ The child has more difficulty sitting at his desk for a long time than other students.

_____ The child does best if he watches someone do something before he tries it for himself.

_____ The child solves problems by trial and error, and will try one solution method many times before he changes his approach.

_____ The child may wiggle around a lot while reading and will change positions frequently if on the floor.

_____ The child takes breaks frequently and may do something else, such as visiting another child for a short while, before returning to the task.

_____ The child has a hard time explaining how to do something step-by-step, and may not keep the logical order.

_____ The child is good at sports and likes several different types of sports.

_____ When describing something, the child uses his hands a lot.

_____ One way for the child to learn is to write something several times or to draw a picture.

_____ *Total*

Verbal Modality

_____ The child reads a great deal.

_____ The child has a good vocabulary and easily picks up words from what he reads.

_____ The child would rather write a story than tell about it.

_____ The child can work at one task for a longer time than most, particularly if it involves reading.

_____ The child has a hard time answering questions and has difficulty sorting out what part of the information answers the question and what is off topic.

_____ The child likes to read out loud.

(Continued)

Table 11.2 (Continued)

_____ The child is well organized, rarely loses his papers, and can find papers easily.
_____ The child finds that math is difficult because he does not understand what he is asked to do and may have trouble understanding the symbols.
_____ The child may get distracted when others are talking or when there are other lessons going on in the classroom.
_____ The child likes handouts and keeps them all.
_____ *Total*
Total the score for each section. A score of 21 points or more in a modality indicates a strength in that area. The highest score among the four sections signifies the most efficient method of information intake. The second highest score indicates the modality that boosts the primary strength.
Note: This inventory is not meant to substitute for assessments designed to identify learning or other disabilities. Such disabilities must also be considered when designing a student's instruction. For example, a child with verbal processing strengths may still be unorganized and easily lose his papers due to other difficulties.

SOURCE: Howard, L. A., & James, A. N. (2003). *What principals need to know about teaching: Differentiated instruction.* Alexandria, VA; National Association of Elementary School Principals, pp. 75–77.

Table 11.3   Learning Style Preference Inventory, Secondary School

Read each statement, and enter the appropriate number for the response that applies to you.
Often (3)   Sometimes (2)   Seldom/Never (1)
Visual Modality
_____ You remember information better if you can look at it (handouts, flashcards).
_____ You need to look at the teacher when the teacher is talking.
_____ You need to study in a quiet place and it helps to turn your back to the class to work.
_____ You can remember where information is on a page, but can't remember what the page says.
_____ You do not remember when you are told directions; you need directions to be written down.
_____ You remember signs and landmarks when you give directions.
_____ You have a hard time understanding jokes and may mix up words that look the same, such as *like* and *bike*.

_____ You doodle and draw pictures on your work.

_____ Even though you pay close attention, you have a hard time remembering what the teacher said—but do remember what the teacher did.

_____ You use different colored highlighters or use color to sort or code your work.

_____ *Total*

Auditory Modality

_____ You have a messy and cluttered backpack and desk, and your papers tend to be messy.

_____ When you read, it helps to use your index finger to track your place on the line.

_____ You have more trouble following written directions.

_____ You can remember directions better if the teacher says them.

_____ You have trouble writing; it is easier for you to tell a story or give oral reports.

_____ You mix up homonyms because they sound the same (*hear* and *here*).

_____ You like to be read to rather than read for yourself.

_____ You can easily tell when someone is upset or excited by the way their voice sounds.

_____ You have a hard time reading small print and like larger print, even though your vision is fine.

_____ You rub your eyes often or squint when you read, even though your vision is fine.

_____ *Total*

Kinesthetic Modality

_____ You often begin work before you read the directions or before the teacher finishes reading the directions.

_____ You have difficulty sitting at your desk for a long time.

_____ You prefer to watch someone do something before you try something new, rather than reading or hearing the directions.

_____ You like to try to figure problems out for yourself and may have a hard time changing the way you solve problems.

_____ You have a hard time sitting still while you are reading and may prefer to read on the floor.

(Continued)

Table 11.3 (Continued)

_____ You prefer to take frequent breaks and like to change tasks often to stay focused.

_____ You have a hard time explaining the steps of how to do something and may get the steps out of order.

_____ You like sports and are good at several different types of sports.

_____ You use your hands a lot when you are describing something.

_____ One way for you to learn is to write something down several times or draw a picture or chart.

_____ Total

Verbal Modality

_____ You read a great deal.

_____ You have a good vocabulary and easily pick up words from the context.

_____ You would rather write a story than tell about it.

_____ You can work at one task longer than most other people, particularly if reading is involved.

_____ You may have a hard time answering questions because you include too much information and have difficulty sorting out what is important and what is not.

_____ You like to read out loud.

_____ You are well organized, rarely lose papers, and can find your schoolwork easily.

_____ You find math difficult because you have trouble with what the question asks you to do and are not always sure of what the symbols mean.

_____ You may get distracted when others are talking or when there are other lessons going on in the classroom.

_____ You keep all the papers that you get from your teacher.

_____ Total

Total the score for each section. A score of 21 points or more in a modality indicates a strength in that area. The highest score among the four sections signifies the most efficient way for you to access information. The second highest score indicates the modality that boosts your primary strength.

SOURCE: Adapted from Howard & James. (2003), pp. 75–77.

Resources

List of books for boys

BOOKS FOR BOYS AGES 6–9

All About Sam, by Lois Lowry
The Boy, the Bear, the Baron, the Bard, by Gregory Rogers
Captain Raptor and the Moon Mystery, by Kevin O'Malley
Chalk Box Kid, by Clyde Robert Bulla
Dinosaurs Before Dark (Magic Tree House 1), by Mary Pope Osborne
Freedom Summer, by Deborah Wiles
Henry Huggins, by Beverly Cleary
Horrible Harry in Room 2B, by Suzy Kline
The Legend of Spud Murphy, by Eoin Colfer
Lucky Leaf, by Kevin O'Malley
Math Curse, by Jon Scieszka
Meanwhile?, by Jules Feiffer
Merlin and the Making of the King, by Margaret Hodges
The Monster in the Third Dresser Drawer, and Other Stories About Adam Josh, by
    Janice Lee Smith
Odd Boy Out: Young Albert Einstein, by Don Brown
Puss 'n Boots: The Adventures of That Most Enterprising Feline, by Philip
    Pullman
Runny Babbit: A Billy Sook, by Shel Silverstein
Sideways Stories From Wayside School, by Louis Sachar
Zen Shorts, by Jon Muth

BOOKS FOR BOYS AGES 9–13

Abner and Me (Baseball Card Adventures series), by Dan Gutman
Al Capone Does My Shirts, by Gennifer Choldenko

The Amulet of Samarkand (The Bartimaeus Trilogy, Book 1), by Jonathan Stroud

Artemis Fowl, by Eoin Colfer

The Best Christmas Pageant Ever, by Barbara Robinson

Billy the Kid: A Novel, by Theodore Taylor

The Book of Three, by Lloyd Alexander

Bud, Not Buddy, by Christopher Paul Curtis

Bunnicula: A Rabbit-Tale of Mystery, by Deborah Howe and James Howe

Crispin: The Cross of Lead, by Avi

The Dark Is Rising, by Susan Cooper

Freak the Mighty, by Rodman Philbrick

Harry Potter and the Sorcerer's Stone, by J. K. Rowling

Hatchet, by Gary Paulsen

Holes, by Louis Sachar

Hoot, by Carl Hiaasen

The House of Dies Drear, by Virginia Hamilton

James and the Giant Peach, by Roald Dahl (and other books by Dahl)

Jip: His Story, by Katherine Paterson

The Last Shot: A Final Four Mystery, by John Feinstein

Maniac Magee, by Jerry Spinelli

Mrs. Frisby and the Rats of Nimh, by Robert O'Brien

The Sea of Trolls, by Nancy Farmer

Truckers, by Terry Pratchett

A Wrinkle in Time, by Madeleine L'Engle

BOOKS FOR BOYS AGES 13–18

The Adventures of Huckleberry Finn, by Mark Twain

Brave New World, by Aldous Huxley

The Chosen, by Chaim Potok

A Confederacy of Dunces, by John Kennedy Toole

The Count of Monte Cristo, by Alexander Dumas

The Curious Incident of the Dog in the Night-Time, by Mark Haddon

Dracula, by Bram Stoker

The Emperor of Ocean Park, by Stephen L. Carter

For Whom the Bell Tolls, by Ernest Hemingway

The Great Santini, by Pat Conroy (Conroy's *My Losing Season* is also good)

High Fidelity, by Nick Hornby

Hitchhiker's Guide to the Galaxy, by Douglas Adams

House Made of Dawn, by Scott Momaday

The Hunt for Red October, by Tom Clancy

Into Thin Air: A Personal Account of the Mt. Everest Disaster, by Jon Krakauer

Jurassic Park, by Michael Crichton

Killer Angels, by Michael Shaara

The Kite Runner, by Khaled Hosseini

A Lesson Before Dying, by Ernest Gaines

Lord of the Flies, by William Golding

The Lord of the Rings and *The Hobbit,* by J. R. R. Tolkien

Montana, 1948, by Larry Watson

Ragtime, by E. L. Doctorow

The Red Badge of Courage, by Stephen Crane

Robinson Crusoe, by Daniel Defoe

Sherlock Holmes: The Complete Novels and Stories, by Sir Arthur Conan Doyle

Slaughterhouse Five, or the Children's Crusade: A Duty Dance With Death, by Kurt Vonnegut

Taps: A Novel, by Willie Morris

Undaunted Courage: Meriwether Lewis, Thomas Jefferson and the Opening of the West, by Stephen Ambrose

---

SOURCE: A larger list has been compiled by the International Boys' School Coalition, www.boysschoolcoalition.org

References

Ackerman, P. L., Bowen, K. R., Beier, M. E., & Kanfer, R. (2001). Determinants of individual differences and gender differences in knowledge. *Journal of Educational Psychology, 93*(4), 797–825.

Agnew, S., & Ross, C. (1988). *Boys don't cry: Boys and sexism in education.* Philadelphia: Open University Press.

Alexander, G. M. (2003). An evolutionary perspective of sex-typed toy preferences: Pink, blue, and the brain. *Archives of Sexual Behavior, 32*(1), 7–15.

Anderson, K. G. (1997). Gender bias and special education referrals. *Annals of Dyslexia, 47*, 151–162.

Anderson, P. A., & Morganstern, B. (1981, April). *Accuracy in identifying facial expressions as a function of communication context.* Paper presented at the annual meeting of the Eastern Communication Association, Pittsburg, PA.

Andrews, J. A., Duncan, S. C., & Hops, H. (1994, February). *Explaining the relation between academic motivation and substance use: Effects of family relationships and self-esteem.* Paper presented at the biennial meeting of the Society for Research on Adolescence, San Diego, CA.

Askew, S., & Ross, C. (1988). *Boys don't cry: Boys and sexism in education.* Buckingham, England: Open University Press.

Armstrong, T. (1996). ADD: Does it really exist? *Phi Delta Kappan, 77*, 6.

Bailes, J., Guskiewicz, K., & Marshall, S. (2003, April). *Recurrent sport-related concussion linked to clinical depression.* Paper presented at the annual meeting of the American Association of Neurological Surgeons, San Diego, CA.

Bailey, D. F. (2003). Preparing African American males for postsecondary options. *Journal of Men's Studies, 12*(1), 15–24.

Bailey, D. F., & Paisley, P. O. (2004). Developing and nurturing excellence in African American male adolescents. *Journal of Counseling and Development, 82*(1), 10–17.

Barnett, M. A., Quackenbush, S. W., & Sinisi, C. S. (1996). Factors affecting children's, adolescents', and young adults' perceptions of parental discipline. *Journal of Genetic Psychology, 157*(4), 411–424.

Baron-Cohen, S. (2003). *The essential difference: The truth about the male and female brain.* New York: Basic Books.

Barretti, M. R. (1993). *Increasing the success of learning disabled high school students in their transistion to the community college through the use of support services.* Nova University: Fort Lauderdale, FL.

265

Baum, S. (1990). *Gifted but learning disabled: A puzzling paradox* (ERIC Digest No. E479). Reston, VA: ERIC Clearinghouse on Handicapped and Gifted Children and Council for Exceptional Children.

Benenson, J. F. (1993). Greater preference among females than males for dyadic interaction in early childhood. *Child Development, 64,* 544–555.

Beneson, J. F., Liroff, E. R., Pascal, S. J., & Della Cioppa, G. (1997). Propulsion: A behavioural expression of masculinity. *British Journal of Developmental Psychology, 15,* 37–50.

Bennett, C. K., & Bennett, J. A. (1994, April). *Teachers' attributions and beliefs in relation to gender and success of students.* Paper presented at the annual meeting of the American Educational Research Association, New Orleans, LA.

Bennett, R. E., Gottesman, R. L., Rock, D. A., & Cerullo, F. (1993). Influence of behavior perceptions and gender on teachers' judgments of students' academic skill. *Journal of Educational Psychology, 85*(2), 347–356.

Berk, L. E. (1997). *Child development* (4th ed.). Boston: Allyn & Bacon.

Berninger, V. W., & Fuller, F. (1992). Gender differences in orthographic, verbal, and compositional writing: Implications for assessing writing disabilities in primary grade children. *Journal of School Psychology, 30,* 363–382.

Biddulph, S. (1997). *Raising boys.* Berkeley, CA: Celestial Arts.

Biederman, J., Wilens, T., Mick, E., Faraone, S. V., Weber, W., Curtis, S., et al. (1997). Is ADHD a risk factor for psychoactive substance use disorders? Findings from a four-year prospective follow-up study. *Journal of the American Academy of Child and Adolescent Psychiatry, 36*(1), 21–29.

Billing, J. (1980). *Direct versus indirect competition* (Viewpoints/Reports). Chapel Hill: University of North Carolina. (ERIC Document Reproduction Service No. ED195502)

Bishop, K. M., & Wahlsten, D. (1997). Sex differences in the human corpus callosum: Myth or reality? *Neuroscience and Biobehavioral Reviews, 21*(5), 581–601.

Blazer, B. (1995). Classroom adjustments to support students with attention and learning weaknesses. *Intervention in School and Clinic, 30*(4), 248.

Bleach, K. (1997, February 14). Where did we go wrong? *The Times Educational Supplement,* p. 14.

Bonta, B. D. (1997). Cooperation and competition in peaceful societies. *Psychological Bulletin, 121*(2), 299–320.

Bornholt, L. J., Goodnow, J. J., & Cooney, G. H. (1988). *Perceptions of achievement: The effects of gender, school type, and grade* (Research/technical report). Sydney, Australia: Macquarie University. (ERIC Document Reproduction Service No. ED 305989)

Branch, A. J. (2001). Increasing the numbers of teachers of color in K–12 public schools. *The Educational Forum, 65*(3), 254–261.

Breznitz, Z. (2003). The speech and vocalization patterns of boys with ADHD compared with boys with dyslexia and boys without learning disabilities. *Journal of Genetic Psychology, 164*(4), 425–452.

Burnham, D. K., & Harris, M. B. (1991). Effects of real gender and labeled gender on adults' perceptions of infants. *Journal of Genetic Psychology, 153*(2), 165–183.

Bushweller, K. (1994). Turning our backs on boys. *American School Board Journal, 181,* 20–25.

Cahill, B., & Adams, E. (1997). An exploratory study of early childhood teachers' attitudes toward gender roles. *Sex Roles, 36*(7/8), 517–529.

Cahill, L. (2003). Sex- and hemisphere-related influences on the neurobiology of emotionally influenced memory. *Progress in Neuro-Psychopharmacology and Biological Psychiatry, 27*(8), 1235–1241.

Canada, G. (1999/2000). Raising better boys. *Educational Leadership, 57*(4), 14–17.

Carson, B., & Murphey, C. (1990). *Gifted hands: The Ben Carson story.* New York: Zondervan.

Casey, M. B., Nuttall, R. L., & Pezaris, E. (1997). Mediators of gender differences in mathematics college entrance test scores: A comparison of spatial skills with internalized beliefs and anxieties. *Developmental Psychology, 33*(4), 669–680.

Caspi, A. (1995). Puberty and the gender organization of schools: How biology and social context shape the adolescent experience. In L. J. Crockett & A. C. Crouter (Eds.), *Pathways through adolescence: Individual development in relation to social contexts* (pp. 57–74). Mahwah, NJ: Erlbaum.

Cassidy, S., & Eachus, P. (2000). Learning style, academic belief systems, self-report student proficiency and academic achievement in higher education. *Educational Psychology, 20*(3), 307–322.

Centers for Disease Control (2004). *Youth on line: Comprehensive results.* Retrieved April 26, 2005, from http://www.cdc.gov/HealthyYouth/pdf/YRBSpress-release.pdf

Christakis, D. A., Zimmerman, F. J., DiGiuseppe, D. L., & McCarty, C. A. (2004). Early television viewing and subsequent attentional problems in children. *Pediatrics, 113*(4), 708–713.

Collins, M. W., Lovell, M. R., Iverson, G. L., Cantu, R. C., Maroon, J. C., & Field, M. (2002). Cumulative effects of concussion in high school athletes. *Neurosurgery, 51*(5), 1175–1181.

Collins-Standley, T., Gan, S.-l., Yu, H.-J. J., & Zillman, D. (1996). Choice of romantic, violent, and scary fairy-tale books by preschool girls and boys. *Child Study Journal, 26*(4), 279–301.

Connell, R. W. (1996). Teaching the boys: New research on masculinity, and gender strategies for schools. *Teachers College Record, 98*(2), 206–235.

Connellan, J., Baron-Cohen, S., Wheelwright, S., Batki, A., & Ahuluwalia, J. (2000). Sex differences in human neonatal social perception. *Infant Behavior and Development, 23,* 113–118.

Corso, J. (1959). Age and sex differences in pure-tone thresholds. *Journal of the Acoustical Society of America, 31*(4), 498–507.

Currie, M. (2004). Doing anger differently: A group percussion therapy for angry adolescent boys. *International Journal of Group Psychotherapy, 54*(3), 275–294.

Davies, P. L., & Rose, J. D. (1999). Assessment of cognitive development in adolescents by means of neuropsychological tasks. *Developmental Neuropsychology, 15*(2), 227–248.

Davis, J. E. (2001). Transgressing the masculine: African American boys and the failure of schools. In W. Martino & B. Meyenn (Eds.), *What about the boys?* (pp. 140–153). Buckingham, England: Open University Press.

Davis, P. J. (1999). Gender differences in autobiographical memory for childhood emotional experiences. *Journal of Personality and Social Psychology, 76*(3), 498–510.

de Agostini, M., Paré, C., Goudot, D., & Dellatolas, G. (1992). Manual preference and skill development in preschool children. *Developmental Neuropsychology, 8*(1), 41–57.

DeBaryshe, B. D., Patterson, G. R., & Capaldi, D. M. (1993). A performance model for academic achievement in early adolescent boys. *Developmental Psychology, 29*(5), 795–804.

de Courten-Myers, G. M. (1999). The human cortex: Gender differences in structure and function. *Journal of Neuropathology and Experimental Neurology, 58*(3), 217–226.

Don, M., Ponton, C. W., Eggermont, J. J., & Masuda, A. (1993). Gender differences in cochlear response time: An explanation for gender amplitude differences in unmasked auditory brain-stem response. *Journal of the Acoustical Society of America, 94*(4), 2135–2146.

Doyle, R. (1999, October). Men, women and college. *Scientific American, 281,* 40.

Du, Y., Weymouth, C. M., & Dragseth, K. (2003, April). *Gender differences and student learning.* Paper presented at the annual meeting of the American Educational Research Association, Chicago.

Dubas, J. S., Graber, J. A., & Petersen, A. C. (1991). The effects of pubertal development on achievement during adolescence. *American Journal of Education, 99,* 444–460.

Duke, P. M., Carlsmith, J. M., Jennings, D., Martin, J. A., Dornbusch, S. M., Gross, R. T., & Siegel-Gorelick, B. (1982). Educational correlates of early and late sexual maturation in adolescence. *Journal of Pediatrics, 100*(4), 633–637.

Duncan, G. (1999). The education of adolescent black males: Connecting self-esteem to human dignity. In L. E. Davis (Ed.), *Working with African-American males.* Thousand Oaks, CA: Sage.

Dunn, M. S., Barte, R. T., & Perko, M. A. (2003). Self-reported alcohol use and sexual behaviors of adolescents. *Psychological Reports, 92,* 339–348.

Dwyer, F. M., & Moore, D. M. (2001). The effect of gender, field dependence and color-coding on student achievement of differential educational objectives. *International Journal of Instructional Media, 28*(3), 309.

Eccles, J. S., Lord, S., & Midgley, C. (1991). What are we doing to early adolescents? The impact of educational contexts on early adolescents. *American Journal of Education, 99*(4), 521–542.

Elder, R. W., Shults, R. A., Swahn, M. H., Strife, B. J., & Ryan, G. W. (2004). Alcohol-related emergency department visits among people ages 13 to 25 years. *Journal of Studies on Alcohol, 65*(3), 297–301.

El-Sayed, E., Larsson, J.-O., Persson, H. E., Santosh, P. J., & Rydelius, P.-A. (2003). "Maturational lag" hypothesis of attention deficit hyperactivity disorder: An update. *Acta Paediatrica, 92,* 776–784.

Epstein, D. (1999). Real boys don't work. In D. Epstein, J. Elwood, V. Hey, & J. Maw (Eds.), *Failing boys? Issues in gender and achievement* (pp. 96-108). Philadelphia: Open University Press.

Evans, E. M., Schweingruber, H., & Stevenson, H. W. (2002). Gender differences in interest and knowledge acquisition: The United States, Taiwan, and Japan. *Sex Roles, 47*(3/4), 153–167.

Everett, D. (2003, July). *Boys and literacy: Three ideas that work.* Paper presented at the annual conference of the International Boys' Schools Coalition, Sydney, Australia.

Faust, M. S. (1977). Somatic development of adolescent girls. *Monographs of the Society for Research in Child Development, 42*(1), 1-90.

Feagans, L. V., Kipp, E., & Blood, I. (1994). The effects of otitis media on the attention skills of day-care-attending toddlers. *Developmental Psychology, 30,* 701–708.

Fearon, I., McGrath, P. J., & Achat, H. (1996). 'Booboos': The study of everyday pain among young children. *International Association for the Study of Pain, 68,* 55–62.

Felson, R. B., & Burchfield, K. B. (2004). Alcohol and the risk of physical and sexual victimization. *Criminology, 42*(4), 837–859.

Fennema, E., Peterson, P. L., Carpenter, T. P., & Lubinski, C. A. (1990). Teachers' attributions and beliefs about girls, boys, and mathematics. *Educational Studies in Mathematics, 21*(1), 55–69.

Fenzel, L. M., Peyrot, M. F., & Premoshis, K. (1997, March). *Alternative model for urban middle-level schooling: An evaluation study.* Paper presented at the annual meeting of the American Educational Research Association, Chicago.

Finegold, A. (1992). Sex differences in variability in intellectual abilities: A new look at an old controversy. *Review of Educational Research, 62*(1), 61–84.

Ford, D. Y., & Moore, J. L. I. (2004). Creating culturally responsive gifted education classrooms: Understanding "culture" is the first step. *Gifted Child Today, 27*(4), 34–39.

Ford-Harris, D. Y., Schuerger, J. M., & Harris, J. J. I. (1991). Meeting the psychological needs of gifted black students: A cultural perspective. *Journal of Counseling and Development, 69*(6), 577–580.

Friedman, L. (1995). The space factor in mathematics: Gender differences. *Review of Educational Research, 65*(1), 22–50.

Frydenberg, E., & Lewis, R. (1993). Boys play sport and girls turn to others: Age, gender, and ethnicity as determinants of coping. *Journal of Adolescence, 16,* 253–266.

Furr, L. A. (1998). Fathers' characteristics and their children's scores on college entrance exams: A comparison of intact and divorced families. *Adolescence, 33*(131), 533–542.

Gardill, M. C., DuPaul, G. J., & Kyle, K. E. (1996). Classroom strategies for managing students with Attention-Deficit/Hyperactivity Disorder. *Intervention in School and Clinic, 32*(2), 89–94.

Gardner, H. (1983). *Frames of Mind: The Theory of Multiple Intelligences.* New York: Basic Books.

Garibaldi, A. M. (1992). Educating and motivating African American males to succeed. *Journal of Negro Education, 61*(1), 12–18.

Geary, D. C. (1998). *Male, female: The evolution of human sex differences.* Washington, DC: American Psychological Association.

Gentry, M., Gable, R., & Rizza, M. G. (2002). Students' perceptions of classroom activities: Are there grade-level and gender differences? *Journal of Educational Psychology, 94*(3), 539–544.

Gettinger, M., & Seibert, J. K. (2002). Contributions of study skills to academic competence. *School Psychology Review, 31*(3), 350–365.

Giedd, J. N., Blumenthal, J., Jeffries, N. O., Castellanos, F. X., Liu, H., Zijdenbos, A., et al. (1999). Brain development during childhood and adolescence: A longitudinal MRI study. *Nature Neuroscience, 2*(10), 861–863.

Giedd, J. N., Castellanos, F. X., Rajapakse, J., Vaituzis, A. C., & Rapoport, J. L. (1997). Sexual dimorphism of the developing human brain. *Progress in Neuro-Psychopharmacology and Biological Psychiatry, 21*(8), 1185–1201.

Gneezy, U., & Rustichini, A. (2004). Gender and competition at a younger age. *American Economic Review, 94*(2), 377–381.

Goldstein, M. A. (2003). Male puberty: Physical, psychological, and emotional issues. *Adolescent Medicine, 14*(3), 541–553.

Goran, M. I., Nagy, T. R., Gower, B. A., Mazariegos, M., Solomons, N., Hood, V., et al. (1998). Influence of sex, seasonality, ethnicity, and geographic location on the components of total energy expenditure in young children: Implications for energy requirements. *American Journal of Clinical Nutrition, 68,* 675–682.

Gose, B. (1997, June 6). Liberal-arts colleges ask: Where have the men gone? *Chronicle of Higher Education,* pp. A35-A36.

Goyette, K., & Xie, Y. (1999). Educational expectations of Asian American youths: Determinants and ethnic differences. *Sociology of Education, 72*(1), 22–36.

Graham, S., Berninger, V. W., Weintraub, N., & Schafer, W. (1998). Development of handwriting speed and legibility in grades 1–9. *Journal of Educational Research, 92*(1), 42–52.

Graham, S., Harris, K. R., & Fink, B. (2000). Is handwriting causally related to learning to write? Treatment of handwriting problems in beginning writers. *Journal of Educational Psychology, 92*(4), 620–633.

Grantham, T. C., & Ford, D. Y. (2003). Beyond self-concept and self-esteem: Racial identity and gifted African American students. *High School Journal, 87*(1), 18–29.

Gregory, G. H. (2003). *Differentiated instructional strategies in practice: Training, implementation, and supervision.* Thousand Oaks, CA: Corwin Press.

Griffin, B. W. (2002). Academic disidentification, race, and high school dropouts. *High School Journal, 85*(4), 71–81.

Grossman, H., & Grossman, S. H. (1994). *Gender issues in education.* Boston: Allyn & Bacon.

Gur, R. C., Alsop, D., Glahn, D., Petty, R., Swanson, C. L., Maldjian, J. A., et al. (2000). An fMRI study of sex differences in regional activation to a verbal and a spatial skill. *Brain and Language, 74,* 157–170.

Hall, C., & Coles, M. (1997). Gendered readings: Helping boys develop as critical readers. *Gender and Education, 9*(1), 61–68.

Hall, J. A. Y., & Kimura, D. (1995). Sexual orientation and performance on sexually dimorphic motor tasks. *Archives of Sexual Behavior, 24*(4), 395–407.

Hall, W., & Solowij, N. (1998). Adverse effects of cannabis. *The Lancet, 352,* 1611–1616.

Halpern, D. F. (2000). *Sex differences in cognitive abilities* (3rd ed.). Mahwah, NJ: Erlbaum.

Harasty, J., Double, K. L., Halliday, G. M., Kril, J. J., & McRitchie, D. A. (1997). Language-associated cortical regions are proportionally larger in the female brain. *Archives of Neurology, 54*(2), 171–176.

Harmon, K. G. (1999). Assessment and management of concussion in sports. *American Family Physician, 60*(3), 887.

Harris, S., Nixon, J., & Ruddock, J. (1993). School work, homework, and gender. *Gender and Education, 5*(1), 3–15.

Hartley, J. (1991). Sex differences in handwriting: A comment on Spear. *British Educational Research Journal, 17*(2), 141–145.

Hartnett, D. N., Nelson, J. M., & Rinn, A. N. (2004). Gifted or ADHD? The possiblities of misdiagnosis. *Roeper Review, 26*(2), 73–76.

Hawley, R. A. (1991). About boys schools: A progressive case for an ancient form. *Teachers College Record, 92*(3), 433–444.

Heacox, D. (2002). *Differentiating instruction in the regular classroom.* Minneapolis, MN: Free Spirit.

Henrie, R. L., Aron, R. H., Nelson, B. D., & Poole, D. A. (1997). Gender-related knowledge variations within geography. *Sex Roles, 36*(9/10), 605–624.

Herlitz, A., Airaksien, E., & Nordstrom, E. (1999). Sex differences in episodic memory: The impact of verbal and visuospatial ability. *Neuropsychology, 13*(4), 590–597.

Heyman, G. D., & Legare, C. H. (2004). Children's beliefs about gender differences in the academic and social domains. *Sex Roles, 50*(3–4), 227–239.

Hill, N. E., Castellino, D. R., Lansford, J. E., Nowlin, P., Dodge, K. A., Bates, J. E., et al. (2004). Parent academic involvement as related to school behavior, achievement, and aspirations: Demographic variations across adolescence. *Child Development, 75*(5), 1491–1509.

Hines, M. (2004). *Brain gender.* New York: Oxford University Press.

Hirt, E. R., McCrea, S. M., & Boris, H. I. (2003). "I know you self-handicapped that last exam": Gender differences in reactions to self-handicapping. *Journal of Personality and Social Psychology, 84*(1), 177–193.

Holland, S. H. (1996). Project 2000: An educational mentoring and academic support model for inner-city African American boys. *Journal of Negro Education, 65*(3), 315–321.

Holland, V. (1998). Underachieving boys: Problems and solutions. *Support for Learning, 13*(4), 174–178.

Honigsfeld, A., & Dunn, R. (2003). High school male and female learning-style similarities and differences in diverse nations. *Journal of Educational Research, 96*(4), 195–207.

Hortacsu, N. (1995). Parents' educational levels, parents' beliefs, and child outcomes. *Journal of Genetic Psychology, 156*(3), 373–383.

Howard, L. A., & James, A. N. (2003). *What principals need to know about teaching: Differentiated instruction.* Alexandria, VA: National Association of Elementary School Principals.

Howard, T. C. (2003). "A tug of war for our minds": African American high school students' perceptions of their academic identities and college aspirations. *High School Journal, 87*(1), 4–17.

Howland, J., Hingson, R., Mangione, T. W., Bell, N., & Bak, S. (1996). Why are most drowning victims men? Sex differences in aquatic skills and behaviors. *American Journal of Public Health, 86*(1), 93–96.

Hubbard, L., & Datnow, A. (2005). Do single-sex schools improve the education of low-income and minority students? An investigation of California's public single-gender academies. *Anthropology and Education Quarterly, 36*(2), 115–131.

Huesmann, L. R., Moise-Titus, J., Podolski, C., & Eron, L. D. (2003). Longitudinal relations between children's exposure to TV violence and their aggressive and violent behavior in young adulthood: 1977–1992. *Developmental Psychology, 39*(2), 201–221.

Iijima, M., Arisaka, O., Minamoto, F., & Arai, Y. (2001). Sex differences in children's free drawings: A study on girls with congenital adrenal hyperplasia. *Hormones and Behavior, 40,* 99–104.

Jackson, T., Iezzi, T., Gunderson, J., & Nagasaka, T. (2002). Gender differences in pain perception: The mediating role of self-efficacy beliefs. *Sex Roles, 47*(11), 561–568.

James, A. N., & Richards, H. C. (2003). Escaping stereotypes: Educational attitudes of male alumni of single-sex and coed schools. *Psychology of Men and Masculinity, 4*(2), 136–148.

Jonassen, D. H., & Grabowski, B. (1993). *Handbook of individual differences, learning, and instruction.* Mahwah, NJ: Erlbaum.

Jones, P., & Fiorelli, D. C. (2003). Overcoming the obstacle course: Teenage boys and reading. *Teacher Librarian, 30,* 9–13.

Kelly, J. P. (2001). Loss of consciousness: Pathophysiology and implications in grading and safe return to play. *Journal of Athletic Training, 36*(3), 249–252.

Killgore, W. D. S., Oki, M., & Yurgelun-Todd, D. A. (2001). Sex-specific developmental changes in amygdala responses to affective faces. *Neuroreport, 12*(2), 427–433.

Killgore, W. D. S., & Yurgelun-Todd, D. A. (2001). Sex differences in amygdala activation during the perception of facial affect. *Neuroreport, 12*(11), 2543–2547.

Kimura, D. (2000). *Sex and cognition.* Cambridge: MIT Press.

Kindlon, D., & Thompson, M. (1999). *Raising Cain: Protecting the emotional life of boys.* New York: Ballantine.

Kirby, E. A., & Kirby, S. H. (1994). Classroom discipline with Attention Deficit Hyperactivity Disorder children. *Contemporary Education, 65*(3), 142–144.

Kleine, D. (1994). Sports activity as a means of reducing school stress. *International Journal of Sport Psychology, 22*, 366–380.

Knez, I. (1995). Effects of indoor lighting on mood and cognition. *Journal of Environmental Psychology, 15*, 39–51.

Kronenberger, W. G., Mathews, V. P., Dunn, D. W., Wang, Y., Wood, E. A., Giauque, A. L., et al. (2005). Media violence exposure and executive functioning in aggressive and control adolescents. *Journal of Clinical Psychology, 61*(6), 7525–7737.

Kubberod, E., Ueland, O., Tronstad, A., & Risvik, E. (2002). Attitudes toward meat and meat-eating among adolescents in Norway: A qualitative study. *Appetite, 38*(1), 53–62.

Lamberg, L. (1998). Girls' and boys' differing response to pain starts early in their lives. *Journal of the American Medical Association, 280*(12), 1035–1036.

Langerman, D. (1990). Books and boys: Gender preferences and book selection. *School Library Journal, 36*(3), 132–136.

Lawler, B. (2000). Gifted or ADHD: Misdiagnosis? How can we be certain a correct diagnosis has been made? *Understanding Our Gifted, 13*(1), 16–18.

Lewinsohn, P. M., Rohde, P., & Seeley, J. R. (1996). Alcohol consumption in high school adolescents: Frequency of use and dimensional structure of associated problems. *Addiction, 91*(3), 375–390.

Lewis, A. (1992). *Urban youth in community service: Becoming part of the solution.* Washington, DC: Office of Educational Research and Improvement. ERIC Digest No. 81.

Liederman, J., Kantrowitz, L., & Flannery, K. (2005). Male vulnerability to reading disability is not likely to be a myth: A call for new data. *Journal of Learning Disabilities, 38*(2), 109–129.

Limber, S. P. (2003). Efforts to address bullying in U.S. Schools. *American Journal of Health Education, 35*(5), S-23–S-29.

Linn, M. C., & Petersen, A. C. (1985). Emergence and characterization of sex differences in spatial ability: A meta-analysis. *Child Development, 56*, 1479–1498.

Littlewood, A. (1995). The worst class in school? In R. Browne & R. Fletcher (Eds.), *Boys in schools: Addressing the real issues—behavior, values, and relationships* (pp. 54–64). Sydney, Australia: Finch.

Lonsdorf, E. V., Eberly, L. E., & Pusey, A. E. (2004, April 15). Sex differences in learning in chimpanzees. *Nature, 428*, 715–716.

Lorente, F. O., Peretti-Watel, P., Griffet, J., & Grelot, L. (2003). Alcohol use and intoxication in sport university students. *Alcohol and Alcoholism, 38*(5), 427–430.

Lovell, M. R., Collins, M. W., Iverson, G. L., Johnston, K. M., & Bradley, J. P. (2004). Grade 1 or "ding" concussions in high school athletes. *American Journal of Sports Medicine, 32*(1), 47–54.

Lowen, J. W., Rosser, P., & Katzman, J. (1988, April). *Gender bias in SAT items.* Paper presented at the annual meeting of the American Educational Research Association, New Orleans, LA.

Lutchmaya, S., & Baron-Cohen, S. (2002). Human sex differences in social and non-social looking preferences at 12 months of age. *Infant Behavior and Development, 25,* 319–325.

Lynn, R., & Irwing, P. (2002). Sex differences in general knowledge, semantic memory and reasoning ability. *British Journal of Psychology, 93*(4), 545–556.

Mac an Ghaill, M. (1994). *The making of men: Masculinities, sexualities, and schooling.* Buckingham, England: Open University Press.

Maccoby, E. E. (1998). *The two sexes: Growing up apart, coming together.* Cambridge, MA: Harvard University Press.

Maccoby, E. E., & Jacklin, C. N. (1974). *The psychology of sex differences.* Stanford, CA: Stanford University Press.

MacFadden, A., Elias, L., & Saucier, D. (2003). Males and females scan maps similarly, but give directions differently. *Brain and Cognition, 53*(2), 297–300.

Majeres, R. L. (1999). Sex differences in phonological processes: Speeded matching and word reading. *Memory and Cognition, 27*(2), 246–253.

Martino, W. (1995). It's not the way guys think! In R. Browne & R. Fletcher (Eds.), *Boys in schools* (pp. 124–138). Sydney, Australia: Finch.

Mathews, V. P., Kronenberger, W. G., Wang, Y., Lurito, J. T., Lowe, M. J., & Dunn, D. W. (2005). Media violence exposure and frontal lobe activation measured by functional magnetic resonance imaging in aggressive and nonaggressive adolescents. *Journal of Computer Assisted Tomography, 29*(3), 287–292.

Maxwell, C. D., Robinson, A. L., & Post, L. A. (2003). The nature and predictors of sexual victimization and offending among adolescents. *Journal of Youth and Adolescence, 32*(6), 465–477.

McClure, E. B. (2000). A meta-analytic review of sex differences in facial expression processing and their development in infants, children, and adolescents. *Psychological Bulletin, 126*(3), 424–453.

McCormick, L. H. (2003). ADHD treatment and academic performance: A case series. *Journal of Family Practice, 52*(8), 620–626.

McFadden, D. (1998). Sex differences in the auditory system. *Developmental Neuropsychology, 14*(2/3), 261–298.

McGuinness, D. (1976). Away from a unisex psychology: Individual differences in visual sensory and perceptual processes. *Perception, 5,* 279–294.

Meadows, B. (2005, March 14). The web: The bully's new playground. *People, 63,* 152–155.

Messner, M. A. (1992). *Power at play: Sports and the problem of masculinity.* Boston: Beacon Press.

Moore, J. L. I., Ford, D. Y., & Milner, H. R. (2005). Underachievement among gifted students of color: Implications for educators. *Theory Into Practice, 44*(2), 167–177.

Morgan, S. L., & Mehta, J. D. (2004). Beyond the laboratory: Evaluating the survey evidence for the disidentification explanation of black-white differences in achievement. *Sociology of Education, 77*(1), 82–101.

Morisset, C. E., Barnard, K. E., & Booth, C. L. (1995). Toddlers' language development: Sex differences within social risk. *Developmental Psychology, 31*(5), 851–865.

Murphy, J. (2001). Boys will be boys: A public librarian leads her first book group for the opposite sex. *School Library Journal, 47*(1), 31.

Naglieri, J. A., & Rojahn, J. (2001). Gender differences in planning, attention, simultaneous, and successive (pass) cognitive processes and achievement. *Journal of Educational Psychology, 93*(2), 430–437.

National Assessment of Educational Progress. (2006). *Long term trend assessment in reading and writing, 2002: Major results.* Retrieved July 20, 2006, from http://nces.ed.gov/nationsreportcard

National Center for Education Statistics. (1997). *Profiles of students with disabilities as identified in NELS:88.* (NCES No. 97254). Retrieved July 26, 2006, from http://nces.ed.gov/surveys/nels88

National Center for Education Statistics. (2004). *Indicators of school crime and safety: 2004.* Retrieved July 24, 2006, from http://nces.ed.gov

National Center for Education Statistics. (2005). *Digest of educational statistics: 2003.* Retrieved October 2, 2006, from http://nces.edu.gov/pro grams/digest

National Center for Education Statistics. (2006). *Digest of education statistics: 2006.* Retrieved July 20, 2006, from http://nces.ed.gov/programs/digest

Neall, L. (2002). *Bringing the best out in boys: Communication strategies for teachers.* Stroud, England: Hawthorne Press.

Nemes, J. (1999). Gender and hearing: New studies find auditory differences between the sexes. *Hearing Journal, 52*(4), 21–28.

Newman, R. M. (2000, July 6). Dyscalculia.Org. Retrieved April 25, 2005, from http://www.dyscalculia.org

Nordin, S., Broman, D. A., Garvill, J., & Nyroos, M. (2004). Gender differences in factors affecting rejection of food in healthy young Swedish adults. *Appetite, 43*(3), 295–301.

Office of Special Education Programs. (2005). Individuals with Disability Education Act. Retrieved May 25, 2005, from http://thomas.loc.gov

Ogbu, J. U. & Simons, H. D. (1998). Voluntary and involuntary minorities: A cultural-ecological theory of school performance with some implications for education. *Anthropology & Education Quarterly, 29*(2), 155–188.

Ogbu, J. U. (2003). *Black American students in an affluent suburb: A study of academic disengagement.* Mahwah, NJ: Erlbaum.

Ogbu, J. U. (2004). Collective identity and the burden of 'acting white' in Black history, community, and education. *Urban Review, 36*(1), 1-35.

Oka, S., Miyamoto, O., Janjua, N. A., Honjo-Fujiwara, N., Ohkawa, M., Nagao, S., et al. (1999). Re-evaluation of sexual dimorphism in human corpus callosum. *Neuroreport, 10*(5), 937–940.

Ólafsdóttir, M. P. (1996). Kids are both girls and boys in Iceland. *Women's Studies International Forum, 19,* 357–369.

Olweus, D. (2001, March 1). Bullying at school: Tackling the problem. *OECD Observer,* 24–26.

Osborne, J. W. (1997). Race and academic disidentification. *Journal of Educational Psychology, 89*(4), 728–735.

Overman, W. H., Bachevalier, J., Schuhmann, E., & Ryan, P. (1996). Cognitive gender differences in very young children parallel biologically based cognitive gender differences in monkeys. *Behavioral Neuroscience, 110*(4), 673–684.

Pakkenberg, B., & Gundersen, J. G. (1997). Neurocortical neuron number in humans: Effect of sex and age. *Journal of Comparative Neurology, 384,* 312–320.

Paradise, J. L., Rockett, H. E., Colborn, D. K., Bernard, B. S., Smith, C. G., Kurs-Lasky, M., et al. (1997). Otitis media in 2253 Pittsburgh-area infants: Prevalance and risk factors during the first two years of life. *Pediatrics, 99*(3), 318–233.

Parsons, J. E. (1981, April). *Attributions, learned helplessness, and sex differences in achievement.* Paper presented at the annual meeting of the American Educational Research Association, Los Angeles.

Pelham, J., William E., Murphy, D. A., Vannatta, K., Milich, R., Licht, B., Gnagy, E. M., et al. (1992). Methylphenidate and attributions in boys with attention-deficit hyperactivity disorder. *Journal of Consulting and Clinical Psychology, 60*(2), 282–292.

Peters, M., & Campagnaro, P. (1996). Do women really excel over men in manual dexterity? *Journal of Experimental Psychology, 22*(5), 1107–1112.

Peterson, A. C. (1986, April). *Early adolescence: A critical development transistion?* Paper presented at the annual meeting of the American Educational Research Association, San Francisco.

Peugh, J., & Blenko, S. (2001). Alcohol, drugs and sexual function: A review. *Journal of Psychoactive Drugs, 33*(3), 223–232.

Phillips, A. (1994). *The trouble with boys.* New York: HarperCollins.

Pinker, S. (1997). *How the mind works.* New York: W. W. Norton.

Pinker, S. (2002). *The blank slate.* New York, New York: Viking.

Pollack, W. (1998). *Real boys: Rescuing our sons from the myths of boyhood.* New York: Random House.

Pope, H. G., Jr., Gruber, A. J., Hudson, J. I., Huestis, M. G., & Yurgelun-Todd, D. A. (2001). Neuropsychological performance in long-term cannabis users. *Archives of General Psychiatry, 58*(10), 909–915.

Pottorff, D. D., Phelps-Zientarski, D., & Skovera, M. E. (1996). Gender perceptions of elementary and middle school students about literacy at school and home. *Journal of Research and Development in Education, 29*(4), 203–211.

Preboth, M. (2000). Marijuana use among children and adolescents. *American Family Physician, 61*(9), 2887.

Ramirez, A. Y. (2001). "Parent involvement is like apple pie": A look at parental involvement in two states. *High School Journal, 85*(1), 1–9.

Raspberry, W. (1999, March 5). Learning about boys from elephants. *The* [Charlottesville, VA] *Daily Progress,* p. A6.

Reis, S. M., Callahan, C. M., & Goldsmith, D. (1994). Attitudes of adolescent gifted girls and boys toward education, achievement, and the future. *Gifted Education International, 9*(3), 144–151.

Rodney, L. W., Rodney, H. E., Crafter, B., & Mupier, R. M. (1999). Variables contributing to grade retention among African American adolescent males. *Journal of Educational Research, 92*(3), 185–195.

Roopnarine, J. L. (1986). Mothers' and fathers' behaviors toward the toy play of their infant sons and daughters. *Sex Roles, 14*(1/2), 59–68.

Roulstone, S., Loader, S., Northstone, K., Beveridge, M., & Team, T. A. (2002). The speech and language of children aged 25 months: Descriptive data from the Avon longitudinal study of parents and children. *Early Child Development and Care, 172*(3), 259–268.

Sadker, M., & Sadker, D. (1994). *Failing at fairness: How our schools cheat girls.* New York: Touchstone/Simon & Schuster.

Safer, D. J., Zito, J. M., & dosReis, S. (2003). Concomitant psychotropic medication for youths. *American Journal of Psychiatry, 160*(3), 438–449.

Safer, D. J., Zito, J. M., & Fine, E. M. (1996). Increased methylphenidate usage for attention deficit disorder in the 1990s. *Pediatrics, 98*(6), 1084–1088.

Sankofa, B. M., Hurley, E. A., Allen, B. A., & Boykin, W. W. (2005). Cultural expression and black students' attitudes toward high achievers. *Journal of Psychology, 139*(3), 247–259.

Sarkar, S., & Andreas, M. (2004). Acceptance of and engagement in risky driving behaviors by teenagers. *Adolescence, 39,* 687–700.

Sax, L. (2001). Reclaiming kindergarten: Making kindergarten less harmful to boys. *Psychology of Men and Masculinity, 2,* 3–12.

Sax, L. (2005). *Why gender matters.* New York: Doubleday.

Sax, L. (2006). Six degrees of separation: What teachers need to know about the emerging science of sex differences. *Educational Horizons, 84*(3), 190–200.

Schneider, F. W., & Coutts, L. M. (1985). Person orientation of male and female high school students: To the educational disadvantage of males? *Sex Roles, 13*(1–2), 47–63

Schneider, M., Marschall, M., Teske, P., & Roch, C. (1998). School choice and culture wars in the classroom: What different parents seek from education. *Social Science Quarterly, 79*(3), 489–501.

Schwartz, W. (2001). *School practices for equitable discipline of African American students* (ERIC Digest No. 166). New York: ERIC Clearinghouse on Urban Education.

Scieszka, J. (2003). Guys and reading. *Teacher Librarian, 30,* 17–18.

Sciutto, M. J., Nolfi, C. J., & Bluhm, C. (2004). Effects of child gender and symptom type on referrals for ADHD by elementary school teachers. *Journal of Emotional and Behavioral Disorders, 12*(4), 247–253.

Shaywitz, B., Shaywitz, S. E., Pugh, K. R., Constable, R. T., Skudiarski, P., Fulbright, R. K., et al. (1995, February 16). Sex differences in the functional organization of the brain for language. *Nature, 373,* 607–609.

Shaywitz, S. E. (1998). Dyslexia. *New England Journal of Medicine, 338*(5), 307–312.

Shaywitz, S. E., Shaywitz, B., Fletcher, J. M., & Escobar, M. (1990). Prevalence of reading disability in boys and girls. *Journal of the American Medical Association, 264,* 998–1002.

Shucard, J. L., & Shucard, D. W. (1990). Auditory evoked potentials and hand preference in 6-month-old infants: Possible gender-related differences in cerebral organization. *Developmental Psychology, 26*(6), 923–930.

Smart, D., Sanson, A., & Prior, M. (1996). Connections between reading disability and behavior problems: Testing temporal and causal hypotheses. *Journal of Abnormal Child Psychology, 24*(3), 363- 383.

Smith, B. H., Molina, B. S. G., & Pelham, Jr., William E. (2002). The clinically meaningful link between alcohol use and Attention Deficit Hyperactivity Disorder. *Alcohol Research & Health, 26*(2), 122–129.

Smith, M. W., & Wilhelm, J. D. (2002). *"Reading don't fix no Chevys": Literacy in the lives of young men.* Portsmouth, NH: Heinemann.

Solowij, N., Stephens, R. S., Roffman, R. A., Babor, T. R. K., & Miller, M. (2002). Cognitive functioning of long-term heavy cannabis users seeking treatment. *Journal of the American Medical Association, 287,* 1123–1131.

Sousa, D. (2001). *How the special needs brain learns.* Thousand Oaks, CA: Corwin Press.

Steele, C. M. (1997). A threat in the air: How stereotypes shape intellectual identity and performance. *American Psychologist, 52*(6), 613–629.

Stephen, A. (1998, May 29). Shame you're not a girl, son. *New Statesman, 127*(4387), 20.

Stephens, R. S., Roffman, R. A., & Simpson, E. E. (1994). Treating adult marijuana dependence: A test of the relapse prevention model. *Journal of Consulting and Clinical Psychology, 62*(1), 92–99.

Stormont-Spurgin, M. (1997). I lost my homework: Strategies for improving organization in students with ADHD. *Intervention in School and Clinic, 32*(5), 270–274.

Stumpf, H. (1998). Gender-related differences in academically talented students' scores and use of time on tests of spatial ability. *Gifted Child Quarterly, 42*(3), 157–171.

Swartz, J. (2005, March 6). Schoolyard bullies get nastier online. *USA Today.* Retrieved October 26, 2006, from http://www.usatoday.com

Swift, E. M. (1991). Sports in a school curriculum: Four postulates to play by. *Teachers College Record, 92*(3), 426–432.

Tallent-Runnels, M. K. (1994). A comparison of learning and study strategies of gifted and average-ability junior high students. *Journal for the Education of the Gifted, 17*(2), 143–160.

Tarter, R. E., Kirisci, L., Mezzich, A., Cornelius, J. R., Pajer, K., Vanyukov, M., et al. (2003). Neurobehavioral disinhibition in childhood predicts early age at onset of substance abuse disorder. *American Journal of Psychiatry, 6*, 1078–1085.

Taylor, S. E., Klein, L. C., Lewis, B. P., Gruenewald, T. L., Gurung, R. A. R., & Updegraff, J. A. (2000). Biobehavioral responses to stress in females: Tend-and-befriend, not fight-or-flight. *Psychological Review, 107*(3), 411–429.

Thies, A. P. (1999). The neuropsychology of learning styles. *National Forum of Applied Educational Research Journal, 13*(1), 50–62.

Thomas, P. (1997). Doom to the red-eyed Nyungghns from the planet Glarg: Boys as writers of narrative. *English in Education, 31*(3), 23–31.

Tibbetts, S.-L. (1977). Sex-role stereotyping and its effects on boys. *Journal of the NAWDAC, 40*(3), 109–111.

Tomlinson, C. A. (1999). *The differentiated classroom: Responding to the needs of all learners*. Alexandria, VA: Association for Supervision and Curriculum Development.

Tomlinson, C. A. (2001). *How to differentiate instruction in mixed-ability classrooms* (2nd ed.). Alexandria, VA: Association for Supervision and Curriculum Development.

Townsend, B. L. (2000). The disproportionate discipline of African American learners: Reducing school suspensions and expulsions. *Exceptional Children, 66*(3), 381–391.

Vaidya, S. R. (2004). Understanding dyscalculia for teaching. *Education, 124*(4), 717–720.

Velle, W. (1987). Sex differences in sensory functions. *Perspectives in Biology and Medicine, 30*(4), 490–522.

Webb, J. T. (2000, August). *Misdiagnosis and dual diagnosis of gifted children: Gifted and LD, ADHD, OCD, oppositional defiant disorder*. Paper presented at the American Psychological Association annual convention, Washington, DC.

Wehmeyer, M. L., & Schwartz, M. (2001). Disproportionate representation of males in special education: Biology, behavior, or bias? *Education and Treatment of Children, 24*(1), 28–45.

West, P. (2002). *What IS the matter with boys?* Marricksville, Australia: CHOICE Books.

What the numbers say. (2000). *Curriculum Review, 42*(3), S3.

Wiggins, G., & McTighe, J. (1998). *Understanding by design*. Alexandria, VA: Association for Supervision and Curriculum Development.

Wilberg, S., & Lynn, R. (1999). Sex differences in historical knowledge and school grades: A 26-nation study. *Personality and Individual Differences, 27*, 1221–1229.

Wilkinson, L., Scholey, A., & Wesnes, K. (2002). Chewing gum selectively improves aspects of memory in healthy volunteers. *Appetite, 38*, 235–236.

Willingham, W. W., & Cole, N. S. (1997). *Gender and fair assessment*. Mahwah, NJ: Erlbaum.

Witelson, S. F. (1989). Hand and sex differences in the isthmus and genu of the human corpus callosum. *Brain, 112*, 799–835.

Witelson, S. F., Glezer, I. I., & Kigar, D. L. (1995). Women have greater density of neurons in posterior temporal cortex. *Journal of Neuroscience, 15*(5), 3418–3428.

Witelson, S. F., & Kigar, D. L. (1988). Asymmetry in brain function follows asymmetry in anatomical form: Gross, microscopic, postmortem, and imaging studies. In F. Boller & J. Grafman (Eds.), *Handbook of neuropsychology* (Vol. 1, pp. 112–142). New York: Elsevier.

Wuethrich, B. (2001, March). Getting stupid. *Discover, 22,* 56–63.

Yeakey, C. C. (2002). America's disposable children: Setting the stage. *Journal of Negro Education, 71*(3), 97–107.

Younger, M., & Warrington, M. (1999). "He's such a nice man, but he's so boring, you have to really make a conscious effort to learn": The views of Gemma, Daniel and their contemporaries on teacher quality and effectiveness. *Educational Review, 51*(3), 231–241.

Yurgelun-Todd, D. A., Killgore, W. D. S., & Cintron, C. B. (2003). Cognitive correlates of medial temporal lobe development across adolescence: A magnetic resonance imaging study. *Perceptual and Motor Skills, 96,* 3–17.

Index

CORWIN PRESS

The Corwin Press logo—a raven striding across an open book—represents the union of courage and learning. Corwin Press is committed to improving education for all learners by publishing books and other professional development resources for those serving the field of PreK–12 education. By providing practical, hands-on materials, Corwin Press continues to carry out the promise of its motto: **"Helping Educators Do Their Work Better."**